Michel Fokine

Twayne's Dance Series

Don McDonagh, Editor

George Balanchine
by Don McDonagh

Choreographer and Composer:
Theatrical Dance and Music in Western Culture
by Baird Hastings

Denishawn: the enduring influence
by Jane Sherman

Michel Fokine

Dawn Lille Horwitz

Twayne Publishers

Michel Fokine
Dawn Lille Horwitz

First Printing

Book production by Marne B. Sultz
Book design by Barbara Anderson

Typeset in 10 pt. Sabon by Compset, Inc.
with Snell roundhand display type supplied
by Typographic House.

Printed on permanent/durable acid-free
paper and bound in the United States of America

Library of Congress Cataloging in Publication Data

Horwitz, Dawn Lille.
Michel Fokine.

(Twayne's dance series)
Bibliography: p. 193
Includes index.
1. Fokine, Michel, 1880–1942.   2. Choreographers—
Russian S.F.S.R.—Biography.   3. Ballet dancers—
Russian S.F.S.R.—Biography.   I. Title.   II. Series.
GV1785.F65H67   1985   792.8′2′0924 [B]   85-928
ISBN 0-8057-9603-7

For My Parents,
My Husband,
and My Children

Contents

Editor's Foreword

Michel Fokine was the best-known choreographer in Europe and the United States prior to the outbreak of World War I. The five interrupted years (1909–12, 1914) spent with the Ballets Russes de Serge Diaghilev saw him produce a score of ballets of which half a dozen became the cornerstone of his reputation as a revolutionary creative force. His career continued, however, until 1942, the year of his death.

During the nearly four decades of his artistic life he worked continuously in the United States, Europe, and South America producing over eighty ballets, sequences for musical comedy, pageants, and incidental dances for dramas. Little has been written about the bulk of this work until now.

Fokine had the deserved reputation of being a revolutionary, but it is one of the pleasures of Dr. Horwitz's book to have that term explained in the specific manner to which it applies to Fokine. That he was the cutting edge of the reestablishment of ballet as a serious art during the first year of the century is undeniable. For many, however, he became the embodiment of the traditional Imperial Ballet, a seeming contradiction that becomes comprehensible in the light of his own dance training and belief in the untapped expressive qualities of the classic ballet vocabulary.

It is in the examination of the years before Fokine joined Diaghilev's company and the many years after, particularly those years spent in the United States, that the thread of Fokine's artistic development becomes clear. He did not so much break with the past as reshape it in response to the artistic imperatives of the turn of the century. To a great extent the creative ideas that Fokine had at the start of his career were those that he had at the end of it.

These ideas about the unity of dancing, music, and stage decoration were startling but quickly became received wisdom since they were so clearly right. The unusual thing was that they became received wisdom so quickly. In 1919, when Fokine came to the United States, he was welcomed as the living representative of the Imperial Russian Ballet tradition and not as a wild revolutionary intent on destroying all that came before him in his quest for new directions.

When he became the heralded creator of a new choreographic era after the first Diaghilev season in 1909, it took only five years before he was welcomed back by the Imperial Theater system in St. Petersburg as its honored ballet master. Diaghilev was never taken back, and Stravinsky, who composed two of the scores for Fokine's most successful ballets, had to wait until the 1960s to be honored by his native land. Clearly Fokine's contribution was of a special sort that pointed in new directions but did not rudely turn its back on tradition.

His substantial commitment to teaching persisted throughout his life. He was the youngest member of the faculty ever to be appointed at the Maryinsky School, a testimony to his skill. After his arrival in the United States he regularly gave classes, both on a private and a group basis. Members of these classes received performing experience in one or another of the small concert companies that Fokine organized between 1919 and 1938. Since he was never able to establish a permanent company the more talented dancers were eventually absorbed by other more stable performing groups.

Throughout his career he was in demand by ballet companies wishing to perform the works of his Diaghilev years. He traveled, taught, and coached them indefatigably. Generations of dancers had the opportunity to experience contact with him firsthand and through that exposure touch the tradition of which he was the most famous representative. It was natural when the American Ballet Theatre (originally Ballet Theatre) was being organized that Fokine was asked to remount his most famous works. In addition he was commissioned to create new ballets, one of which, *Bluebeard,* was a resounding popular success.

Given the opportunity to work within the frame of a solid ballet company, his banked creative fires glowed warmly once again. He was at work in 1942 when he died. Public taste had changed greatly between the time of his first arrival in the United States in 1919 because of his own efforts and the number of ballet companies that had visited and others that had been formed subsequently. Ballet was no longer an exotic curiosity but a recognized art form. Fokine had not been able to establish the academy he had hoped to form in the United States but his example as choreographer and teacher helped those who did. The balanced story of these successes and failures is the matter of Dr. Horwitz's graceful and detailed study of his career.

Don McDonagh

Preface

Michel Fokine, often referred to as "the father of Modern Ballet," was an outstanding dancer, and as a choreographer whose works are still performed, he has attained a lasting reputation. But it is his principles of reform, which changed traditional nineteenth-century ballet into a twentieth-century art and affected not only his own creations but those of the entire Western world, that attract primary attention. Had he never choreographed or danced, Fokine would still be remembered for these concepts alone. In stressing the use of the human body as a means of natural expression and insisting upon the organic unity of a production, he became the pivotal creator of the early Ballets Russes, which, in turn, influenced so many other artists.

Through his choreography for several student performances and charity benefits in Russia Fokine came to the attention of Serge Diaghilev. The history and accomplishments of the Ballets Russes are tremendous subjects in themselves; it is enough to note here that when Fokine left Diaghilev for the first time in 1912 (he returned briefly in 1914), the company had nineteen ballets in its repertory, fourteen of them choreographed by Fokine. In the ballets he created for this unique assemblage of performers, artists, writers, and composers, he was able to realize his reforms.

Fokine returned to Russia after the outbreak of World War I and left again in 1918 for Scandinavia, where he was working when he received an offer from the American impresario Morris Gest to choreograph the Broadway musical *Aphrodite*. Even though he had never been in the United States, Fokine's name and his ballets were known, both through numerous reports from Europe and performances by others.

The formation of the Ballets Russes, with Fokine playing a leading role, marked the entrance of dance into the twentieth century, an era that has witnessed an active investigation by the Western world of the relationship between man and his outward means of expression. The inquiry occurred in the United States also, but as the artistic development of this new country was at a different stage from that of Europe, so was the art of dance. America in the first two decades of the twentieth century had almost no dancers trained in ballet technique. There had been a few outstanding American dancers during the first half of the nineteenth century, such as George Washington Smith, Augusta Maywood, and Mary Ann Lee. Both of the women studied and performed in Europe as well as the United States. It was during this romantic period that ballet enjoyed its first great surge of popularity in this country, which welcomed many European artists, among them Fanny Elssler. The second half of the century was dominated by such musical spectacles as *The Black Crook,* and Italian ballerinas such as Rita Sangalli and Marie Bonfanti. Occasionally the ballet at the Metropolitan Opera in New York featured a guest artist such as the Danish Adeline Genée or LaScala's Cia Fornaroli, both of whom appeared a few years prior to the tour of the Diaghilev company. But it was Anna Pavlova who was really responsible for stimulating the interest of the American public in ballet, dancing almost anywhere they would have her.

The American public, in fact, saw most of its dance in vaudeville and musical comedy. It is therefore not surprising that Morris Gest hired Fokine to create dance for a musical, or that so much of the work of the Russian ballet master during more than twenty years in the United States was in the area of popular entertainment.

This Russian-born, Russian-educated artist, who loved and respected his native country and its art forms throughout his life, began his career there, played a major role in introducing Russia and dance to the rest of Europe, and finally acted in a pioneering role in his new country, where he faced a less sophisticated audience. Here he brought ballet to large sections of the population and also participated in the developmental years of Ballet Theatre, adding new triumphs and frustrations to an already remarkable career.

This book is based upon personal interviews, assorted clippings, press releases, programs, articles, Fokine's own writings, references by others, and three books that deal solely with Michel Fokine: Cyril Beaumont's *Michel Fokine and His Ballets* (1935), Michel Fokine's *Memoirs of a Ballet Master* (1961), and *Against the Tide* (1962), the Russian version of his memoirs edited by Yuri Slonimsky. Beaumont's book covers only the years up to 1925, although in an appendix he makes a brief summary of Fokine's activities through 1931. Fokine died before completing his memoirs, and, as published, only the years covering his association with Diaghilev were written by him. Vitale Fokine completed the volume, using his father's notes and papers, helped by Anatole Chujoy. The Russian version of *Memoirs* contains many letters written by Fokine, as well as the outline he originally made for this autobiography. Here he indicated his plan to write at length about the American years. It is our loss that he did not live to fulfill this intention.

Acknowledgments

Many libraries and historical societies in the United States were contacted for information concerning Fokine, and several conducted extensive searches. The Free Library of Philadelphia and the Detroit Public Library copied and sent a great deal of material.

The resources of the Dance and Theatre Collections of the New York Public Library at Lincoln Center provided the most material and the staffs of both were exceptionally helpful. All films mentioned were viewed at the Dance Collection. Mary Ann Jensen and Florence Downer of the William Seymour Collection at Princeton and Dina Abramsowicz of the Yivo Institute for Jewish Research were generous with their time, as were the staffs of the Theatre Collection of the Museum of the City of New York, the Ballet Theatre Foundation, the Grand Army Plaza Public Library in Brooklyn, and the Metropolitan Opera Archives. The reference librarians at the Bay Shore/Brightwaters Public Library, Long Island, were encouraging in their enthusiasm and amazing in their ability to locate materials all over New York State.

Special thanks to Phyllis Fokine, who gave up vacation time, evenings, and weekends to share her archive on her father-in-law; to Selma Jeanne Cohen and Jeanette Roosevelt, each of whom provided the encouragement to begin this project; to George Dorris, who often supplied the solution to a problem; to Naima Prevots, who located material in Los Angeles; to Dale Harris, Michael Kirby, Francis Mason, Sally Sommers, and especially Brooks McNamara, who read the original manuscript; and to my family for thinking it was a great idea.

Chronology

1880   Born, St. Petersburg, Russia, 26 April.

1889   Enters Imperial Ballet School, Maryinsky Theatre, St. Petersburg.

1898   Graduates from Imperial School and joins the Maryinsky Ballet.

1902   Appointed as instructor at the Imperial Ballet School, Junior Division.

1904   Submits outline for a ballet, *Daphnis and Chloë*, which includes his principles for reform of ballet, to the Directorate of the Imperial Theatres.

1905   Marries Vera Antonova; *Acis and Galatea*, his first ballet, created for his students; *Dying Swan* created for Anna Pavlova.

1906   *La Vigne*, his first ballet for professional artists.

1907   *Chopiniana* (student performance); *Le Pavillon d' Armide*, first work for the Maryinsky Ballet and first collaboration with Benois.

1908   Second and third versions of *Chopiniana* (later, *Les Sylphides*).

1909   Ballets Russes: *Prince Igor, Cléopâtre*.

1910   Ballets Russes: *Le Carnaval, Firebird, Schéhérazade*.

1911   Ballets Russes: *Le Spectre de la Rose, Petrouchka*.

1912   Ballets Russes: *Daphnis and Chloë*; resigns from Ballets Russes.

1914   Returns to Ballets Russes: *La Legend de Joseph, Le Coq d'Or;* basic principles of reform published in the *Times* of London, 6 July.

1916   Russia: *Sorcerer's Apprentice* (charity performance), *Jota Aragonesa* (Maryinsky).

1918   Leaves Russia, never to return. Tours Scandinavia and settles in Denmark.

1919   First visit to America. *Aphrodite*.

1920   *Mecca*. Performances in the United States.

1921   Settles permanently in New York and opens first studio; *The Rose Girl, Thunderbird, Le Réve de la Marquise*.

1922 *Frolicking Gods* and *Farjandio;* first choreography for movie theaters at Mark Strand, New York, 15 October; dances for *Johannes Kreisler.*

1923 Moves into house with studio at 4 Riverside Drive, New York; dances for *Casanova* and *Hassan.*

1924 Fokine American Ballet Company at Metropolitan Opera House, New York, 26 February with new works *Les Elfes* and *Medusa;* dances for *the Miracle.*

1926 Dances for *The Tenth Commandment.*

1927 First performances by Fokine Company at Lewisohn Stadium, New York.

1929 In Hollywood to teach and perform at Hollywood Bowl.

1931 Teatro Colón, Buenos Aires: five months as Artistic Director.

1933 Last performance by both Fokines, Eaton Auditorium, Toronto, 23 January.

1935 Choreographs ballets for Olga Spessivtzeva and Ida Rubinstein.

1936 René Blum's Les Ballets de Monte Carlo: *L'Epreuve d' Amour* and *Don Juan.*

1937 Col. de Basil's Ballet Russe: *Coq d'Or* (new version).

1939 *Paganini* for de Basil; signs contract with Ballet Theatre.

1941 Ballet Theatre: *Bluebeard.*

1942 Ballet Theatre: *Russian Soldier, Helen of Troy.* Dies, 22 August, in New York City.

Chapter One

The Formative Years (1880–1908)

IN ANY CONSIDERATION OF Michel Fokine, dancer, choreographer, and dance reformer, it is necessary to understand that the reason behind almost every decision that the Russian ballet master made—artistic or practical—can be traced to his ideas concerning the need for a "new" ballet.

From the very beginning of his career, Fokine realized that the classical ballet, as it was being produced in Russia at the turn of the century, had become stagnant and almost absurd because of its constantly repeated formula: three to five acts; spectacular pas de deux; obligatory folk-dance scene; identical mime interludes; emphasis on the technique of the ballerina; and the fact that the music, decor, and steps were not only unrelated to each other but often to the story and period of the ballet as well. Russian ballet, he felt, was not fulfilling its potential as an art form.

In 1904 he submitted to the director of the Imperial Theatres a scenario for a ballet based on *Daphnis and Chloë*. In the notes acompanying it was his plan to reform the ballet. Although these suggestions were never acknowledged, they were the result of all the twenty-four-year-old artist had experienced up to that point, and for the rest of his life he would refer to these principles, basing most of his artistic choices upon them. Fokine's ideas were first published in the *Times* of London on 6 July 1914, and were formally presented to the Russians by means of a more literary article in the Russian periodical *Argus* in 1916. An editorial comment accompanying the latter called it Fokine's first public answer to the antagonists of the new ballet.[1]

Fokine's five basic principles of reform were designed to transform the old ballet into the new. In effect, they would allow ballet to lead the changes occurring in twentieth-century theater by making ballet an expressive art that would mirror life. First, Fokine believed, ready-made movements out of the classroom should be abandoned for those that were appropriate to the country and period of action. Second, dramatic action should unfold in terms of movement. Third, sign language (i.e., codified mime) should be abandoned and the whole body should be expressive. Fourth, the entire corps, not just the soloists, should express the theme. Finally, the music should be a unifying force, carrying forth the dramatic action, and the decor should be as creative as the movement while appropriate to the period and theme.

To Fokine, the new ballet—as opposed to the traditional Russian model—was concerned with man's natural beauty, and its purpose, he felt, was to express feelings rather than just to look pretty and show off the ballerina. Hence dance could no longer use the fixed movements and unexpressive gestures found in traditional ballet. He felt that the form must express the theme of the work and that all elements must be integrated in a kind of total theater. He believed that the rigid rules of ballet technique had their value in training a dancer, but not in choreography, except where stylistically valid. He deplored the fact that ballet had become acrobatic, with emphasis on turnout and the lower limbs. He believed that the importance of both the upper body and of natural movements, such as runs and walks, had been forgotten along with expression.

Fokine felt that dance was the development and idealization of natural truthful gestures and that it should depict the natural beauty found in life, as well as the emotional and psychological forces present in all humans. To him, gestures reflected the psychic life of a race. He was not opposed to distortion for artistic purposes, pointing out, however, that the painter Vrubel knew how to draw a healthy human body and therefore had the right to paint mutilated demons. He could even be humorous, noting the appearance in every traditional ballet of the "mama" urging her son to get married.

Throughout his career Fokine wrote numerous articles on the "new" ballet (by which he meant the Fokine ballet), all of which were really elaborations on his basic canons. Many writers have pointed out that what he advocated was not new, and, in fact, had been proposed by Jean Georges Noverre in 1760. Fokine was quite familiar with Noverre's writings, but by 1904 he felt the need for similar reforms since Noverre's had been forgotten. Fokine had the courage to voice his ideas, often passionately, and he pursued them throughout his life. Arnold Haskell says simply that he took a dying academic formula and made it into a living art.

Portrait of Michel Fokine, St. Petersburg, circa 1884. *Courtesy Phyllis Fokine Archive.*

Mikhail Mikhailovich Fokine was born on 26 April 1880, in St. Petersburg, Russia. The son of a prosperous merchant and a German-born mother, he was the youngest of five children, four boys and one girl, all of whom were exposed to the theater very early. In his memoirs, Fokine, noting the influence of his entire family, attributes his love of the theater to his mother and his love of ballet and art to his brother Nicholai, a cavalry officer and the member of his family who had the greatest influence on him.[2] Another brother, Vladimir, became an actor specializing in comedy and farce. His third brother, Alexander, was a sports lover and businessman who later founded the Troitsky Miniature Theatre.

Fokine seems to have had an active, happy childhood, with a broad exposure to the life and people around him—he was the lively, mischievous, and often spoiled baby of the family. The Fokines had a summer home on Krestovsky Island, where they belonged to a yacht club. His sister, Sophia, was friendly with a girl at the club who was a student at the Imperial School of Ballet in St. Petersburg, and it was through this friendship that the family and Michel became aware of the possibilities of a dance career.

In 1889 when Michel Fokine was accepted by the Imperial School (his mother had taken him to the auditions secretly because of his father's objections) he entered willingly. His life there until his graduation in 1898 was, as he recalled it, a very positive one under a staff he respected, with his own hard work relieved by his genius for pranks. Because of their rigorous theater training, the students at the Imperial School often approached their academic subjects superficially, to Fokine's regret. He nevertheless managed to acquire a thorough knowledge of art and music, both through others and on his own, becoming in time a proficient painter and a musician who played the piano and the mandolin. His dance training, however, left nothing to be desired.

Fokine's first teacher was Platon Karsavin. He recalls his initial six months of training as limited to barre work only, and the second six months repeating the same simple exercises in the center. The two years of physical development with Karsavin (who would later disapprove of the eighteen-year-old Fokine's romantic relationship with his daughter Tamara Karsavina) were later remembered by Fokine as having little to do with the art of dance. Fokine found relief from the rigors of Karsavin's regime by participating in and observing performances at the different Imperial Theatres. In his second year with Karsavin he was put in the more advanced group and was also accepted as a boarder at the school, with all expenses paid.

Fokine was promoted to Nikolai Volkov's class in 1891, and although he studied under this strict, despotic, pedantic, and often dull teacher only a short time (Volkov died after a few months), he would always remember his dedication to discipline, his fanatical insistence on exact positions, and his complete obliviousness to his student's individuality. Fokine writes in his memoirs, "I feel that in a large degree, I owe to Volkov my ability in later years to squeeze out hard work from artists. . . . I also inherited from him my antipathy to sloppy technique and haphazard dancing." Alexander Shiriaiev, who replaced Volkov, was open and easygoing, the opposite of his predecessor. Fokine writes that he mastered the technique of classic dance under his guidance, although Shiriaiev's forte was actually character dance.

Fokine's next teacher, from 1893 to 1896, was Pavel Gerdt, who he remembers as perfectly built, graceful, elegant, and magnificent. Gerdt had been an exceptional dancer and was an excellent mime. His method of teaching was to demonstrate and have his pupils learn by imitation. Fokine, recalling Gerdt's distinctive walk, points out that "one had to know how to study under him to be able to draw all possible benefits from this epitome of elegance," and he probably influenced the future choreographer more than any other teacher. (Fokine attributes much of Pavlova's success to Gerdt as well.) Later, when Fokine was in the company, he shared a dressing room with his former teacher, who also danced in some of his ballets. Fokine states emphatically in his memoirs that his criticism of some of the traditions of ballet did not extend to animosity toward the older dancers and teachers, contrary to what others later wrote about his quarrels with Gerdt.

When Gerdt retired as a teacher, his classes were taken over by Nicholai Legat, who still studied with his father, Gustav Legat, a pupil of Christian Johansson. Fokine's later criticism of Legat, who he recalls as an extremely talented individual with a creative, gay personality in private, was that in class he found him a slave to tradition, opposed to any change. His blind adherence to tradition was a useful foil for his student, who was just beginning to question the accepted practice.

Fokine studied with Johansson himself after he joined the Maryinsky Theatre Ballet Company and was eligible to take the professioal classes of the octogenarian, who had been a pupil of the Dane August Bournonville. The system and material were much the same as that of Legat's classes and were strict and pedantic in approach, but Fokine felt he was at the source of classic dance and held the great teacher in reverence and awe. The classes required tremendous concentration: the white-haired old man would demonstrate the steps with his hands; everyone would attempt the combination; they would gather around him for corrections; finally they would perform it again. To Fokine, Johansson was "a living museum of choreographic art" who taught technique as the foundation that eventually allowed the student the freedom of individual creativity. It was this lack of flexibility in expressiveness that Fokine had begun to see in the productions in which he started appearing at the age of eleven.

Fokine graduated from the Imperial Ballet School of the Maryinsky Theatre in 1898. In a class that included Lubov Egorova, Julie Sedova, and Mikhail Oboukhov, he won the first prize and was taken into the company at a salary and level above that of the corps de ballet. This was a tribute to his outstanding abilities as a dancer—his strong, yet graceful and expressive technique, in addition to his talents as a mime. He was Anna Pavlova's first partner, and Tamara Karsavina states that he was an exceptional artist who eventually had to make a choice between performing and choreographing. Bronislava Nijinska refers to him as a "premier danseur."

As a soloist in the Maryinsky Ballet, Fokine danced much less frequently than he would have as a member of the corps. He had to share his roles with the Legat brothers, Nicholai and Serge, with Georgi Kyaksht, and with Vladimir Oboukhov, the Legats' nephew. He was last in line; in his memoirs he observes that, since he lacked relatives in the company and patrons and friends among the influential balletomanes, he had to accept the traditional hierarchy and wait for someone to be ill. He eventually danced Bernard de Ventadur in *Raymonda,* the Bluebird in *Sleeping Beauty,* and the pas de trois in *Swan Lake,* among other roles. This wait was perhaps fortunate because it gave him time to read voraciously, study music, paint, travel, visit museums, and develop his own ideas more firmly.

In 1902 Fokine was appointed an instructor of the junior classes in the girls' department of the Imperial Ballet School. This was a great honor for someone so young—he was the youngest dancer ever asked to be on the faculty—and he presented the fundamentals of ballet in a disciplined and mechanical manner, acutely aware of the responsibility this honor entailed. He writes that he realized that his ballet reforms could not begin here and reiterates his strong belief in the foundations of classic ballet as the basis for any creative structure. He eventually taught the older girls and in 1908 began teaching the boys. Among his pupils were Lydia Lopokhova, Alexander Gavrilov, and Bronislava Nijinska. The last named says that she loved Fokine's classes and was sorry when she had to change teachers.

Michel Fokine first had the opportunity to choreograph when, like anyone teaching a senior class, he had to stage a ballet for his students' examination performance. In 1905 he chose to create a work himself instead of rehearsing one from the repertory. For the next few years he would choreograph a number of ballets for examination performances, for charity performances, and a few for the Imperial Theatre. In these works he began to apply his new ideas, and several were the basis for later ballets of historical and/or artistic significance.

Acis and Galatea, a Greek ballet to music by Andreas Kadletz, which Lev Ivanov had choreographed some years earlier, hardly fits these categories, but for his first creation Fokine carefully researched Greek mythology and art in an attempt to find an authentic form. His original plan, based on this research, was turned down, and he was instructed to compose a more traditional ballet. This work, with its nymphs and its Dance of the Fauns, in which one of the twelve boys was Nijinsky, was, by his own account and that of Bronislava Nijinska, innovative in that his groupings were asymmetrical, with the dancers on different levels. Fokine says that he also managed to change the customary female costumes so that they bore some resemblance to those of the ancient Greeks, and that the fauns performed no ballet steps but were more like beasts, even doing some tumbling. He considered the work successful and an apt expression of his principles. It was the first of his Greek ballets, and the fauns would later reappear in the Venusberg ballet, created in 1910 for the opera *Tannhäuser* at the Maryinsky Theater.

The following year Fokine created a ballet based on Shakespeare's *A Midsummer Night's Dream* for the examination performance. He used Mendelssohn's music of this title plus part of his violin concerto. The work included elves, among them Nijinsky, and the women were arranged in groups to resemble garlands of flowers.

That same year (1906) Fokine was asked by the dancers of the theater to stage a ballet for them to perform at a benefit for the Grebolovsky School. For this, his first opportunity to work with the professional artists, he staged one act from the three-act ballet *La Vigne* to music composed in 1883 by Anton Rubinstein. Fokine's version takes place in a wine cellar where the qualities of the wine are danced as a group of drinking companions uncorks them. Lydia Kyaksht was champagne, performing a series of turns on a rising trap door; Maria Petipa, Hungarian wine (in a czardas); and Tamara Karsavina, Vera Fokina, and Michel Fokine himself took other parts in the ballet, which ended in an orgy.

It was after this performance that Fokine received a note from Marius Petipa congratulating him on his composition and predicting that he would be a great ballet master. Fokine later wrote, "Never in my entire career as a ballet master did any compliment for my work please me more than this note from the great ballet master," and he always stressed his admiration for Petipa's French elegance, good taste, and undiminished talent. Fokine felt that his own desire to create in a new way did not lessen the significance of Petipa's work, saying, "My principle was to create, but not to destroy."

In February 1907 Fokine was asked by Victor Dandré to produce a program for a charity performance and the result was *Eunice*, a two-act ballet to music by Vladimir Shtcherbashev and *Chopiniana* to a suite by Chopin. (The latter will be discussd in chapter 2.) *Eunice* had a libretto by Count Stenbock-Fermor, which was based on episodes from *Quo Vadis*, the novel by Henryk Sienkiewicz, and combined Greek and Egyptian dances, with some additional references to Rome. Fokine later re-flected that the ballet was very experimental in its attempt to re-create authentically the dances of antiquity, and he felt he was successful in certain choreographic innovations, in staging effects, and in the costumes and makeup of the performers.

Eunice is another example of an early ballet in which the ideas and sketches for later works can be seen. The rather flimsy libretto revolves around the "entertainment" at a banquet given by the Roman patrician Petronius, featuring several slaves, including Eunice and Acte. Among the divertissements was a sword dance by Eunice (Mathilda Kchessinska) performed in the middle of eight swords stuck into the ground with the points up, Acte's (Anna Pavlova) Dance of the Seven Veils, a dance performed on top of large wine skins, another with lighted torches, and one by three Egyptian girls (Fokina, Sedova, and Rutkovskaya) whose darkened bodies were seen in profile.

Fokine says he distributed Pavlova's veils so that they were not bulky and each revealed a different part of the body as it unwound. The Torch Dance for the corps, in which there were real torches on stage, he regards as the outstanding success of the ballet and the first of his ecstatic dances. He also says that he substituted expressive movements to further the telling of the story. The costumes included Greek chitons and, since bare legs and/or feet were not allowed, toes with pink nails were painted on the dancers' tights. Karsavina, who took over Pavlova's role when Pavlova took Kchessinska's, calls the work a compromise between the Hellenic tradition and the balletic tradition.

Fokine reports a backstage visit from the influential balletomane General Nicholai Bezobrazov during one of the final rehearsals of the ballet. Rumors had spread, and the General pleaded with the choreographer to introduce his innovations gradually—to dress the corps as Egyptians, but at least keep the principles en pointe and in tutus. Fokine says he listened respectfully, did what he wished, and that afterward the General was one of his supporters.

In 1907, when he again had to produce something for the final examinations, Fokine turned to the composer Nicholai Tcherepnin, whose suite from "Le Pavillon d'Armide" he had heard at a concert. Tcherepnin explained that it was actually the second act of a three-act ballet, the libretto for which had been written by the painter Alexandre Benois, his wife's uncle. It had been given to the Directorate of the Imperial Theatre, who had apparently forgotten about it. Fokine and Tcherepnin decided to present this one scene under the title *The Animated Gobelins,* and the students danced it on 15 April, wearing costumes that Fokine had select-ed, as he always did for such performances, from the wardrobe of the Maryinsky Theatre. The highlight of the work was the Dance of the Jest-ers, led by Georgi Rosai, in what Fokine considered the most technically difficult dance he ever created, involving jumps with bent legs, which end-ed in a sitting position on the floor and then rebounded into more jumps.

A few days after the school program, which also featured Nijinsky, Fokine was asked by Alexander Krupensky, the assistant director of the Imperial Theatres, if he would stage the full ballet for the Maryinsky. The choreographer was overjoyed to be given his first opportunity to work with the artists of the Theatre, on the Imperial stage, under sponsorship of the Imperial Directors. He requested that Benois be asked for the com-plete libretto, and Krupensky soon sent it to him. Keith Money, in his book on Pavlova, says that Fokine began work immediately, and when he was put in charge of a group of young dancers from the Maryinsky who were sent on a tour to Moscow in May, he presented part of this work as scenes from a new ballet.

The story of *Le Pavillon d' Armide* concerns a journeying Vicomte forced by bad weather to seek refuge in the castle of a Marquis, who is also a magician. He is sheltered in a domed annex, known as Armide's Pavilion, in which is hung a beautiful Gobelins tapestry, depicting an an-cestress of the Marquis costumed as the witch Armide. Beneath the tap-estry is a clock supported by the figures of Love and Time. The Vicomte falls asleep, to be awakened at midnight as Love drives Time away and the Hours appear. Gradually the tapestry comes to life and the Vicomte joins the revelry at the King's court, falling in love with Armide. Before morning the figures disappear. Time vanquishes Love, the tapestry is re-stored, and the Vicomte sleeps. He is awakened by the Marquis, whom he recognizes as the King of his dream. He passionately rushes up to the tapestry and, filled with horror, tries to escape, but falls dead as a result of the enchantment.

When Fokine read the original libretto, he felt that it could be con-densed into a one-act ballet—a form that strengthened his principles of artistic unity and coherence. Vladimir Teliakovsky, the director of the Im-perial Theatres, and Krupensky agreed with him. It was many years later that he learned how upset Benois was at the condensation, blaming the destruction of his dream of a full evening ballet on Krupensky. Benois also felt, however, that the working relationship among himself, Tcherepnin, and Fokine was excellent, that Fokine's choreography realized precisely his own concept of eighteenth-century art and "Hoffmannish" mystery, and that in Fokine fate had brought him together with the very person he needed. He also says that *Eunice* was an experiment, but even the dancers recognized *Pavillon* as a mature work. Serge Grigoriev, a friend of Fokine's and later an indispensable part of the Diaghilev organization, writes that the ballet still showed some influences of Petipa and Fokine himself says it was filled with waltzes because Teliakovsky liked them.

The three creators evolved a style of working in which they met for discussion, the music was played, Fokine outlined his choreography, and Benois developed the dramatic side. The next day was spent in rehearsal with the dancers. For a while, all went well. Then Krupensky and Benois had an argument and the dancers were divided in their allegiance, with those on Krupensky's side becoming uncooperative, arriving late to rehearsals, and voicing criticisms aloud—all of which resulted in constant cast changes. There were also problems with costumes (Benois designed them and supervised construction) and Kchessinska backed out as a performer, affording Pavlova the opportunity to take over her role. Matters were not helped by all the special effects contributed by both collaborators, including trap doors and a flock of mechanical sheep. The first performance was canceled as a result of a letter Benois sent to a newspaper, accusing the administration of sabotaging the ballet in what he later referred to as a "cabal" against Fokine and himself. This letter ignored a previous misunderstanding between Benois and Teliakovsky, as well as a "coolness" between Benois's friend Serge Diaghilev and the director. (In fact, on one occasion when he was attending a rehearsal of the ballet, Diaghilev was removed from the theater by guards.)

Le Pavillon d'Armide finally received its premier performance on 25 November 1907, and met with moderate success, remaining in the repertory of the company for some time. Although Fokine had added to the number of his adversaries, he and Benois became close friends and decided that their further work would be outside the "bureaucratic" world.

By the following year Fokine was even clearer in his aims and how to accomplish them; he had learned from his experiences and was developing a reputation on several levels. On 8 March 1908, for a charity performance at the Maryinsky Theatre, he staged *Egyptian Nights* and the second version of *Chopiniana*. He had been doing some research in the Library of the Imperial Theatre when he found the libretto for *Egyptian Nights*, which had been written by Petipa, to music by Anton Arensky. It was choreographed in 1900 by Lev Ivanov for a visit by the Shah of Iran, but never performed, and Fokine felt that it would be an excellent vehicle for further illustrating his reforms.

The first scene of *Egyptian Nights* takes place on the banks of the Nile and the scenery shows a temple and, in the distance, pyramids and a sphinx. Berenice is a young woman very much in love with her betrothed, the hunter Amoun. But when he sees Cléopâtre, he falls passionately and irrationally in love with her and willingly offers his life for a night of love. When dawn comes and the return of Anthony is announced, the queen orders the poisoned cup for her young lover; he drinks it and is carried off. After Anthony and Cléopâtre sail away, however, it is revealed that the High Priest has substituted a sleeping potion and Amoun awakens to be forgiven by Berenice.

Fokine says that the dancers were very cooperative—but for a charity performance such as this they were usually all his admirers and followers, and their acceptance of his ideas was to be expected. Pavlova danced the leading role, Gerdt was Anthony, Alexei Bulgakov the High Priest, Nijinsky and Olga Preobrajenska were slaves, and Fokine himself danced Amoun. The role of Cléopâtre was played by Elizaveta Tihme, a student at the drama school, because he felt an actress was best suited for this part. Fokine staged the dances using angular lines and flattened palms, with the bodies in profile, keeping in mind that this was a drama in which everything was to contribute equally to the whole.

Because of this concept of unity he rejected most of the costumes that had been created for the original production, finding them very un-Egyptian, and selected what he could from the hodgepodge of other old costumes. Leon Bakst, who helped with the staging and lighting, designed a few new ones. The dancers all wore dark body makeup, a requirement that caused much complaining when the ballet was later taken into the repertoire of the Maryinsky Company. Benois was present throughout the production period and it was his idea to place Cléopâtre on a couch and to have the lovemaking scene discreetly hidden by veils. Lincoln Kirstein considers this ballet the first real occasion for the public presentation of Fokine's theories and says it "created a sensation directly comparable to the romantic revolution of the first night of *Ernani*."[3]

By this time in his career Fokine had been innovative enough to be noticed in his most traditional profession, and he had succeeded well enough as a young dancer and teacher to be resented. He felt that the older teachers condemned him because, although he tried to avoid experimentation in teaching, he did begin to emphasize such things as music, expressive use of the head, and épaulement. His artistic run-ins with the directorate were not in themselves of serious consequence, but he did manage to get caught in the midst of others' plays for power. The Benois/Krupensky dispute is one example of this. It is also possible that because of his own talents (which even his adversaries acknowledged) and his propensity to express his ideas vehemently and, perhaps, dogmatically, he attracted or repelled other strong and often influential personalities. Fokine relates an incident that occurred immediately after he choreographed *Acis and Galatea*. He was asked by Alexander Sanin, the regisseur of the dramatic troupe at the theater, to choreograph a dance in a new production. Fokine had already started rehearsals when Krupensky told Sanin he needed official permission for this. Sanin, insulted, immediately resigned, creating an incident in which Fokine's name was featured.

His demands, passionate outbursts at rehearsals, and his habit of asking performers to do things that made them feel uncomfortable (not all were creatively challenged by the newness of his approach) eventually caused a division between Fokine followers and others. Karsavina says that Fokine was irritable at rehearsals and often shouted until he was hoarse. Outwardly, he appeared antagonistic to tradition, evoking disapproval from the older members of the ballet company. She herself was shocked by his intolerance although inspired by his enthusiasm, and says that the senior dancers were openly hostile toward her for dancing in his ballets.[4] Pavlova, who had been a staunch supporter and admirer of Fokine since their student days, was becoming more independent as an artist, though wielding less influence within the Imperial Circle. Pavlova's growing independence was necessitated by the fact that her competitor Kchessinska was surrounded by a large and powerful circle of admirers, who spared no pains to assist her in getting what she wanted and thwarting the efforts of those she did not wish to succeed—including, eventually, Fokine and Diaghilev.

Politically, Fokine became almost dangerously involved in 1905 when he, Karsavina, and Pavlova were among the twelve delegates chosen by their fellow dancers to present a resolution listing the demands of the dancers in the negotiation of a new contract between the performers and the Imperial Maryinsky Theatre. The Directorate, pointing out that they were under the patronage of the czar, became incensed, called their action a breach of discipline, and demanded that all the dancers sign a loyalty oath. Most of them, feeling they had no choice, signed, leaving their twelve delegates in limbo. Serge Legat was one of those who signed. Shortly afterward he killed himself, an act many associated with his politics and his belief that he was a traitor. Life in the company continued, but this entire incident had deep emotional repercussions, created even more divisions, and separated Michel Fokine from the traditional ballet establishment even further.

Although he initially may have felt that he was operating in isolation, Fokine soon discovered through his friendship with Benois that this was not so. The painter was a founding member of a group of friends, all of whom had attended a private college called Mays at the end of the nineteenth century. They had formed a club for the presentation of papers and discussions, taking the name "Pickwickians." In addition to Benois, who had the widest background and was their mentor, the original group included Constantine Somov, an artist, Walter Nouvel, who was very interested in opera and literature, and Dimitri Filosofov, whose expertise was in history. Later came Charles Birlé, an attaché at the French Consulate, Leo Rosenberg (who soon took his mother's name and became Léon Bakst), Alfred Nourok, and Serge Diaghilev, a cousin of Filosofov's.

Although the composer Tcherepnin eventually joined the group, and the critic Valerian Svetlov and General Bezobrazov did also, the link among these men was their desire to make art a vital and creative means of expression. It was Diaghilev, the least intellectual, but most businesslike "country cousin," who eventually crystallized the group, almost all of whom were Europeans, with his idea in 1899 for the magazine *Mir Iskusstva* (The World of Art), which brought European as well as Russian art to the attention of Russians. Other members of the circle founded a society to present concerts of French and German compositions that had never been heard in Russia.

The group also supported theater and dance, anxious to reconcile the Russian heritage with Westernism in these areas as well as in painting and music. Here they had musical predecessors as far back as the 1860s when the Kuchka or "mighty five"—Balakirev, Borodin, Cui, Moussorgsky, and Rimsky-Korsakov—rejected a separation of the arts and desired to reform musical language, favoring realism, truth, nationalism, folk tales, and legends in their attempt to become part of the European movement. They were succeeded by the Belyayev Circle, which met at the home of the Russian art patron Mitrofan Belyayev—Glazounov, Liadov, Borodine, Scriabin, Blumenfeld. Of these, Glazounov, probably the most successful Russian composer after Tchaikovsky, carried on the national music traditions, using Russian melodies and rhythms to reflect the country's life and folklore in orchestrations that were smooth flowing and almost romantic in their unity and lyricism.

In the dance world, aside from Fokine, a great generation of Russian performers had emerged—Kchessinska, Trefilova, Preobrajenska, Egorova, Pavlova, Nijinsky—balancing the prior influence of Brianza, Legnani, Cecchetti, and Zucci, all of whom were foreigners.

Thus by the time Benois began inviting Fokine to the meetings of the old Pickwickians there were many people and ideas waiting for a force to unite them. Because those in charge of the Imperial Theatres did not wish to encourage them, they were forced to go elsewhere. After *Armide* Fokine started meeting with the group on a regular basis, and Benois started to think about bringing the Russian ballet to Europe.

Fokine writes that during his first evenings with the group he discovered that they had no understanding of the possibilities inherent in the dance, but that after *Armide* their interest and sympathy began to grow. He also points out that *Mir Iskusstva* rarely mentioned ballet. Actually they had tried working with Nikolai Legat as early as 1901 *(Sylvia)*, but found him too traditional. Benois, who felt that his friendship with Fokine was of the highest significance for the future of the Ballets Russes, was the first to recognize Fokine's abilities. Prince Peter Lieven implies that Fokine was never a member of the "inner circle" of friends and creators, who felt him an authority on one thing only—the dance.

Benois realized that the ideas that resulted in the Ballets Russes were conceived not by dance professionals but by artists whose dreams were connected with the entire world of art, and that in Fokine (and Stravinsky) they found men with dreams similar to theirs. He wrote, "We did not aim at astounding the world with sensational innovations; our chief wish was to make the European public participate with us in something that we loved."

If Fokine's dream was to merge with those of others, thus creating a new dimension in art, his own accomplishments and personal rebellion up to this point should not be forgotten. He had absorbed the tradition that produced him, carefully analyzed it in relation to contemporary ideas and art, saw the need for reforms, and put them into practice in both his teaching and choreography. He also affected others enough to have divided them into those who agreed with him and those who adhered to the set concepts of the Imperial Theatre System. A logical next step would make Fokine part of the Ballets Russes adventure.

Chapter Two

The Diaghilev Ballets Russes
(1909–1912, 1914)

THE DIAGHILEV BALLETS RUSSES has been written about extensively—by many of those involved with it, by critics, by historians—most of whom looked back on it and all of whom remember things quite differently.[1] Varied as the views of the Ballets Russes are, most seem to agree that the idea for the venture originated with Alexandre Benois and that he was responsible for suggesting the first year's program and for giving Fokine a strong position. There is also a consensus that of the seventeen works created by Fokine and presented by the Ballets Russes from 1909 to 1914, the major ones are *Le Pavillon d'Armide, Les Sylphides, Cléopâtre, Prince Igor, Firebird, Schéhérazade, Petrouchka, Le Spectre de la Rose,* and *Carnaval.* This chapter is an attempt to place Michel Fokine in the context of this company and to understand the major works he created there in relation to those that preceded and those that eventually followed them—with the full realization that each ballet could sustain at least a chapter in itself.

Michel Fokine was vacationing in Switzerland in the summer of 1908 when he received a letter from Benois saying that he was trying to persuade Serge Diaghilev to take some ballet to Paris in addition to the opera that he had just successfully presented there. When the magazine *Mir Iskusstva* discontinued publication in 1904, Diaghilev, with the ideas and active support of his circle, had also staged several art exhibits in both Paris and St. Petersburg. His short-lived appointment with the Imperial Theatres had ended with abrupt dismissal in 1901 and his independent and often dictatorial manner had made him many influential enemies;

but his uncanny insights and organizational abilities had given him the position of leadership among his intellectual and artistic friends.

Diaghilev's close circle was in favor of recruiting Fokine as both choreographer and dancer after Benois suggested him. Most of them had met him and all were familiar with his works. Diaghilev, who had been interested in ballet since he had seen the Italian ballerina Virginia Zucchi, had been brought to rehearsals and performances of Fokine's ballets by Benois. The facts were that he had already presented paintings and opera and needed something "different" at this point, that new works and dancers existed in Russia but would never have a real chance to develop as long as Teliakovsky and a conservative group ruled the Imperial Theatres, that the French producer Gabriel Astruc was interested in ballet, and that Fokine's relationship with the Imperial Theatres was becoming strained. All conspired to cause Diaghilev to act on Benois's suggestion.

Fokine and Diaghilev knew each other casually, but their first meeting in 1908 with Benois was also their first real interchange, and Fokine writes that Diaghilev charmed him from the very beginning. The impresario had already decided to bring *Le Pavillon d'Armide.* He accepted Fokine's idea of *Chopiniana,* with a certain number of changes, and was interested in Benois's suggestions of *Egyptian Nights,* although he rejected the Arensky music, and requested that Fokine think about creating something new on a purely Russian theme. It was understood that Fokine was to be a premier danseur as well as ballet master.

When Fokine began rehearsing the artists from the Maryinsky who would perform during their summer break, they worked at Catherine Hall, on the Catherine Canal, and started with the new "Russian" ballet, the Polovtsian Dances from Borodin's opera *Prince Igor.*[2] Most of them were already familiar with *Pavillon* and *Chopiniana,* and *Egyptian Nights* was not finally chosen until later. With Diaghilev, Benois, Bakst, the painter Nicholas Roerich, and many others present at these rehearsals, they are remembered as intensive and exciting, with Fokine's bluntness sparing no one, including himself. When they arrived at the Théâtre du Chalet in Paris, *Prince Igor* and *Pavillon* were seen together on a program that was first performed on 19 May 1909, and *Egyptian Nights (Cléopâtre)* and *Les Sylphides* on 2 June.

Prince Igor, the Polovtsian Dances from Act III of Alexander Borodin's opera *Prince Igor,* was seen this first year as part of a whole act of the opera, with the accompaniment of a complete chorus. These dances are plotless, occasioned because the Polovtsian Chief desires to entertain Prince Igor, whom he has captured and with whom he wishes to conclude a peace treaty. Roerich's set for this primitive nomadic tribe—dome-shaped tents arranged on a number of hills seen at dawn in the light of dying fires—contributed to the ecstatic, virtuosic work that Fokine created after careful research and absorbtion of Borodin's music. The slow, voluptuous, circular dances of the women are contrasted with the impetuous, swift, linear dances of the men. The piece ends with the men hurling themselves into the air at a faster and faster pace, crashing to the floor only to rise again.

Fokine considers this one of the most important of all his works, in which his goal was "to create an excitement arousing dance for the corps," and when Paris saw the ensemble of male dancers whirling and jumping in a wild frenzy to the rhythms so suggestive of Russian primitiveness, they realized the art of ballet had taken a new turn. The choreographer says his choice of steps was dictated solely by the music and that initially Diaghilev did not like the piece, relaying his critical suggestions through others. The leading role of the Polovtsian Warrior was danced by Adolph Bolm (regarded by all, including Fokine, as the best performer in the role) and the cast included Sophie Fedorova and Elena Smirnova. All the dancers are reported to have performed as if possessed, with Benois saying that they "seemed to have been re-incarnated as ancient heroic savages, sensitive steppe maidens and Hindu bayaderes." The audience responded with the same wildness the performers displayed; Fokine claims they rushed forward and tore off the orchestra rail. In other seasons and companies this ballet was performed simply as a dance, without the opera setting and chorus.

Diaghilev's decision to bring *Chopiniana* to Paris seems to have been largely taken alone, although he insisted upon renaming it *Les Sylphides* so that the public would think of the earlier *La Sylphide* and immediately know that this was a romantic ballet. He also ordered new orchestrations of the Chopin music by Liadov, Glazounov, Taneyev, Sokolov, and Stravinsky (whose work on the "Valse Brillante" was his first commission from Diaghilev). Fokine agreed to the changes, with some reluctance.

Les Sylphides was first choreographed by Fokine for the same charity performance at the Maryinsky Theatre in February 1907, at which he presented *Eunice*. He had come across a suite of four Chopin piano pieces orchestrated by Glazounov and requested the composer to orchestrate one other Chopin piece, the Waltz in C Sharp Minor. The "First Chopiniana," as Fokine called it, consisted of five tableaux: the Polonaise featured a Polish ballroom; the Nocturne depicted an ill Chopin having nightmarish hallucinations and saved by his muse;[3] the Mazurka accompanied a Polish wedding; the Tarantella was the excuse for a Neapolitan scene. Only the waltz—which Fokine had wanted because the other pieces suggested character dances—was plotless, accompanying a duet by Pavlova and Oboukhov. This classical pas de deux for two equal partners, which used no virtuosic steps, was created by Fokine because he wanted to show that, although a reformer, he did understand the unique beauty of the classic dance.

When he created and presented his "Second Chopiniana" for a charity performance on 8 March 1908, he had new orchestrations by Maurice Keller. He did keep the C Sharp Minor Waltz intact and in fact expanded the pas de deux to create an entirely new abstract ballet, which was intended to reveal the purely poetic side of the romantic era.[4] For this performance, what Fokine terms the "glorious" cast consisted of Pavlova, Preobrajenska, Karsavina, and Nijinsky. The costumes, based on a sketch Bakst had done the previous year, were the ankle-length tutu of the romantics. It was this ballet, with decor by Benois, that Paris saw as *Les Sylphides*. It has probably been the most frequently performed ballet in the twentieth century and was its first lesson in the freedom possible within the classical idiom.

After the Overture the curtain rises on an ancient ruin where the women are grouped around a man dressed in white and black velvet. The whole is lighted as if in moonlight and the girls dance the light, airy Nocturne. The first Waltz, a joyous, idyllic one, is a solo for a ballerina. The Mazurka, also for a female soloist, opens with grand jetés performed diagonally across the stage, evoking a sense of exuberant, abandoned floating. The second Mazurka, for the danseur, is slow and sustained. The Prelude is a fluid free-style variation of great rhythmic complexity. The pas de deux Waltz begins with the danseur lifting the ballerina and carrying her across the stage from the wings, with the variation increasing in momentum and swiftness, as does the music. Following a briefly silent and empty stage the entire company enters in along diagonals of swiftly fluttering movement, there are four brief solos, another rush of movement, and the curtain falls on the same tableau on which it opened.

In the seamless development of this ballet, which, with its entrances and exits that constantly fuse and dissolve, caused one writer to term it "as satisfying as the elucidation of a Euclidean theorem," there is not a wasted movement. Fokine felt it expressed his sentiments even more clearly than his program of reforms. There are no ready-made combination of steps, no classical poses, no virtuoso steps; no variation begins or ends in the same fashion. The movements, with their constantly flowing arms, recall the illusion of lightness and flight sought by Marie Taglioni and others. The man dances alongside the woman as an equal; the corps is integrated with the solists, wearing the same costume. Sono Osato recalls that when Fokine restaged this ballet in 1937 he told the dancers that nothing mattered except the emotion of the motion.

Karsavina danced in the first Waltz, Pavlova in the fast Mazurka, Nijinsky in the slow Mazurka, Maria Baldina in the Prelude, and Pavlova and Nijinsky in the pas de deux. Except for Baldina, this was the same cast on which the ballet had been set the previous year. The sustained intensity required from all resulted in a performance that caused the critics and the audience to admit that the Russian dances could be more than exotic: they could be romantic. Pavlova was compared to Taglioni, although she did not get the attention expected, partly because the French saw *Les Sylphides* as "merely" a ballet blanc and were not immediately aware of Fokine's changes, and partly because the male roles in all his works were so outstanding that Nijinsky was seen as more unique than she.

Le Pavillon d' Armide, which shared the ballet portion of the first program with *Prince Igor*, featured Pavlova and Nijinsky in the leading roles. Many have speculated that Benois was so strong in his desire to bring ballet to Paris because of his extensive role in creating this work, and many hours were spent in rehearsing the elaborate changes in sets because he insisted upon exact timing. If *Sylphides* proved that the Russians were capable of romanticism, this ballet showed that they could evoke an eighteenth-century atmosphere just as well, bringing a French ambience back to France.

The fourth Fokine ballet was *Cléopâtre*, the renamed *Egyptian Nights*. Essentially it was the same work, but Diaghilev hated the Arensky score and chose new music, which, miraculously, fit the choreography. There was an excerpt from Rimsky-Korsakov's opera *Mlada* for a dance by the slave girls, and one from Glinka's *Russlan and Ludmilla* for the Dance of the Veil, which Karsavina performed. Two new dances were added, a Finale to music from Moussorgsky's opera *Khovanshchina* and a Bacchanale to the Autumn section from Glazounov's "The Seasons." The other changes were that Berenice's name was changed to Ta-Hor; the character of Anthony, who had previously entered on a chariot drawn by white stallions, was eliminated; and the story had a new ending in which Amoun is poisoned.

Fokine, as well as everyone else, highlights two aspects of this ballet: the Bacchanale and the performance of Ida Rubinstein as Cléopâtre. Vera

Fokina and Sophia Fedorova were featured in the former, a dance of frenzy and violence, which ended with the two satyrs and twelve young Greek men and women crashing to the floor. For Fokine this dance was his first successful translation of the bas reliefs on ancient vases into flowing movement, and it was probably the prototype of all the bacchanales that followed. In Ida Rubinstein, a young and wealthy actress and would-be dancer, who had studied privately with Fokine and of whom no one had heard prior to her striking performance as the mysteriously evil and seductive Cléopâtre, the company had a beautiful woman who fascinated Paris. The cast also included Nijinsky as a slave and Fokine as Amoun.

Benois, who says that it was he who insisted upon including *Cléopâtre* in the repertory, is also credited with the idea of having Rubinstein brought on stage wrapped in twelve veils, each of a different color and design, and encased in an ebony and gold casket which was placed on a catafalque carried by eight slaves. (It may be recalled, however, that Fokine used seven veils in the earlier *Eunice*.) Leon Bakst's rich red and pink decor represented a turning point in theatrical decorative art that was sensational, and the entire production, including its "hodgepodge" of music, was an instantaneous success, predating many later Hollywood films of imitative sumptuousness.

The fifth ballet that Diaghilev presented, in addition to opera segments, was *Le Festin*, a suite of different national dances for which Fokine created the Finale. It was based on a Georgian dance, used Glinka's music, and was performed by Fokina and several men. Fokine makes no comment about this work except to note that there was nothing unified in it; in fact, he does not even mention that he choreographed one segment. Gregoriev remembers much time and energy put into a divertissement that never really worked.

If *Le Festin* was unremarkable, it was alone in that first season. From the preopening rehearsals in Paris, when Diaghilev's various friends and others came to watch Fokine frantically working to integrate the Moscow dancers with those from St. Petersburg amid the lighting technicians and carpenters trying to repair the cracks in the stage floor, until closing night, they "really did stagger the world," as Benois said. The critics declared Fokine a great choreographer, *Cléopâtre* and *Prince Igor* were generally agreed to be the most successful ballets from the point of audience popularity, and the effect of the corps de ballet in its ensemble dancing established that body as important in its own right—as Fokine wished. In future years the Diaghilev company would present many other works based on the prototypes those of the first season established: romantic ballets (*Spectre, Carnaval*) would have a model in *Les Sylphides;* spectacular ones with moods of allure and/or abandonment (*Schéhérazade, Thamar*) in *Cléopâtre;* and national ones based on folk and fairytales (*Firebird, Coq d'Or*) in *Festin* and *Prince Igor.* The Greek theme would also recur.

In May 1909 Robert Brussel, the critic for *Le Figaro,* described Michel Fokine as a "thin, highly strung young man" whose "sharp eyes miss nothing . . . watchful, stimulating, he demonstrates, mimes [and] darts from pianist to dancer."[5] Still in this state, exhausted from both choreographing and dancing, but further stimulated by the great success of the first Paris season, Fokine began to plan with the group for the next summer as soon as they returned home. The season of 1910 unveiled three more Fokine creations: *Le Carnaval, Schéhérazade,* and *Firebird.*

Le Carnaval was originally presented early in 1910 at a ball held for the benefit of the magazine *Satyrican.* Fokine was approached by two young men involved with the publication, one of whom was the to-be-famous poet Potemkin, the other Mikhail Kornfeld, who later became the magazine's publisher. The ball, held just prior to Lent, was based on the Carnival theme and Fokine immediately decided to use Robert Schumann's Piano Suite "Le Carnaval," which he had long admired. The choreographer had read Schumann's biography as translated into Russian and had Kornfeld, who knew German, go through the original version with him.

Schumann's score has musical references (to Chopin and Paganini), literary ones (to the characters of the commedia dell'arte), and stage directions that were written in after the score was completed. The basic musical theme of A, E flat (S in German), C, and B (H in German) spells ASCH, the birthplace of Ernestine von Frichen, with whom the young Schumann was in love. The second autobiographical element in the score is the final "Marche des Davidsbündler Contre les Philistines," reflecting the composer's advocacy of the "new" art, as against the conservatism of the old.

The libretto finally put together by Fokine and Bakst really has no plot. Rather, it is a series of light, humorous, and joyous incidents and some moments of poignancy, plus an undercurrent of satire, which intermingle the four basic characters of the commedia—Harlequin, Columbine, Pierrot, and Pantalone—with Florestan, who represents the impulsive side of Schumann's nature, and Eusebius, who is the thoughtful, solitary aspect. There is also Estrella, a portrayal of Ernestine von Frichen; Chiarina, who is Clara Schumann, the composer's wife, as a young girl; and the fluttering lady, Papillon, who is pursued by the hapless Pierrot. There are, in addition, six lighthearted couples who waltz in and out, partaking in various revels centered around the betrothal of Columbine and Harlequin.

For the gallant males, coquettish females, and lovers who teasingly accept and reject each other, Fokine devised numerous pas de deux, pas de trois, and pas seuls, which, as Beaumont observes, are very difficult because they appear so simple in construction.[6] Alongside the sometimes slapstick antics of Harlequin, Pierrot is pathetic in his constant chase after people and emotions that forever elude him. Fokine says that in the final dance (the chasing of the Philistines) everything was built on runs, with Florestan chasing Estrella, Eusebius after Chiarina, and Papillon running away from Pierrot. For the benefit performance, which was created spontaneously in three rehearsals, this last section actually took place in the audience, but when the Diaghilev company performed it, everything remained on stage.

In the cast at the benefit Karsavina was Columbine; Leonide Leontiev, Harlequin; Vasily Kiselev, Florestan; Ludmila Shollar, Estrella; Alexander Shiriaiev, Eusébius; Nijinska, Papillon; Alfred Bekefi, Pantalone; and Vsevolod Meyerhold, of later fame as an innovative stage director, Pierrot. The music for their performance was played on the piano, as written, but by the first performance by the Ballets Russes, which took place in Berlin on 20 May, the score had been orchestrated by Glazounov, Rimsky-Korsakov, Liadov, and Tcherepnin. For this version, as for the Paris premiere, which took place on 4 June, the role of Columbine was danced by Lydia Lopokova, Harlequin by Nijinsky, Pantalone by Cecchetti, and Pierrot by Alexandre Bulgakov. (It was not until 1911 that Karsavina danced Columbine to Nijinsky's Harlequin.)

The simple set, representing the anteroom of a ballroom with two striped divans, and the costumes, all in the style of Biedermeier, were designed by Bakst. It was never clear to the audience whether the dancers were actually commedia characters or dancers at a ball pretending to be them. The masks on the dancers served a double purpose at the charity benefit since the stars of the Imperial Theatre were prohibited from partaking in private performances during the regular theater season.

Nijinska says that they all loved rehearsing for the Diaghilev production and wished the work would never end. Grigoriev, who claims credit for suggesting *Carnaval* to Diaghilev, remembers the solo by Nijinsky where he finished one series of pirouettes by slowing down and then sitting on the final chord. This variation by itself raised the general level of male dancing. Two other outstanding variations were a pas de trois by

Estrella and two friends concerning their virginity, which was soon to be lost, and a duet by Harlequin and Columbine, where his steps were performed to the melody of the flute and clarinet and hers, in counterpoint, to the strings. Lieven feels each scene in *Carnaval* had choreographic, emotional, and dramatic content and that in its simplicity and severity, Fokine showed that he was capable of great artistic subtlety. Benois observed that although Fokine had been nurtured in a different environment than himself and the others, he nourished the same dreams and ideals, and this harmony was particularly apparent in *Carnaval*. The ballet was so successful at the charity performance it was taken into the repetoire of the Maryinsky, but Diaghilev was originally opposed to bringing it to Paris because he felt it was not grandiose enough. As it turned out, it provided a soothing contrast to the other two ballets.

Schéhérazade, the exotic Oriental spectacle that really catapulted Fokine and the Ballets Russes to international fame, was created because Diaghilev decided he wanted a work set to Rimsky-Korsakov's symphonic poem of the same name. Composed in 1888, the four-movement suite, a free musical interpretation of some of the tales from *The Thousand and One Nights,* is rich in color and sound, and Diaghilev obviously projected a breathtaking extravaganza.

The story of the ballet, based on the first of the Arabian tales, tells of the Shah and his brother, who go off on a hunt leaving the Shah's favorite wife, Zobeïde, and the rest of his harem in charge of the chief eunuch, who is convinced by the women to free all the slaves, with whom they indulge in a voluptuous orgy. The early return of the suspicious Shah and the subsequent slaying of all, including Zobeïde and the object of her affections, the Golden Slave, provides the base for a ballet of continuous movement and a strong element of violence. Who the actual author of this libretto was is still a matter of debate: Benois thought it was he (the story line was written on the score by him) and he was astonished and angered on opening night in Paris (4 June 1910) to find Bakst given full credit for libretto and decor. Fokine recalls Bakst suggesting a version in which the Shah has the bodies of his harem and their Ethiopian lovers put in sacks and cast into the sea, an ending that he and the rest of the "committee" rejected. In all probability it was a group creation and it is entirely possible that Diaghilev used the program credit as an occasion to set Bakst and Benois against each other, thereby giving himself some much-needed power.

Fokine, stating that the authorship is really irrelevant, claims that the important details were in the staging, and that this ballet marked the first application of his principles of describing actions and emotions entirely through movements and positions of the body. In creating this emotional and often bloody story of uninhibited passions, he had Ida Rubinstein as an acting rather than dancing Zobeïde, Nijinsky as an animal-like and otherworldly favorite slave, Bulgakov as the Shah, and Cecchetti as the Chief Eunuch. Fokine had begun by working with three of the five Odalisques (Fokina, Sophia Fedorova, and Elena Poliakova), making them sit on the floor, moving only their heads, arms, and upper bodies. By all accounts the steps were simple and he produced them with ease, although he credits the results to his superb cast. Stressing the importance of finding the most economical means of expression, he recalls Rubinstein's ability to communicate everything in a single pose (as for instance her stillness while observing the slaughter around her and awaiting her own inevitable death); Nijinsky's large, yet soft and half-feline leaps and great energy; and the single gesture with which Bulgakov as the Shah orders Zobeïde's execution after the sight of Nijinsky's body arouses his intense jealousy. Fokine knew little about the actual dance of the Orient at this point, and studied Persian miniatures in preparation.

Both Nijinska and Marie Rambert, who was one of the wives on the South American tour, say that in certain sections of the work, particularly the beginning of the orgy, Fokine did not give specific directions, but told each wife exactly where to go and whom to embrace. The ballet builds into the intensity of the orgy scene in the middle, with its leaping and flying individuals interwoven with groups and contrasted with sensuous poses. Its climax occurs during a pause in the music, which is used to halt the dancers momentarily and then untangle them at an accelerated pace.

Although many purists complained that Rimsky-Korsakov's music was not used as intended (one section was cut and the bacchanale was danced to the movement that referred to the sea) it was a perfect counterpart to the choreography. The entire work was tied together and given theatrical validity by Bakst's luscious and dazzling decor, which, with its rich greens, blues, and oranges, evoked instant applause from the audience and started an Oriental craze that affected fashion and furniture designers throughout the Western world. *Schéhérazade*'s tumultuous reception can probably be credited to a combination of its themes of lust, slaughter, and vengeance; the new mime of Fokine involving the entire body; the striking performances; the evocative music; Bakst's harmonic rendering of the exotic; and the emphasis on color rather than form. From an audience point of view, it was the quintessence of the first period of the Diaghilev Ballets Russes, and as late as 1925 in a contest in London was voted the most popular Diaghilev ballet, even though it was not on the ballot.

Michel Fokine as the Golden Slave in *Scheherezade*, Diaghilev Ballets Russes, date unknown. *Courtesy Phyllis Fokine Archive.*

The Firebird, the other outstanding ballet of the company's second season, was the first complete production of the Ballets Russes in the sense that the music, by Igor Stravinsky, was commissioned, and the close collaboration among the composer, the choreographer, and the decorative artist, Alexander Golovine, represented the true equality of the arts that Fokine had sought. Diaghilev, Fokine, and the "committee" had, from the beginning, agreed on the necessity of a piece based on Russian folklore, and work was begun with the idea that it would be presented the first season. Because *The Firebird* was not ready and he had already announced it by name, Diaghilev presented the Bluebird pas de deux from *Sleeping Beauty* in 1909 (Fokine rehearsed it!) calling it *Firebird*. The "real" work, however, which represents a landmark in the history of modern ballet, was not presented until 24 June 1910.

The libretto is generally attributed to Fokine, who states adamantly that it is solely his and that he evolved it by weaving together elements from different Russian folktales and narrating the results on several occasions at the evening gatherings at Benois's home. Stravinsky is one of those who say it was a group effort, but since he was not brought in until after the original libretto was complete (Liadov was given the original script and agreed to write the music but when he did not fulfill his obligation, Diaghilev suggested Stravinsky) he may well be referring to the group meetings where finishing touches were added. The resulting story combines several tales from the collection of the writer Alexandr Afanasiev, with one about the enchanter Kostchei. It fulfilled Fokine's long-held desire to create a ballet based on a Russian fairytale.

The ballet opens on the garden of the magician Kostchei, with its surrounding wall, its trees filled with golden apples, and its stone monsters. Suddenly an extraordinary creature, a bird, agitatedly flies in, closely followed by a hunter, Prince Ivan, who catches her. He accepts a magic feather in exchange for freeing her and is soon distracted by the sight of the twelve captive Princesses, who enter and begin to play with golden apples. The most beautiful Princess tells Ivan of the spell cast upon them and he falls in love with her. When a sudden burst of sound from the orchestra causes them to leave hastily, he tries to follow but is soon surrounded by Kostchei and his horde of monsters, who attempt to petrify him. Ivan remembers the magic feather. This summons the Firebird, who makes them all dance until they collapse, and then shows Ivan the hidden egg containing the soul of Kostchei. The shell is broken, Kostchei dies, all are freed, and Ivan and the Princess are reunited. The ballet ends with a procession celebrating love and the forthcoming marriage. In the original cast, Karsavina was the Firebird (a role originally intended for Pavlova, who did not return to the company), Bulgakov was Kostchei, Fokina was the Princess Unearthly Beauty, and Fokine danced Ivan.

The story contains all the old symbols—a prince, a princess, a magician, a dance-unto-death—but what is new is the total liberation from evil. Hence there is a reminder of tradition, but a noticeable veering away from it—an approach found in the music as well. The bird, which expresses the joy of flight, is really a bird, not a human transformed into a bird. With its mystic powers, it is outside human reference. Fokine staged this role en pointe with many jumps, but no turnout. He says the arms, which sometimes open up like wings and at other times hug the head and body, had an Oriental element. The princesses were in bare feet. The monsters, with their grotesque movements and spinning jumps that landed in squats, are recalled by the choreographer with pleasure. Fokine feels that the "newness" of this ballet rests on two elements: there are no "conversations" in it and the working process evolved by himself and Stravinsky was unique.

The collaboration between the choreographer and the composer is one upon which both commented. Fokine, noting that never again did he work so closely with a composer, adds that the ballet is dear to him "for the memories of the excitement and joy" he shared with Stravinsky. The latter, for whom *Firebird* was the first of many ballets, admits that Fokine taught him much and that he has worked in the same manner with choreographers ever since. Their method, once Stravinsky was familiar with the libretto, began with Fokine miming the scenes. Later Stravinsky would return with his themes and sketches and the choreographer would create on the spot, inspired by the music, as the composer expanded his ideas at the piano. The result of such close collaboration is reflected in such sequences as the bird assigning each group of demons a different theme in their dance-unto-death: each theme is given a characteristic musical motif.

Stravinsky's score, which creates a magic atmosphere and imitates the sounds of thunder and the wings of a bird, nevertheless bears some resemblance to both Rimsky-Korsakov (his teacher) and Tchaikovsky, combining Russian melodies and new sounds. *Firebird* was the beginning of his own break from tradition. Perhaps because his "new" approaches outstripped Fokine's innovations, perhaps, too, because of his long friendship with Diaghilev, Stravinsky became negative and vindictive in his later declarations about Fokine. In his autobiography he writes that the choreography in *Firebird* is complicated and overburdened with detail and that the artists have difficulty in coordinating their steps with the music. To this, Grigoriev retorts that the dancers said the score did not sound like music. In answer to Stravinsky's comment that he prefers the clear-cut lines of *Prince Igor,* Fokine himself responds that the nightmarish scene of the monsters should give the feeling of disorder—a necessity for nightmares.

Stravinsky was also known to have had his own visualizations of the movements to be performed to his music and for him the ideal synchronization did not follow a story line (as in his two collaborations with Fokine) but formed a structural relationship between music and choreography (as in his later collaborations with Balanchine). The fact that Fokine usually picked traditional nineteenth- and early twentieth-century music (often Russian), if given the chance, would suggest that he was not comfortable with the dissonances of modern music. Grigoriev claims that in 1913 he gladly relinquished the choreography of *Le Rossignol* because he did not like the music, and Anton Dolin says that in 1931 he declined an invitation to create a work to *Apollo Musagetes*: both scores were Stravinsky's. It is possible that the composer sensed Fokine's basic aversion to his musical idiom and took it personally. As early as March 1912, Stravinsky, writing to his mother about *Le Sacre du Printemps* and still under the impression that Fokine was to choreograph it, dismissed the choreographer as an exhausted artist who had not even dreamed of the new forms to be created.

Although Diaghilev did not like some of Golovine's costumes and had Bakst make new designs, he did get a production that was Russian from beginning to end. The critics, in their enthusiasm, were most impressed by the unity of all the elements. The set evoked an atmosphere of a fairyland. The dancing—by both soloists and ensemble—was considered impeccable.

Benois and Lieven, among others, criticize the *Firebird* story as a jumble of incohesive tales that, in the end, is not convincing, and they find it hard to believe in Ivan and the Princess. Chief among its faults, Benois feels, is its failure to transcend the children's story to become the fairy tale for adults to which its creators aspired. Of its choreography, Nijinska recalls that Fokine himself had trouble remembering its intricacies when he restaged the work in 1912 after a two-year hiatus; yet Osato says that in 1936 it remained so brilliant that it kept a weary company (de Basil's) awake. There seems to be no question that *Firebird* was difficult, required superb acting as well as dancing, and, if not taken seriously, could degenerate into a series of lackadaisical steps with dancers practically counting out loud—as it did in the dozens of productions by as many companies over the years. Fokine also laments the destruction of Golovine's three-dimensional set in 1922: Gontcharova's painted replacement eliminated so many details that much of the movement became meaningless. In 1910, however, *Firebird* was a hit from every point of view, and led the way for new collaborations in the art of dance.

Because of financial problems, Diaghilev dropped opera completely this second season and, to supplement Fokine's ballets, included *Giselle* in the repertory. When Fokine balked at rehearsing it, Diaghilev responded that if he did not, someone else would have to be brought in. Although Fokine acquiesced, the result was not a great success and it seemed to mark the beginning of his problems with the impresario. Reports of Fokine's moody outbursts during this period might be traced to this, to the issue of "Commoedia Illustre," which listed him last among the performers, with no choreographic credit at all, and to the continuing intrigues and jealousies of the ballet world. Karsavina (who replaced Pavlova since the latter had bookings elsewhere, although Diaghilev thought she would be in Paris) writes that after that second season Diaghilev was already beginning to think that Fokine's choreography belonged to the past. She also suggests that by keeping Fokine, Diaghilev felt he was avoiding an open schism and maintaining his company. Meanwhile, in Russia, Petipa died in July, making Fokine's position there a bit more secure, if not yet markedly so. (He staged only one ballet there in 1910, the Venusberg Scene from Wagner's *Tannhäuser,* for a charity benefit in April.)

In late spring of 1911 the Diaghilev Ballets Russes began their third season of performances—a season in which they were again successful in Paris at the Théâtre du Chatelet, they appeared in London for the first time, and they were established as a permanent institution with Monte Carlo as their base. Since his own status was becoming more secure, Diaghilev allowed the break between himself and Fokine to become more visible. He began by offering the ballet master a two-year contract at a high salary, but as a choreographer only—a move interpreted by some as stemming from his desire to eliminate any performer who might compete with his favorite, Nijinsky. Fokine was still officially a member of the Maryinsky, but his reputation as both an artistic and political revolutionary had not diminished, and the Ballets Russes was his major creative outlet. Although he choreographed two major ballets for Diaghilev, *Le Spectre de la Rose* and *Petrouchka,* in addition to *Sadko* and *Narcisse,* the year 1911 is significant because it marks the obvious change and disintegration of Fokine's relationship with the Ballets Russes.

Le Spectre de la Rose, the short ethereal pas de deux for Karsavina and Nijinsky, was based on an idea suggested by the French writer Jean Vaudoyer and created by Fokine in St. Petersburg before the company left for Monte Carlo. The story, based on a poem by Théophile Gautier in which a young girl returns from her first ball and dreams that the spirit of the rose she is carrying visits her, was set to Carl-Maria Von Weber's "Invitation to the Dance" and danced in a blue and white French-doored boudoir. The girl enters and falls asleep. Suddenly, to a lush and buoyant waltz, the spirit of the rose leaps through the open window. First he dances alone, gliding around the room; then he awakens her, and they dance together. She returns to her chair and sleep; he hovers a moment, then disappears through the window.

Spectre, like *Sylphides* an essentially romantic ballet, also makes use of the classical idiom, but the pas de deux does not follow the traditional formula of supported adagio, solo variations, and coda. The movements are fluid and meant to be performed without a turnout, with the girl's runs on half toe, not en pointe. The pirouette turns are performed with asymmetrical arms and the face to the ceiling. Nijinsky imbued the role with his own natural sense of elevation. André Eglevsky, who was coached by Fokine and taught the role to Mikhail Baryshnikov, says the flow of movement is so exhausting that at the end of the ten-minute work he would collapse. The gestures are blended into the constant flow of the movement, which is inspired by, but not tied to, the music. Bakst designed the set as well as the girl's long white gown and the Spectre's pink/purple leotard with the silk leaves and petals, many of which were sewn on at the dress rehearsal with Nijinsky in the costume.

This work, which Karsavina calls "blessed," was meant to be a trifling fill-in ballet, a brief contrast to the other works on the program, and its success took everyone by surprise. It was created spontaneously in two or three rehearsals, in what Karsavina remembers as a blissful mood, and even Diaghilev was calm about the entire production. The only moments of discord occurred when Bakst insisted on including a caged canary in the decor; wherever he hung it, it interfered with the dance—hence expediting its elimination. One fault found in this duet, which helped many audiences further understand and see Fokine's reforms, is that few of the many performers who have since attempted the roles have been able to achieve the fresh, spontaneous, dreamlike quality of Karsavina and Nijinsky. In writing of the poetic dancing of the latter, Fokine laments the apocryphal stories of his final leap and insists that this great artist needs nothing more than the truth told about his portrayal of "a spirit . . . a hope . . . a fragrance that defies description."

Spectre was first seen on 6 June 1911, and exactly one week later, on 13 June, Paris first saw *Petrouchka,* a work often considered the supreme example of storytelling in ballet. It was the climax of Diaghilev's beginning stage, of Fokine's association with him, and of the group's collective achievement. To many, it is *the* masterpiece of the Ballets Russes.

The idea for a ballet about Petrouchka, the half-comic, half-tragic puppet with the human heart—the Russian Pierrot and Punch—was first conceived by Stravinsky as a work for piano and orchestra. After Diaghilev heard the score, he asked the composer to turn it into a ballet and wrote to Benois, asking him to work on a libretto. The three eventually met in Rome and produced the final version, which Benois ultimately wrote. He points out that, to a large extent, the story follows the score exactly, although the precise setting—the annual Butterweek Fair, the Russian version of Mardi Gras—reflected his nostalgic wish to immortalize the St. Petersburg Carnival of his childhood.

Set in 1830, in four scenes, the ballet opens on a square filled with diverse people—peasants, aristocrats, soldiers, gypsies—whose merriment is interrupted by the appearance of the bearded showman who presents his three puppets: the doll-like Ballerina, the opulent Moor, the sad Petrouchka. He makes them move and then perform a mechanical dance. The second scene, in Petrouchka's dark, cold cell, exposes the showman's cruelty, the puppet's awkward love for the uncomprehending Ballerina, and his frustration and despair with life. In scene 3, which takes place in the Moor's warm, red room, this prisoner shows himself quite content to lie about playing with his coconut and accepting the Ballerina's admiration. He becomes angry when Petrouchka enters and chases him with the intent of destroying him. The last scene is a return to the Fair, where festivities are reaching a peak. Suddenly Petrouchka rushes out of the Showman's booth, followed by the Moor, who kills him. The Showman proves to the horrified crowd that the corpse is simply a doll. But as the fair ends, the ghost of Petrouchka appears above the rooftop, threatening and triumphant.

As Lincoln Kirstein notes, none of these characters is new. Petrouchka is related to Pierrot and Punch; the Ballerina to Columbine and Coppelia; the Moor to the medieval wildman and the Turk; the Showman to the doctor of the commedia. The collective crowd could be seen as early as 1844 in *Esmeralda.* Ultimately, it was Fokine's unique treatment of each

Petrouchka, scene i, 1911. *Courtesy Collection of Gerald Ackerman.*

character and vignette, with complete awareness of the qualities projected in Stravinsky's brilliant score, that makes this a truly tragic ballet, created not by emotion and instinct but by intellect and logic. This work belongs to the twentieth century in its break with romanticism, its realization of discord and defeat, and its sensitivity to the psychology of the individual.

The impact of *Petrouchka* was the result not only of the music, the choreography, and Benois's decor (he designed each and every character in the ballet separately) but of the talents and acting abilities of the original cast: Karsavina (the Ballerina), Cecchetti (the Showman), Alexandre Orlov (the Moor), Nijinsky (Petrouchka). Fokine points out that the overall process of creation for this work was entirely different from that of *Firebird*. Rather than a simultaneous, mutual method, each artist showed Petrouchka's suffering in his own way. Expressing his admiration for Stravinsky's music, with its richness of suggestive character and its use of old Russian themes, Fokine nevertheless deems much of the score "non-danceable," and feels the change of rhythms could have been more natural with greater use of repetition for the group dances. The attention to incident, character, and psychological interpretation in the score—the arpeggio for Petrouchka in his cell, the shrieking trumpets for his frustration—did appeal to Fokine, who says they supplied the kind of pictorialization essential to his new ballet.[7]

The steps for the Moor, whose legs are always turned out, are gauche and almost primitive, those for the Ballerina gay and dainty, but never human, and those for Petrouchka, whose legs are always turned in, are almost natural, although at the same time stiff and doll-like. These solos are the ultimate realization of Fokine's theories of expressive dance. The crowd scenes were of great importance to him also. Fokine notes that in the opening scene Stravinsky uses only two musical themes and has the characters appear consecutively, whereas he, Fokine, uses over a hundred themes choreographically (one for each character on stage) and has them appear simultaneously. Fokine also states that, as the choreographer, he wished these scenes to appear spontaneous and free, not as if they were staged.

Although many in the audience did not understand the music, *Petrouchka* was a great success for its blending of all the visual and auditory elements and the brilliant dancing. The handling of the crowds evoked comment from all, with Stravinsky's among the few negative ones. Cyril Beaumont speaks of the "vivid sense of life" animating everything and the group that did not "march to and fro like soldiers at a review in the manner of the old ballet," but jostled each other, exchanged greetings and gossiped.[8] The national dances of the ensemble, which were absorbed into the overall dance drama, and the minute details of "slice of life" realism (like the little girl attracted by the Showman's flute) were all admired. Carl Van Vechten describes Nijinsky's expression of grief as more poignant than that of most Romeos.

It is noteworthy that *Petrouchka*, which utilized all of Fokine's theories and talents, was created under the most difficult conditions. It was originally rehearsed in the hot and stuffy basement buffet of the Teatro Costanza in Rome, with the dancers moving on a dirty red carpet and Stravinsky accompanying them on the piano. Fokine was under tremendous physical strain: he was responsible for rehearsing his old ballets and, in addition to *Petrouchka*, creating two more new ones. Parts of the libretto were still incomplete. Grigoriev, realizing the impossibility of Fokine's task, tried to get Diaghilev to relieve him somewhat, but the impresario was adamant about the ballet master's role in his old works and the need for the new ones.

The situation during the staging in Paris where Fokine had only two hours to set one crowd scene, was even worse. The stage itself was cluttered with Benois's sets, Stravinsky (with whom Fokine argued over the tempi of the music) had drums set up in the prompt corner, and the lighting was done at the very last minute. The latter was to be supervised by Benois, who had an argument with Diaghilev over a portrait in the set, refused to change it, and as a result would not appear. When Diaghilev eventually had Bakst redo the portrait, Benois resigned as artistic director of the company. Hence the friction between Fokine and Diaghilev was increased as other breaks in the organization's unity began to appear.

This occurred at a time when the success of the Ballets Russes was established without a doubt—owing in large part, to *Petrouchka*. For Diaghilev, however, music was now beginning to assume a more important role than the other elements, and he was abandoning his earlier advocacy of a hybrid mixture of composers. To this pragmatic man, his earlier collaborators, including Fokine, had served their purpose, and he was ready to move on.

The two new Fokine ballets of the season were both on the program with *Spectre* on 6 June. *Sadko*, first shown in Rome, was a tableau from one act of Rimsky-Korsakov's opera of the same title, in which the minstrel Sadko enters the underwater kingdom of the Sea King, where his playing causes all to dance. He then escapes, taking the King's daughter as his bride. This opera-ballet, with decor by Boris Anisfeld, was sung by a chorus, danced entirely by the ensemble, and seems to have produced no great impression. It was also called *Le Royaume Sous-marin*.

Diaghilev commissioned Tcherepnin to compose a ballet in the Greek style, and Bakst, who was interested in archaic Greece, wrote the scenario and encouraged the production of *Narcisse*, a ballet that Fokine really did not want to choreograph. He had been anxious to create a work on a Greek theme, and *Daphnis and Chloë*, to a score by Ravel, had been on the production schedule for some time; however, Diaghilev seems to have purposely delayed this, an action many attribute to his desire for a work that would feature Nijinsky.

The libretto for *Narcisse* adheres closely to the Greek myth of Narcissus, who is so enamoured by his own image that he ignores the admiring Echo. She causes the goddess Nemesis to punish the youth by turning him into a flower. There were some wood demons and satyrs at the beginning and end of this work, some Bacchantes, and a brief appearance by some peasants, but the focus was on Karsavina as Echo and Nijinsky as Narcissus. Fokine was more successful with his flowing movements for the grieving Echo than he was with those for Narcissus, who remained rather static in the contemplation of his own beauty in a reflecting pool. Benois and others note that the basic theme was too static for a ballet and the transformations of Narcissus into a flower did not work. The Parisians did not like it (although Bakst's set, originally designed for *Daphnis and Chloë,* was considered quite lovely). Beaumont, however, deems it a beautiful creation, embodying simplicity and economy of gesture.

The following season, Fokine finally did get to choreograph "his" Greek ballet, but by the time it got on stage, his break with Diaghilev was definite and his departure imminent. The year 1912 was to have witnessed the company's first performances in Russia, but the theater in which they were to appear was destroyed by fire, and they were canceled. Fokine, assuming a Ballets Russes season in Russia, had agreed to mount *Carnaval* and to choreograph two new works, using Ballets Russes dancers, for a charity performance at the Maryinsky immediately following the planned Ballets Russes season. Thus, when the company was in Berlin prior to their Monte Carlo opening, Fokine and many of the dancers were back in St. Petersburg fulfilling his commitment. Diaghilev was reportedly furious about this, but at the same time the situation allowed Nijinsky time to rehearse *L'Après-Midi d'un Faune,* a work Diaghilev was encouraging but which he had never officially announced, not wishing to anger Fokine, from whom he expected three new ballets.

Daphnis and Chloë, the last of the new Fokine works to be presented that season, was the most significant artistically and politically. The choreographer had first thought of it in 1904, the score was commissioned from Ravel in 1909, and it was originally scheduled for 1911, but postponed by Diaghilev. Fokine wrote the libretto based on the original tale by the Greek, Longus, about the God Pan and two of his young worshipers, the shepherds Daphnis and Chloë, who are lovers. When Chloë is captured by pirates, Pan intervenes, and there is a happy ending of joyous love. Among the dances is a procession to Pan and a dancing contest between Daphnis and the boorish Darkon.

Staged as an eighteenth-century pastoral, the ballet blended a kind of naive innocence with sensuality (a temptress who entices Daphnis and a scene in the pirate's lair where Chloë is forced to dance) with a certain degree of sentimentality. Diaghilev seems to have had little interest in the work (with *Narcisse* from the previous year and *L'Après-Midi d'un Faune,* it made the third ballet on a Greek theme) and did everything possible to make Fokine postpone it. There was insufficient time for rehearsals, in part because of the premiere of Nijinsky's work at the end of May.

Since the set Bakst had originally designed for *Daphnis and Chloë* had been used the previous year in *Narcisse,* a new one had to be created, which did not meet Fokine's requirements. Costumes were borrowed from other ballets and Diaghilev not only scheduled the work for the end of the season, but indicated it would be the curtain raiser, a decree he eventually changed. Although Fokine had already resigned effective the end of the season, and the company was divided into Fokine/Diaghilev-Nijinsky forces, *Daphnis and Chloë* was finally presented on 5 June with Nijinsky and Karsavina in the title roles and Bolm as Darkon. Fokine himself alternated with Nijinsky in dancing the role for the remainder of the performances.

Both the public and the critical reaction to this work was positive, but a large percentage of its success was probably due to Ravel's score. Played by an orchestra of eighty and sung by a chorus, it was to become a famous piece of music and is probably the reason Diaghilev did not cancel the ballet altogether.

Nijinska, who claims that Fokine was very much aware of what was being done in *L'Après-Midi d'un Faune* and that the dance of Darkon was meant as a travesty of this work, recalls Fokine as strained and tense during this time, often indulging in angry outbursts against Diaghilev. Karsavina describes him as "harried." In spite of this, he created two additional ballets during the spring months of 1912—both with highly acclaimed decor by Bakst, both emphasizing the "exotic" Orient intertwined with sexual passion, and both unsuccessful.

Le Dieu Bleu, to music by Reynaldo Hahn, with a libretto by Jean Cocteau and Frederic de Madrazo, was Fokine's attempt to create dances in the style of India and was influenced by the Siamese dancers he had seen in Paris, and possibly by those who appeared in St. Petersburg earlier in the century. The story concerns a young man who chooses his love rather than the priesthood and how the Blue God (Nijinsky) and Goddess (Karsavina) save them both from death. The sight of Nijinsky appearing at the top of a flight of stairs, which was revealed as an enormous rock split open, was impressive, but neither his dancing nor that of three bayadères and dervishes in white convinced the audience, who did not like Hahn's score either. The ballet was first shown in Paris on 13 May.

Thamar, based on Balakirev's symphonic poem of the same name, was chosen by Diaghilev. Grigoriev says this was dictated by his desire for another ballet on a Russian subject. The story of the twelfth-century Georgian queen Tamara, who entices young men into her castle and, after spending a night with them, has them killed, is reminiscent of *Cléopâtre* and allowed Fokine to reproduce the Caucasian dances first seen in *Prince Igor*. There were warriors in soft boots and women in veils, but nothing especially inspired—due in part, no doubt, to Fokine's depression over Diaghilev's obvious intention to push him out and ease Nijinsky in.

If *Thamar*, first seen on 20 May, was not as much of a failure as *Le Dieu Bleu*, it was hardly a success, and, added to the circumstances surrounding *Daphnis and Chloë*, made Fokine's first departure from the Ballets Russes especially negative. He had choreographed *Islamey* (Balakirev), another Oriental ballet based on *The Arabian Tales*, and *Papillon* (Schumann), a small but charming continuation of *Carnaval*, for a charity performance at the Maryinsky earlier in the year, but he created little after his return to Russia at the end of the summer of 1912 except some dances in two operas. The following year, he choreographed one piece for Ida Rubinstein's company and two for Anna Pavlova's. The latter was still performing the seven-minute *Dying Swan* (Saint-Saëns) that he had spontaneously created for her for a charity performance in 1905, and would do so for decades, making it one of the most famous dances in the world.

Meanwhile, the year 1913 started off as an exciting one for Diaghilev. Now able to choose or create his own choreographers without Fokine's presence, he was planning a new Stravinsky ballet, *Le Sacre de Printemps*, to be choreographed by Nijinsky. The composer had been working on this score since 1910, and Fokine was originally slated as the choreographer. If the previous year had been disastrous for Fokine, this one, with the impact of *Sacre*, which required many hours of rehearsal, had few performances, and was far from a success, ended poorly for Diaghilev. Nijinsky's marriage and subsequent dismissal left Diaghilev with no other choice in 1914 but to ask his former ballet master to return.

Much has been written about this dramatic reconciliation and there are various opinions as to which maestro was more stubborn. Fokine's contract evidently stipulated his return as both choreographer and dancer, gave certain roles to Vera Fokina, and specifically excluded Nijinsky. Whether the latter was Fokine's or Diaghilev's idea is unknown. The impresario was desperate, especially since he had already scheduled one ballet, *La Legende de Joseph*, a vehicle for Nijinsky as both choreographer and performer, and in negotiating contracts for performances he had to have a "name." The other new works in the 1914 repertory of the Ballet Russes were *Papillon*, *Midas*, and *Le Coq d'Or*.

La Legend de Joseph, to Richard Strauss's music, followed a libretto by Hugo von Hofmannsthal and Count Harry Kessler based on the well-known biblical tale of the innocent, pious young man and the greedy, corrupt wife of Potiphar; his spurning of her advances causes his imprisonment and torture, but his devotion causes an archangel to save him. José Maria Sert's plush sets for this work transferred the action to Renaissance Venice and Bakst's costumes (except for Joseph and one or two others) were in the style of the painter Veronese. The work itself was really more of a play with some scattered dances. In the young Leonide Massine, who was making his debut with the Ballets Russes (replacing Nijinsky), Fokine had a good-looking, but not fully trained, dancer, and in Maria Kousnetzova as the wife (a role originally intended for Ida Rubinstein) he had a performer who was more a singer than a dancer.

Joseph was not well received and was criticized for its excessive use of mime. Dame Marie Rambert, a great admirer of Fokine, recalls it as one of his dullest ballets. Benois says the decor was impressive, but the drama was unconvincing, and Massine did not dance well. Fokine was hampered by all of this as well as a poorly planned stage.

Le Coq d'Or was staged as an opera-ballet to Rimsky-Korsakov's suite, with the singers in tiered stands on either side of the stage and the dancers doubling for them and portraying the action. Fokine says he originally suggested this work to Pavlova in 1912, but Benois claims it as his idea. In the end, both did work on it and both were most receptive, as was everyone else, to Nathalie Goncharova's sumptuous decor with its scarlets and yellows depicting everything from a rough palace to a delicate carpet. Vladimir Bielsky's libretto, based on a poem by Pushkin, was a great inspiration to Fokine, who says he loved this work more than any of his other creations.[9] Although *Le Coq d'Or* was the success of the season, and Karsavina, who danced the lead role of the Queen of Shemakhan, recalls it as the most wonderful part she ever performed, Fokine preferred the all-dance version he choreographed in 1937 for de Basil. Gregoriev says it was charming and spontaneous, and Karsavina calls it a "masterpiece." (The second version is discussed in chapter 5.)

Of the other two Fokine works, *Papillon* was presented exactly as the choreographer had mounted it previously in St. Petersburg. *Midas*, a Greek ballet concerning a contest in minstrelsy between Apollo and Pan, had music by Maximilien Steinberg (Rimsky-Korsakov's son-in-law and a friend of Stravinsky), featured Karsavina and Bolm, and, from all reports, was inconsequential. Benois is one of the few who regret the neglect of both of these ballets.

Fokine, completely exhausted from both performing and fulfilling his duties as ballet master, vacationed in Spain after the company completed its London tour and then returned to the Maryinsky, where he was now quite welcome. There are different versions of why Fokine never again worked with Diaghilev. The choreographer maintains that there was a considerable amount of money owed both to him and to Mme Fokina, and that Diaghilev had promised it the next year. Fokine says he refused to go on the American tour of the Ballets Russes in 1916 until this sum was paid. The existence of the debt is probably true. Grigoriev, however, claims that Fokine would not leave Russia in wartime. Otto Kahn, who sponsored the American tour, made a considerable effort to get Fokine to the United States, but was unsuccessful. Diaghilev was probably not greatly concerned, since his own ideas had changed and he was looking for other talents.

Fokine choreographed four ballets for charity performances, one of which, *Sorcerer's Apprentice,* he later remounted in America, and one, *Jota Aragonesa,* for the Maryinsky. He also created dances for the opera *Russlan and Ludmilla.* By the Second Revolution of October 1917, he seems to have been feeling uneasy about living in the midst of a civil war, even though he had been voted into a supposedly secure position at the theater. He therefore accepted an invitation to stage *Petrouchka* at the Royal Theatre in Stockholm.[10] The Fokines eventually settled in Denmark, where Michel Fokine staged large open-air performances and taught extensively. He never again returned to Russia—a decision that affected his life and career.

In all probability, the Diaghilev Ballets Russes could not have existed during its formative seasons without Michel Fokine. It was a fortuitous partnership in history that joined the rebellious traditionalist with the creative dreamers. Diaghilev and his friends found an individual whose artistic beliefs and talents allowed them to see the fruition of their ideas, and Fokine found the perfect outlet for his own creativity. The ballets he choreographed for Diaghilev were sufficient to propel his art and his name into the twentieth century.

Chapter Three

Fokine and the American Popular Theater

Major Broadway Musicals

SINCE HIS ESTRANGEMENT FROM DIAGHILEV closed portions of western Europe to Fokine, and he was obviously not happy in the revolutionary atmosphere of Russia, the United States was a logical place for him to work. In addition, the Fokines had become accustomed to a very high standard of living and the ballet master demanded and received high salaries. There was a great deal of money to be made in America during the 1920s, especially in the area of popular entertainment. Thus the mating of Fokine and Broadway was really not so surprising.

Prior to Fokine's arrival the American public saw most of its dance in vaudeville and musical comedy. It is therefore not unusual that he was hired to create dance for a musical. Although he was fully aware of the nature of the assignment that brought him to this country, Fokine could not have foreseen that the largest part of his contribution to dance in America would be through forms and places accessible to the ordinary citizen, rather than in the opera houses to which he was accustomed.

Anna Pavlova and Adolph Bolm toured the United States in 1920, beginning at the Metropolitan Opera House in New York, and presented *The Dying Swan* and the Bacchanale from *Cléopâtre*. They were so successful that the Met planned to bring the Diaghilev company, but Gertrude Hoffmann beat them to it. In the summer of 1911 this American performer, in her "Saison des Ballets Russes," used Russian dancers who performed unauthorized versions of *Les Sylphides*, *Cléopâtre*, and *Schéhérazade*, with the latter shocking the audience at the Winter Garden Theatre. (Hoffman had seen the Russian dancers in Paris, where she re-

cruited them. Her re-creation of the dances themselves must be attributed
to her own phenomenal visual memory along with some assistance from
the dancers.) In 1915, when Pavlova was on still another tour, she presented *The Seven Daughters of the Ghost King,* which Fokine had created
for her. The Boston critic, H. T. Parker, in reviewing it, noted that all that
had made the Diaghilev Ballet distinctive it owed to Fokine.

When the Ballets Russes finally came to America in 1916 and 1917
there were fourteen ballets in the repertory, eleven of which were Fokine's.
None of the original creators of the roles in his ballets was still in the
company, with the exception of Nijinsky, who danced sporadically in the
1916–17 season, and Fokine himself had not rehearsed the ballets for
several years. In the summer of 1915 advance publicity for the first tour
announced that both Fokines would be appearing. Neither Otto Kahn, a
financial backer of the tour, nor William Guard, the agent he sent to represent him, could persuade the Fokines to join the company. But the public nevertheless saw *Les Sylphides, Carnaval, Cléopâtre, Schéhérazade,
Petrouchka, Firebird,* the Polovtsian Dances from *Prince Igor, Le Spectre
de la Rose, Thamar, Le Pavillon d'Armide,* and *Narcisse.*

Thus when Fokine arrived in this country for the first time, in November 1919, to stage the ballets in the musical *Aphrodite,* he was already
associated, to some degree, with the concept of Oriental splendor. The
American public at the time had comparatively little knowledge of the
East, although it had responded with enthusiasm to what it had seen, notably, apart from the Ballets Russes, Ruth St. Denis and some "exotic"
imitators. This was the beginning of a period of great growth in the American theater, and the extravagance that characterized life during the 1920s
could also be found on Broadway, whose audiences loved extravaganzas
of every sort, particularly exotic Eastern ones. Most of the successful producers were aware of this and were anxious to capitalize on the glamour
of the Fokine name.

Michel Fokine, his wife, Vera Fokina, and their thirteen-year-old son,
Vitale, finally came to this country as a result of successful arrangements
made by the theatrical producer Morris Gest. After two years of negotia-
tions, in competition with other leading producers and managers, Gest
put Fokine under contract. At a salary said to be the highest of any ballet
master in the world, he was to stage the dances for the Broadway musical
Aphrodite, scheduled to open at the Century Theatre in New York on 1
December 1919. The musical had received its first production just prior
to World War I at the Theatre Renaissance in Paris, where Gest had seen
and "coveted" it. The original play by Pierre Frondaie was rewritten for

the New York production by George C. Hazelton, but both men based their work on the well-known, and at one time suppressed, novel by Pierre Louÿs. Staged by E. Lyall Swete, this version had the original music by Henri Fevrier, a French composer known for his operas, and some new scores by Anselm Goetzl, who was also a recognized classical composer, costumes by Joseph and Philip Harker of London, with additional costumes by Leon Bakst, executed in Paris, and choreography by Fokine. The entire production was under Gest's personal supervision.

The opening night audience paid eleven dollars per ticket, and they eagerly anticipated a shocking spectacle, based on their familiarity with the Louÿs novel, what they recalled hearing of the earlier Paris production, and much preopening publicity. Termed "a romance of manners," *Aphrodite* is based on the legend of the statue of Aphrodite by the Greek sculptor Demetrios, which is in the Louvre. It deals with the queen's love for Demetrios and his love for the courtesan Chrysis of Galilee. Demetrios, of ancient Alexandria, worships his statue of the Greek goddess of love to the exclusion of any living female, including Berenike, the young queen of Egypt. But then comes Chrysis, who, before she will accept his love as genuine, requires him to commit three crimes: steal the Rhodopis mirror which once belonged to Sappho and is now owned by Bacchys, a rival courtesan; steal the comb worn by the high priestess of the temple (an act requiring murder); and steal the seven strings of sacred pearls that decorate his own statue of Aphrodite. Demetrios commits the three crimes, then vividly dreams about his statue and the ideals of purity it represents. He awakens, reformed and penitent, repulses Chrysis, and forces her to wear the gifts in public and to pay the inevitable penalty— death.

With a cast of almost 150 performers, the musical was really a pageant that moved continuously from the street to the harbor and to various palaces and gardens, all filled with huge crowds meant to give a sense of Oriental life. The concluding scene, when the crowd surrounds the nude statue of Chrysis perched atop a pedestal, created a furor. Mildred Walker posed as the statue, McKay Morris was Demetrios, Hazel Alden played Berenike, and the silent film star Dorothy Dalton played Chrysis. All of Fokine's ballets occurred in Act II. These included a dance called "Eros, Eros" performed by Theano, one of the votaries of the Temple of Aphrodite, and a male chorus, a full-scale "Bacchanale Ballet," and a solo, "Dance Aphrodasia."

The script of *Aphrodite* describes the dance of Theano, which takes place in the Grove of Aphrodite, as a "supple dance" depicting "an unfortunate love."[1] One review mentions the half-draped male figures moving in and out, but from all available evidence, this interlude, performed by Patterson Dial, served merely to help create the overall atmosphere of the second act. It was followed by a song and a scene, "On the Road to the House of Bacchys." This scene, in the script, is all movement and describes different groups—mannequins, courtiers, city beauties, girls carried by female slaves, horses, Negro torch bearers—coming and going, "Pirouetting and Posturing," to the accompaniment of a bacchanalian song. But all of this was really a preparation for the next scene, which the *New York Dramatic Mirror* described as "the height of the spectacle . . . a ballet superb in its bacchanalian suggestions, which was danced on a floor of rose leaves." This was the Bacchanale Ballet—the reason that Gest had brought Fokine to America.

The script calls for thirty-four dancers, with an additional eighty-two performers on stage. The dancers are "crouched on the floor," covered with rose petals, so that when they spring into their dance "the air is full of rose petals." The script also notes that "voluptuous music dominates the senses" for this ballet.

The setting for the Bacchanale to music by Moussorgsky consisted of a semi-circular raised platform that ran the entire length of the upstage area and a little more than halfway downstage. The platform was probably six to eight feet deep, and six large pillars were spaced equally along its length. Most of the dancing took place on the stage floor in front of the platform. All of the dancers were women with long flowing hair, all were bare legged, and all were dressed in jeweled tops that left the midriff bare, and fairly short skirts (at or above the knee). These costumes were not, as might be expected, designed by Leon Bakst, but by a Miss Alice O'Neil.

The motivation behind this ballet was simply that of revelry and hedonism, which, through continuous movement from statuesque pose to graceful grouping, built in intensity and frenzy until most of the dancers lay strewn on the petal-covered floor and the "spectators" on the platform looked exhausted by the orgy.

Most of the dance was performed with the legs in a natural position, neither turned out in the technical ballet stance nor parallel. Arms and hands were also very natural, the arms often raised upward and slightly to the side, with the head and upper back following in an upward, arched line. Fokine made use of the floor, where he had the dancers lying (either posed or moving), sitting half reclining on one hip, and kneeling. One frequently seen position had a dancer on her knees with her back arched and her arms stretched until they touched the floor. This was usually shown in profile and sometimes the arms were folded across the chest, or one arm framed the face or head. Much of the standing movement was performed either on half toe or ended there, and the two most commonly used leg gestures were a low arabesque and a low back attitude.

The photographs indicate many different groupings and poses in the Bacchanale, giving the impression of constantly moving tableaux. Some show two women stage center facing each other in profile surrounded by the other dancers, who were either kneeling or half reclining. In one pose their heads are lowered, their foreheads are touching, and they are grasping each other at the shoulders.

The dancers are frequently seen divided into three different groups, some facing downstage in a semicircle, others arranged in a circle facing inward. Dancers, singly or in pairs or trios, often look upstage toward those on the platform. In one instance there are six groups of three dancers each spaced around the stage, with the middle dancer in each group leaning backward on the crossed arms of the other two. There are always several different levels indicated at the same time. One pose resembles a rising fountain: there are four women upstage center in a diamond formation, with the downstage dancers in a backbend toward the audience, and the two on either side gesturing toward the fourth, who is reaching upward.

The "Feast of Bacchys" ended with the "Dance of Aphrodasia" to music by Glazounov. This solo, performed by "Mlle Dazie," began when an ostrich was carried onstage on a litter and she emerged from it, wearing a short draped feathery skirt and matching bra, with arms outstretched and body and head arched upward. Her dance, which evoked stares from the ensemble gathered on and in front of the raised platform, included several hip thrusts in which the upper body, head, and arms all followed in a curving line. This dance built to a sensual climax, toward the end of which Chrysis was accused of stealing the mirror of Bacchys and was crucified on stage. During the crucifixion she was actually attached to a long rectangular board in the center of the raised platform.

The press generally agreed that *Aphrodite* was a spectacular pageant, in which all the arts had been called upon, as Louis P. Reid in the *New York Dramatic Mirror* noted, "to decorate this decadent tale out of Egypt." The consensus was that it was gorgeous, but, if not for the costumes and dances, boring. Many agreed with Alan Dale, critic for the *New York Journal,* that it was indecent and irrelevant, which may explain why it was a box-office success for the remainder of the season. Kenneth Macgowan in the *Commercial Advertiser,* observed that "rarely, if ever, in the history of the American stage has so much energy and money brought forth so little of true art." Calling the production a mixture of faults and virtues, he said that Fokine was the one unquestionable touch of genius, although he did not find the dances to be in either Fokine's best or newest manner.

Most of the critics, however, thought Fokine's Bacchanale a superb ballet and the highpoint of the show. Alexander Woollcott of the *Times*, who found the production a mixture of beauty and circus, said that "the beauty [of the ballet] makes you swoon." The *Boston Sunday Post* ran a feature article that called Fokine a genius and speculated that he would discover a potential Pavlova among the American girls in the cast. Fokine later wrote that when he first auditioned the dancers for *Aphrodite* he could not use one out of fifty, because "they didn't know the first principles of how to model the body." After a week of rehearsing, "the girls who were acceptable were black and blue and tired out," but they had found the secret, which was a body that was off center and had curves, but never any right angles.[2]

Aphrodite toured the United States successfully during the season after it opened, but it received nationwide press coverage immediately, not because of the lavishness of the production but because Mayor Hylan of New York asked the License and Police departments to investigate it for being offensive to the public taste. The bared bodies and naked statue made headlines across America. Although some felt it was pure pornography, one reporter noted that there was as much bareness in the audience as on stage, and pointed out that the pinnacle on which the "naked" Chrysis stood was very high and cut off from the view of the audience by a draped curtain. There were enough changes, however, so that on 3 December the *New York American*'s headline read "Aphrodite Made Clean Spectacle."

Fokine was quite accustomed to shocking the public and the press, and it is not surprising that many compared the Bacchanale to his earlier *Schéhérazade*, which was also opulent in set and decor, seductive in atmosphere, and at times sadistic in its explicitness. But he himself very carefully stressed that art was the manifestation of the spirit, and that the aim of the dance was to approach perfection in its beauty.[3] There is a story about his admonition to the dancers in *Schéhérazade* that the men were never to be on top of the women, only next to them. Once, when he saw this rule broken on stage, he rushed behind the scrim in a fury, grabbed the offending boy by the ankle, and dragged him off stage.[4]

Although most notices were favorable, one reviewer felt that the producers had learned nothing from the Russian Ballet, that the show was dull and the Bacchanale ineffective in great part because of the stodgy set. He concluded that "remembering *Schéhérazade,* this orgy scene is particularly flat."[5] Sol Hurok in *S. Hurok Presents* observed that, although it was a great success, *Aphrodite* was not a very good musical, the Bacchanale was not really very exciting, and Fokine was far from happy with it.

After *Aphrodite* opened, Fokine stayed in the United States to fulfill several performance commitments, beginning with one at the Metropolitan Opera House in New York City with his wife on 31 December 1919. Gest then asked him to remain to choreograph the next Comstock and Gest musical, *Mecca,* which opened 4 October 1920, at the Century Theatre. If *Aphrodite* was spectacular, this new effort was to be extraordinary. Gest started the publicity in June 1920, in the *Telegraph,* noting the 13 scenes, 175 stage hands, and 400 in the company, and adding that "I do not believe I will ever attempt such a colossal undertaking again." He did not say that the production would cost somewhere between fifty and sixty thousand dollars, a huge sum for the time, or that part of this cost was the thousand dollars per day he was paying Fokine.

Mecca had a book by Oscar Ashe, author of a previous hit, *Chu, Chin, Chow* (1917), which was also set in the Orient, and music by Percy Fletcher. Like *Aphrodite,* it was staged by E. Lyall Swete. Sets were by Joseph and Philip Harker, and costumes by Percy Anderson, with collaboration by Leon Bakst. The plot, a love story, takes place in ancient Egypt and Arabia. It tells of a Sultan who loves a beggar maid and of the evil plots of a Prince to separate him from his bride and his throne. It involves Chinese spies, dancing girls, Ali Shar, a giant wrestler from Bagdad, and his pilgrimage to Mecca, and hundreds of people in what was basically a pageant of the exotic East. Orville R. Caldwell was the Sultan, Hannah Toback the beggar maid, Gladys Hanson the Prince's sister, and Lional Braham played Ali Shar. The forty-eight female and twelve male dancers were led by Martha Lorber, who had been one of the dancers in *Aphrodite.* (Gest had brought her to Fokine with the warning that he might not consider her because she was an American; she became one of his favorite students.)

There were dances in Act I and a "dance poem" in the first scene of Act II, with no choreographic credit given. But the dance focus of *Mecca* was in the third scene of Act II. Here Fokine choreographed a processional and ballet, "Memories of the Past," which was followed by the Bacchanale that ended the act and was the climax of the show. Both dances took place on a huge flight of steps, which represented the outside of an ancient moss-green Egyptian palace, lit by flaring pink torches.

"Memories of the Past" was introduced by the command "Let my dancers, rousing these stories to life with passionate feet and robed in robes of old bring back some memories of the storied past."[6] The five leading female dancers in this piece portrayed Isis, Goddess of Love, Plaintive Love, Combative Love, Jealous Love, and Triumphant Love, the last danced by Martha Lorber. They were joined by two Arabian groups and a number of Egyptians. Described as containing "lovely movement" and "graceful pantomime," the dance seems merely to have been a celebration of the goddess of love that prepared the audience for the next ballet, the Bacchanale.

At the beginning of the Bacchanale, the script called for the dancers to rush on from various entrances and engage in a wild orgy. The clearest summary was given by the critic Burns Mantle. After describing the stairs, which rose twenty or thirty feet toward the pillared backdrop, a moon above the horizon, and the villain seated on a dozen silk pillows, he wrote:

> The ballet enters on the top flight of steps and proceeds rhythmically toward the bottom. Pretty maidens, not more than a quarter clothed, as was the way in Egypt. . . . Down the steps they advance by fours and eights and sixteens. . . . The boys come out to meet them and there is a wild bacchanale.
>
> In the mixings of the dance there is an ordered but seemingly abandoned promiscuity. There are wild pirouettings. And finally there is the grand finale with the exhausted dancers falling wherever the falling is softest.[7]

The dance groupings and poses in *Mecca* are very much like those in *Aphrodite,* and in photographs it is quite easy to confuse one with the other. Even the costumes are similar. All of the dancers in *Mecca* are barefoot, and their lying, kneeling, and half-reclining positions are reminiscent of the earlier musical. *Mecca,* however, seems to have more two-dimensional movement, which often shows the dancers in profile. Upraised arms with upper back arch, full backbends from a kneeling position, and side tilts led by the hip are all present. There are also circle formations with everyone facing inward, reaching upward, and rising on one or both feet, often with several dancers in the center. The fountainlike grouping of four dancers stage center, with others lying or half-reclining around them, is the same as in *Aphrodite.* It is impossible to reconstruct the floor patterns or time sequences in relation to the music.

What does appear different in *Mecca* is the fact that in many of the poses and larger groupings the bodies are so sculpted and intermingled that it is difficult to tell where one ends and another begins. Also, the

The Bacchanale in *Mecca. Courtesy Billy Rose Theatre Collection, The New York Public Library at Lincoln Center, Astor, Lenox, and Tilden Foundations.*

dances, which were fast-paced and furious, were performed on the stairs, which allowed Fokine to break up the horizontal movement with vertical. In addition, his dancers themselves were on all levels, and when they were on their backs and stomachs their arms and legs were still moving.

Martha Lorber and Serge Pernikoff, the leading dancers, were featured in a duet. The most famous photograph of this pair shows her head hanging downward over a balustrade, with her hair loosely flowing about it, with him lying next to her and looking down into her face. According to a later account, the other dancers showered her with rose leaves at this point.[8] One pose shows them side by side, one of his arms circling her waist, the other holding a wine cup, while she holds a sword in her raised arms. He is seen in another photograph supporting her while she does a backbend, feet off the floor and hair touching it. In several other photographs they are on different levels—one kneeling, the other standing. Her costume, of a fabric that resembles fishnet, is really a two-piece bathing suit with a very short sheer skirt, plus a long train that he is pulling off in one photograph. His costume consists of jeweled shorts and an abbreviated top, a headband, and armbands.

The critics regarded *Mecca* as what it was—an extravagant Oriental spectacle that employed an amalgam of Arabian Nights stories, old familiar melodies, and magnificent scenery and costumes, illuminated by the imaginative genius of Morris Gest and Michel Fokine. Burns Mantle acknowledged that it was the biggest thing in the way of spectacle America had ever seen. Weed Dickinson in the *Telegraph* recalled a bit of alleged nudity in *Aphrodite* that had brought in the mayor, and noted the acceptance one year after of the "gorgeous, barbaric nakedness" of *Mecca*. A later historian wrote that it "pleased the Hippodrome–Radio City Music Hall mentality and ran for five months."[9] Even the critics who did not like the musical singled out the Fokine ballets for praise. Alan Dale said that the settings and accessories were gorgeous, the story and dialogue terrible, and the theater too dark to read the synopsis of the plot, but that the "admirably arranged" Bacchanale was "riotously provocative," and seemed to capture the audience. *Theatre Magazine* called the sensational dancing of the corps de ballet all there was to the spectacle, and the Bacchanale a "terpsichorean orgy danced by half a hundred naked men and women" which was "gorgeous, magnificent, superb."[10] Heywood Broun, writing in the *Tribune*, said the chief credit should go to Fokine; the Bacchanale was the most striking incident in the performance.

Several writers noted that the audience stood up and cheered at the close of Act II, and that the most applause at the final curtain calls went to Fokine. A reporter for the *Kansas City Post* wrote that Fokine had created the most brilliant stage spectacle witnessed in New York in a decade, and the consensus was that the Russian was a genius who had introduced an element of great art into what was otherwise just an extravaganza.

This belief in the artistic validity of Fokine's work countered thoughts that there was anything indecent about the half-naked men and women who moved about the stage. The beauty of the Bacchanale struck all who witnessed it, and they especially noted the passion, which was evoked with much discretion and without vulgarity. Reid, in the *New York Dramatic Mirror,* wrote that it "took one's breath in its startling eroticism, its sensuousness, its spontaneity. It was more than a fleshly riot. It was a fleshly revolution, at the end of which all participants had succumbed."

In an unidentified newspaper article published the day before the opening, Fokine was quoted as saying that he regarded his ballet in *Mecca* as his most important work since *Schéhérazade.* This may well have been merely a publicist's exaggeration but others made comparisons to the Diaghilev ballet. With the exception of Burns Mantle, most reviewers felt that Fokine had outdone his previous effort in a musical, and in the process had brought that form of popular entertainment to new heights.

Fokine's two soloists, Martha Lorber and Serge Pernikoff, were dancers whose training (or perhaps their talent plus his coaching) placed them on a level that was higher than most Broadway dancers. Gest, watching Fokine at a rehearsal, was quoted as saying that he thought the Imperial Ballet School in Petrograd had been lifted bodily and brought across the Atlantic.

In an interview in the *New York World* after the show had opened, Fokine was questioned about the young and untrained American women he had used. He answered that he considered them fresh material and that he had choreographed with their abilities in mind. He also said that he had tried to describe the different moods of love, adding, "I'm afraid Americans will consider me a specialist in bacchanales. I've staged about 1,000 of them, but this one has a reason—the ecstasies of love, the intoxication . . . what better subject may be attempted by a choreographer?" *Mecca,* like *Aphrodite,* toured America after its Broadway season, and Fokine, his ballets, and the American dancers were lavishly publicized and praised throughout the country.

When the Shuberts opened a new theater on 11 February 1921—the Ambassador on West 49th Street—their presentation was *The Rose Girl,* a musical in two acts with music by Anselm Goetzl, book and lyrics by William Carey Duncan, and sets by William Weaver. The production was under the overall direction of Lee Shubert and starred Charles Purcell, plus the ballerina Lydia Lopokova in a special ballet conceived and staged by Fokine.

The plot, with scenes on the Riviera and in Paris, concerns a country girl who wishes to be an opera star and is helped by a wealthy widow, meets a count whose intentions are less than honorable, falls in love with the count's nephew, and ends up in the rose gardens of a perfume firm.

Preopening publicity put great emphasis on the dance featuring Lopokova, brought over from Europe to lend "motive and power" to the production in a ballet that was one of the few things reviewers found commendable. *The Rose Girl*, which ran for fourteen weeks in New York and then toured, seems to have had an ordinary book, unoriginal if tuneful songs, and a cast of variable talent. It was all fashioned in the old comic opera mold and was a poor first tenant for the "costliest, handsomest, and best appointed playhouse yet built by the Messrs. Shubert."[11]

The Shuberts must have realized this fact since Fokine, whose name was not mentioned in the early advertisements, was brought in roughly two weeks before the opening—which had to be put off a day because more dressing rooms were needed to accommodate the members of the Fokine company. The dance, "The Ballet of Perfumes," used the music of Johannes Brahms, to which Lopokova danced, and a song entitled "Some Day" by Anselm Goetzl. It opened the second act, but little information about it is available with the exception of its length—approximately seven minutes—and the fact that eight of the twelve ensemble dancers ascended and descended by means of traps in the stage. One reviewer also mentioned that the dancers were "charmingly" divided into three groups, and that each was "admirably posed."

It was the almost unanimous opinion of the critics, however, that this ballet was injected into a plot to which it bore no relationship. Although many considered the interruption to be the chief appeal of *The Rose Girl*, others were disappointed by both the choreography and Lopokova's performance. The *Sun* suggested that its readers drop in to see the ballet, a "jewel" with Lopokova as a "central brilliance," but warned that the musical did not rank high as entertainment. The *World* noted the new musical and its distinctive ballet, but ended by saying it was the theater itself that chiefly arrested attention.

Lopokova, who had been seen five years earlier as a star of the Ballets Russes, was a disappointment. It was not because she was any less of a dancer, but because, as Alexander Woollcott suggested, she was presented as a ballet artist amid alien surroundings. The producers were chastised for forgetting that the story of a musical play is as important as the decor, and Fokine for the obvious and old-fashioned business of raising and lowering the dancers through the trap door, which Heywood Broun in the *New York Tribune* said suggested "a group of unlucky pedestrians caught on top of a freight elevator." The *Dramatic Mirror and Theater World* critic, who felt that the ballet was tiny but charming, was surprised at how Fokine could do such fine things with untrained American girls "who did not look so bad, even behind Lopokova."

If some of the critics found the ballerina's dancing unsure and nervous, and Fokine's ballet without a clearly defined point of view, this could have been because they were brought in at the last minute, probably in an attempt to upgrade the show. In March 1921, when *The Rose Girl* was on tour at the Garrick Theatre in Philadelphia, Lee Shubert was advised that Lopokova "agreed" to leave the show and that permission was requested to cut out the Fokine ballet and to put in its place a stick dance performed by Rose Rolando. (Miss Rolando, a member of the original cast, performed a dance in the first act and had received good notices and was reported as receiving the most spontaneous audience approval of any performer.)[12]

This final action on the part of the Shuberts could be interpreted as acknowledgment that the dance truly did not bear any relationship to the overall production and did not succeed in glamorizing the second act. Many years later Fokine cited the ballet in *The Rose Girl* as one of those he would like to forget.[13]

Charles Dillingham had taken over the huge, 5,697-seat Hippodrome from the Shuberts in 1915, and by presenting variety bills featuring stars from all levels of entertainment had made it tremendously successful. He hired both the Fokines to dance in a ballet for his revue, *Get Together,* which opened 3 September 1921. Michel Fokine was hired to choreograph it.

The ballet *Thunderbird* was the fifth and closing scene of the first act. Appearing in two shows a day, it was performed almost four hundred times, although the Fokines were not in every performance, being replaced by understudies, and by November were not appearing at all. The revue also featured elephants, dogs, a crow, comedians, and an ice ballet entitled *The Red Shoes.* Incidental to *Thunderbird,* but interesting in itself, is the fact that when the Fokines arrived on the Mauretania in July, immigration officials would not permit them to land. The Russian quota had been reached and it took Dillingham several days to get them ashore.

Vera Fokina as the Thunderbird in *Thunderbird. Courtesy Phyllis Fokine Archive.*

The book for *Thunderbird* was attributed to Vera Fokina, the scenery and costumes were by Willy Pogany, and the music was by Balakirev, Borodin, Rimsky-Korsakov, and Tchaikovsky. The story, linked to an ancient Aztec legend, begins with Aztec warriors performing ritual dances around a fire after a successful hunt. A storm arises and a flock of thunderbirds, led by Nahua, a Toltec Princess whom a wicked magician has made into a bird, appear. Aztlan, the Aztec chief, falls in love with Nahua, and tries to catch her. She is caught by a golden tree and Aztlan, going toward her, is temporarily turned into a stone by her beauty. The other warriors, hearing piercing bird cries, start to shoot the birds with bows and arrows, and Aztlan, throwing himself in front of Nahua to protect her, is mortally wounded. But the tree begins to blossom, releasing her, and she performs a healing dance to save him. The Master of Mystic Forces unites them, after which the tribe greets them with an Aztec war dance.

The large cast of thunderbirds, wizards, warriors, Aztec wives, Aztec girls, bears, tigers, and others featured Vera Fokina as both Nahua and the Thunderbird, Michel Fokine as Aztlan, and Earl Barroy as the Master of Mystic Forces. The corps was led by Albertina Vitak and included Desha.

Photographs in the Hippodrome souvenir program show several of the "members of the Fokine Ballet Corps," as well as the Fokines. One picture of Mme Fokina shows her in pointe shoes, posed in a classical attitude devant, and others barefoot and in playful poses. These photographs, as well as many others of the company, permit the speculation that the female dancers, when they were birds, wore classical pointe shoes and when they were Aztecs did not. Paul Trueman, who was both a thunderbird and an Aztec girl, recalls that they begged the management for weeks for new pointe shoes and when they finally arrived they had cement boxes!

The most revealing record of this ballet is a photograph labeled "Dance of the Enchanted Birds." Here Fokina is surrounded by a large circle, made slightly oval in its spread across the stage, and composed of twenty-three members of the corps. Fokine regards her from an upstage position outside the circle. Another version of what appears to be the same section shows the corps in a zigzag pattern across the entire stage, with the dancers in groups of threes and fours.

At first glance, one almost might think that this was a scene from *Swan Lake*. All the women are wearing pointe shoes and their costumes are based on the classical tutu. Princess Nahua's costume includes an elongated bodice to the hipline and is covered with blue and white beads. The skirt, which ends just above the knees, is embellished with white feathers.

Her large headpiece, also made of feathers, has hanging pieces embroidered with beads and resembles an American Indian headdress, with a slight suggestion of *The Dying Swan*. The corps also wears white tutus and their headpieces, of white feathers just covering the earlobe, are reminiscent of *Swan Lake* and *Dying Swan*. Aztlan's costume is a one-piece tunic that ends at midthigh and has short sleeves. His legs are bare and on his feet are soft slippers, the back of which continues a short distance up his calf before lacing. On his head is a band with a feather.

Although one critic praised *Thunderbird* as an exquisitely beautiful ballet, and the *World* called Fokina a "wild and free thing," the sight of whom "would probably turn Pavlova green with envy," other critics devoted most of their space to revealing the story. Alan Dale's report, which centered on a "multi-colored ballet" that "littered" the Hippodrome stage and ended with a description of Aztec warriors around sacrificial fires, could be considered tongue in cheek. Alexander Woollcott called it "pretentious," although noting that the early scenes were charming. He added that Fokina was lovely to look at, if not startling as a dancer, but concluded that, on the whole, the ballet was a bore and suffered badly in comparison to the ice ballet that ended the second act. Others considered the two ballets (Fokine's and the one on ice) the "hits" of the revue, and compared Fokine's contribution favorably to his work in *Aphrodite* and *Mecca*. In many cases, however, his dancing and eloquent pantomime fared better than his choreography, which was considered by many to be too diffuse and a weak reflection of his earlier work, notably *Firebrid*. A report that Mme Fokina "had an opportunity to reveal again the fluttering bird-like movement of her dance of 'The Dying Swan'" underscored the comparison to that ballet.[14] *Swan Lake* was not mentioned in the press, although the association is instantaneous. The anachronism of an Aztec legend set to traditional Russian music was not belabored either.

Miss Trueman says that all the dancers knew that what they were doing was an old Russian ballet reworked. The libretto, which one critic referred to as being "gallantly attributed" to Mme Fokina, seems to have been a mixture of *Firebird, Swan Lake,* and *Dying Swan,* plus several Russian folk tales, all placed in the mold of a South American Indian setting. Sol Hurok later referred to it as a "pseudo-Aztec affair," set to a musical "pastiche."

The sixteenth *Ziegfeld Follies* opened in the New Amsterdam Theatre on 5 June 1922, and ran well into 1923, with sixty-seven weeks in New York City and forty on the road. Staged by Ned Wayburn, it had a book

The corps de ballet of *Thunderbird,* stage right, with Vera Fokina at the extreme right, which was really stage center. *Courtesy Dance Collection, The New York Public Library at Lincoln Center, Astor, Lenox, and Tilden Foundations.*

by Ring Lardner and Ralph Spence. Among the principals were Will Rogers, Gilda Gray, Evelyn Law, the Tiller Girls from England, and the comedy team of Gallagher and Shean. This version, which was called the "pinnacle" of Follies productions, cost $300,000 to stage, with $67,000 alone spent on tryout revisions. Although dance had always been a part of the Follies, the 1922 edition really represented the first time that ballet was noticeably present. Fokine's two contributions, *Frolicking Gods* and *Farljandio,* received a great deal of publicity and attention, and were generally hailed as daring.

Frolicking Gods was the twelfth scene in the first act, and was danced to Tchaikovksy's *Nutcracker Suite.* The story is set in a Paris museum of art in 1851 and involves a pair of lovers who lose their way and are accidentally locked inside. The familiar tale of marble statues that come to life and enjoy themselves when not seen by visitors become a reality. The statues, displaying what one newspaper called "an occasional scantiness of attire," come down off their pedestals, and involve the lovers in their rollicking dance. A guard hears noises in the museum, finds the lovers undressed like ancient Greeks, and takes them to the police. The *Evening Telegram* described Martha Lorber, who danced the girl, as having her finery stripped from her, and labeled the ballet "an intoxicating Bacchanale." Another critic suggested that it was her beauty alone that thrilled the statues to life.

Serge Pernikoff was the boy, and among the cast of thirty-two was Nellie Savage as one of the Three Graces and Albertina Vitak as a Bacchante. There were also Caryatides, two Fauns, a Satyr, two Hermes, an Apollo,

The corps de Ballet of *Thunderbird*, stage left, with Michel Fokine as Aztlan behind the fourth girl on the right. *Courtesy Dance Collection, The New York Public Library at Lincoln Center, Astor, Lenox, and Tilden Foundations.*

Venus, Hercules, an Amazon, and various muses and menades. From reports and available photographs it is clear that this was a lighthearted ballet, choreographed from a slightly satirical point of view. The statues started off standing on their pedestals, posed both as classical Greek statuary and eighteenth-century figurines, showing once again Fokine's eye for capturing a gesture in stillness. After they descended from their bases, they made full use of the stage. In one instance, a dancer is seen lying on the floor, with one leg crossed over the other. Several dancers are half reclining on the floor, a couple is seen hanging backward over a pedestal, and there is at least one example of a man supporting a woman while she is arched in a full backbend. One photograph in particular recalls *L'Après-Midi d'un Faune*, which is not surprising, since many of the statues were Greek and the characters included two fauns.

The scenery was designed by Joseph Urban and the costumes by James Reynolds, who also conceived and designed the ballet that opened the second act, *Farljandio*. This title may be translated as "revenge," and the ballet, set to music by Victor Herbert, who also conducted the orchestra, takes place in the mountain town of Accio, "a haunt of the Gypsies." The show is built around the "Dance of Allure," which, according to program notes, existed in the tenth century and is still danced by Gypsy brides at their weddings.

This ballet, evidently filled with life and color, was vivid in a tragic Sicilian sense and included an abduction. One report described it as "a convulsive dance, ending in the usual Sicilian death leap." Another called it a "divertissement with Russian dressing."[15] Martha Lorber danced the

role of Arijo, the bride; John Scott was Beppo, the groom; and Serge Pernikoff was Gino, a rival. There was a jilted lover, and Albertina Vitak and
Nellie Savage were the solo dancers in a cast of thirty-three.

The scenery was a painted backdrop representing Gypsy caves and the
costumes resembled authentic Sicilian dress. The women were seen wearing long, almost ankle-length skirts, and many of the men wore big hats
along with vests and knee-length breeches. *Vogue* described the costumes
as being of "preposterous loveliness." The different groupings involve several variations on the semicircle, including one akin to that seen in many
classical ballets in which solos and duets alternate with dances by the entire group. The corps is seen on different levels—standing, kneeling, and
sitting. One scene shows a man on one knee, with his arms outstretched
toward one of the women in the group, and in another we see a couple
on the ground.

The collaboration of the artist James Reynolds on both of these ballets
indicates the importance that Ziegfeld attached to them. Reynolds had
left John Murray Anderson to work on the Follies, and his sense of style
and color in both costumes and decor was greatly admired. Although he
was responsible for the costumes only in *Frolicking Gods,* which in their
delicate coloring and wispy feeling suggested nakedness, *Farljandio* was
his idea completely, and his designs for this dance were vivid and earthy.
Heywood Broun said that *Farljandio* was not well danced. (He thought
that *Frolicking Gods* was one of the best things of that sort Ziegfeld had
ever done.) He commented on the contrast between the gorgeous shawl
worn by the bride while she danced with the groom and the dark silhou-
ette of his rival in the background.

The critics were generally impressed with the beauty and artistry of
both ballets, and most agreed with the *Evening Globe* that they made the
sixteenth Follies "the most exciting and fantastic of the series." The gods
were considered charming and delicately eerie, and the gypsies were compared to the best of the Ballets Russes. Yet, although Martha Lorber
was cited over and over for her beauty and talent, several reviewers felt
that the Tiller Girls, from England, far outdanced their American
counterparts.

Fokine was only too well aware of this lack of serious training in American dancers, a subject he publicly discussed with frequency. Ten years
after the Follies, in 1932, in an article entitled "Sex Appeal in Dance" he
stressed that sex is not the basic raison d'être of the dance. He said that
the Follies girls were always divided into two groups, one that had to
work hard and possess knowledge and talent; the other, the show girls,

that needed only sex appeal. He worked with the former group, although no amount of work and talent could make up for the missing technique, which it was too late to teach.

Six years passed before Fokine choreographed another musical entertainment on Broadway. The level of musical theater had been steadily rising during the 1920s, and the 1927–28 season was particularly noteworthy, with such shows as *Good News, Sidewalks of New York,* and *Funny Face.* It is perhaps for this reason that *Rosalie,* starring Marilyn Miller, was regarded as only a slight attraction. *Variety* (18 January 1928) dubbed it a production "that reminds one of the yesteryear Shubertian musicals," and did not even mention Fokine, who also did not receive masthead billing in the program.

Produced by Florenz Ziegfeld, it had music by George Gershwin and Sigmund Romberg, a book by William McGuire and Guy Bolton, lyrics by P. G. Wodehouse and Ira Gershwin, and it opened at the New Amsterdam Theatre on 10 January 1928. Charles Dillingham was one of the directors of the theater at the time.

The story, told in two acts and eleven scenes, concerns Romanza, a kingdom in Eastern Europe. Two American aviators, one played by Jack Donahue, find themselves in this tiny principality, which resembles Hapsburgian Vienna. Mr. Donahue falls in love with Princess Rosalie, played by Marilyn Miller. By means of various contrivances, the royal party, after a trip on the S.S. *Ile de France,* comes to West Point, where Mr. Donahue is a cadet officer. Here marches are staged in front of the barracks, Academy rules broken, lovers-lane meetings are arranged, and there is an infiltration of the cadet ranks by Miss Miller in disguise. Finally, in Paris, the lovers are united in the ballroom of the Club of Ex-Kings, and Rosalie dances in the "Ballet of Flowers," arranged by Fokine.

This ballet, to music that is unidentified on the program, took place in a lavish red and gold setting of candles and tall narrow arches. The *Sun* mentioned "an exquisite glade of crystal" in relation to the evening's dance climax, probably referring to the tableaux of the Goddesses of Crystal, which Fokine created to precede the actual ballet. There were nine goddesses, representing Ancient Crystal, as well as Crystal Flowers, Jewels, Mirrors, Braid, Fringe, Wings, Mosaics, and Stained Glass. The "Ballet of Flowers," in which Miss Miller, assisted by the ensemble, was required to perform in classical technique, was scarcely reported in the press.

Billboard deemed the fair Miller at her best in the Fokine ballet and the general feeling expressed was that this was an elegant ballet in an especially elegant setting. In fact, Joseph Urban's sets received as much attention as any other aspect of this production.

Other Productions On Broadway and Off

Starting in 1921 Fokine spread his talent and influence further still by choreographing minor productions on and off Broadway, by arranging dances for established popular entertainers, as well as for numerous charity balls and society functions, and by creating incidental dances for major plays. In many cases it is difficult to determine what was a fresh creation and what was a reworking of an older project. To whatever he turned his attention, though, Fokine brought his authority as an acknowledged master of innovative choreography and the inheritor of the Imperial Russian ballet tradition.

Gertrude Hoffmann, the dancer and, later, choreographer, who, with her Hoffmann Girls, had performed all over the world, had already crossed paths with Michel Fokine many times. She originally achieved notoriety for her "Dance of the Seven Veils" and was involved in a famous lawsuit in which she was accused of imitating and stealing from the dancer Maude Allan—and indeed she did! But her most flagrant plagiarism occurred in June 1911, when, under the auspices of Comstock and Gest, she presented a "Saison de Ballets Russes" that included *Les Sylphides, Cléopâtre, Schéhérazade, Carnaval, Prince Igor,* and *Firebird,* with no credit given to Fokine or anyone else.

During the first week of October 1921, Gertrude Hoffmann and her American Ballet were allotted forty-five minutes on the bill at B. F. Keith's Palace Theatre in New York. With three dances choreographed by Fokine, they were the hit of the program. The three ballets by Fokine were a *Mazurka,* the *Pas Espagnol,* and a work called *Shayton's Captive.*[16]

Shayton's Captive, the opening number of Miss Hoffman's program, to music by Glazounov (from "Raymonda"), is yet another Oriental tale. It is the story of an Evil Spirit (Shayton) who brings the Sheik's favorite from the harem, chained in a huge jewel box. In a dance of "mad abandon" she tricks her captor, and locks him in the trunk before joyously escaping. During the dance, Shayton whips the already scantily clad captive (Zeralda) and tears off her clothes.[17]

Variety (7 October 1921) called the entire act the best Hoffmann had ever given vaudeville, and most other reviewers concurred, not forgetting to give Fokine a share of the credit. *Zit's Weekly News* (8 October 1921) noted that the *Mazurka* was arranged by Fokine ("and everyone knows who he is") and said that *Shayton's Captive* was "the most gorgeous dancing pantomime that has been introduced in years." When Hoffman toured her act on the Keith circuit throughout the country she and Fokine continued to receive praise. The *St. Louis Star* (8 November 1921), commenting on the choreographer's "handiwork," said that *Shayton's Captive* "reminds one of the Bacchanalian revels in the Morris Gest spectacles."

The publicity for Hoffmann's act stressed the fact that all of her dancers were American, that she wished to establish an "American Ballet Company," and that E. F. Albee had pledged his support to this idea. As she toured the large cities of the East and Midwest, Hoffmann auditioned local dancers for the American Ballet.

Fokine sent a telegram to Keith, congratulating him on the idea for an American ballet, and saying that, due to the chaotic conditions in Russia, America had become the home of concert and operatic arts and could become the home of ballet. He added that his recent tours had convinced him that Keith was doing "a great service to the art world" and ended by saying, "Please convey to Miss Hoffmann my congratulations and best wishes for the success of her work. I am glad that an American has been chosen to head this first all-American Ballet." One newspaper, commenting on Miss Hoffmann's concept, observed, "It is true, however, that if her company is all-American, Miss Hoffmann has had the assistance of one of the greatest Russian masters of the dance."[18]

She had his assistance again in 1923 in the musical revue *Hello Everybody*, which appeared in Shubert theaters throughout the country, commencing at the Shubert Crescent in Brooklyn on 8 January. Max Hoffmann, Gertrude's husband, wrote some of the songs and conducted the orchestra, as he always did for her and as he frequently did for other productions with which Fokine was involved.

There were four ballets by Fokine in *Hello Everybody* as it originally opened. (When the revue was on the road it often underwent changes and sometimes one of the ballets was eliminated.) The four works were a waltz to "Blue Danube" (Strauss), a Russian Dance, an Apache Dance, and something listed as "Sylphide" but probably a version of *Les Sylphides*.

Whether the waltz, a solo for Miss Hoffmann, was the one to which Fokine referred on his list of ballets to be forgotten is not known. But it was not listed on the program for the performances in Newark. Hoffmann did have another ballet solo to Sousa's "Stars and Stripes," which was created by Adolph Bolm, and it is possible that she felt it necessary to lessen her own already heavy performance load. The Apache Dance, featuring Hoffmann and Willie Lander, to music by Max Hoffmann, was, according to the *Newark Star Eagle* (23 January 1923), typical of its genre: "A creation of Michel Fokine is the dark, dank, throbbing murder under the bridge on the Seine. Gertrude sings 'My Man' and—well, he appears on the scene and she stabs him. Woe betide the Apache!" The Russian Dance Scene closed the first act, and was the ballet that was emphasized in the press release sent out by the Shubert organization, which described it as "a big Russian ballet calling for the services of nearly all the company."

To date, no press or other comment has been found on *Les Sylphides,* in which Miss Hoffmann was originally partnered by Leon Barte. The length of the entire program (fifteen scenes in Act I and twelve in Act II), however, suggests that Fokine staged only part of the ballet for this revue.

The relationship between Fokine and Hoffmann is not completely clear. She stole his ballets and profited greatly from them. He must have been aware of this, yet he choreographed for her, and she and many of her "girls" studied with him. In addition, she promoted herself as the leader of the American company he wanted to establish. He publicly supported this fiction, even when the press reported that she was interviewing students in all parts of the country for her American ballet company. There may also have been some social contact between the Fokines and the Hoffmanns: the latter were reported as special guests of the former at a performance at Lewisohn Stadium in 1935.[19]

Fokine's influence on American entertainers was not restricted to Hoffmann. Another popular dancer who studied with Fokine was Gilda Gray. She appeared in the Follies and later went on to Hollywood and a brief film career. Known as the "Shimmy Girl" (reflecting her specialty number), Gray was also one of the first performers to sing southern "blues" songs. She presented an act at the Rendez-Vous Supper Club in New York in 1922, which included a ballet created for her by Fokine and entitled *Russian Toys.* The music was a piece by Rimsky-Korsakov called "Fantasy on Russian Themes." Under the title *Igrouchka* this ballet was later revived by Fokine for the Ballet Russe de Monte Carlo with Alexandra Danilova as the girl. Under its original name it was also included on numerous programs by the Fokines and their students.

The story of *Russian Toys* centers on a goose girl who is loved by a farm boy and becomes convinced of his passion only when he tries to drown himself in the village stream. In a contemporary *Vogue* photograph, Gray is shown with several other dancers and six geese. The per-

Gilda Gray in *Russian Toys*, as seen in *Vogue*.

formers are wearing rather opulent folk costumes (Miss Gray with an elaborate headdress) and the caption describes the "slender and sinuous Gilda Gray in a quaint and unusual folk dance at the Rendez-Vous, a smart midnight cabaret restaurant." When Miss Gray died in 1960 the *Times* (3 January 1960) recalled *Russian Toys* and added, "No doubt the reason Fokine did not use the shimmy was that stickler as he was for ethnological fidelity, he could find no shimmy in Russian folk tradition."

This ballet was also seen in April 1929, on a program presented at the John Golden Theatre in New York by a dancer-actress named Anna Robenne, who, according to the few available clippings, was a Russian dancer who had performed with the Imperial Russian Ballet. She was first seen in America in April 1925, in a recital at the Manhattan Opera House. In December of that year, she presented a program of waltzes at Carnegie Hall and apparently did not perform again until 1927, when she appeared at the 48th Street Theatre with Anatole Vilzak as her partner.

The *Times* (29 April 1929) reported that, with one exception, the entire program at the Golden consisted of dances composed for Miss Robenne by Fokine, who also created several of the costumes. *Russian Toys* was deemed the most successful of the dances, none of which was brilliant "but served well to exhibit her abilities which are limited." Miss Robenne was called "pretty and charming" but it was noted that she performed irregularly and was lacking in discipline.

In February 1926, the magazine *Dance* contained an announcement concerning Miss Robenne that reflects the thinking of at least some Americans of the time concerning dance:

As it has been rumored that Anna Pavlova will not visit our shores this year, a number of wealthy backers have decided to produce an American ballet. Just now the opening date decided upon is November, when the ballet is booked for Washington. Madame Anna Robenne, a Russian dancer who recently made her debut in this country, is said to have been chosen for the premiere danseuse. This is disappointing inasmuch as it really takes away from the company all claim to the name of "American Ballet." We are still waiting for that long promised production—an American Ballet of Americans, by Americans and for Americans!

The company did not become a reality, and Robenne seems to have danced little after the program of Fokine's works.

Fokine also choreographed one dance for Rose Mendell, a performer and teacher, who gave a recital with her pupils at the Selwyn Theatre in April 1923, as well as for a dancer named Amera Tamar. The latter, with a company of three other people (a troupe one writer called "somewhat of a novelty") performed at the Majestic Theatre in Paterson, New Jersey, in August 1924, in a program of dance sketches choreographed by Fokine. The sketches were "Italiana," "Harlequin," "Tragedie Egyptienne," "Romance of Winter," "A Song of India," and "Spanish Street Scene."[20] With no further information, it is only possible to guess from the titles that for Tamar's sketches Fokine took sections of previously choreographed ballets and dances, or at least ideas from them.

Virginie Mauret, who came to study with Fokine in 1922, after studying with Adolph Bolm, gave many concerts, both with an ensemble and as a soloist. In February 1923, Fokine choreographed a piece for three girls from her group, as part of a children's program on a Saturday afternoon, which was accompanied by a symphony orchestra. Later, in 1926, when she was the ballet mistress at the Roxy, he created a solo for her to "Zigeunerweizen" by the composer Sarasate, which she danced at the theater.

Another endeavor that has escaped notice was a monodrama that never opened, entitled *Skygirl*. A three-act play by Ivan Narodny about life fifty thousand years in the future, it contained one speaking role; the remainder was pantomime. It featured Martha Lorber as the only woman in an asexual society and included music by Tcherepnin and Lajos Serly (who conducted the orchestra). Fokine seems to have been responsible for some of the pantomime as well as the dances for the cast of fourteen.

What appears to have been the one and only performance of this novelty was called a "dress rehearsal" and took place on 9 July 1923, at Harbor Hill, the country estate of Clarence Mackay. A benefit for the Mental Hygiene Committee of the State Charities Aid Society, it attracted a large society audience, but it was never produced in either New York or Moscow, as intended.[21]

Sweet Little Devil, a musical, opened at the Astor Theatre in New York on 21 January 1924, having previewed in Boston and Providence under the title *A Perfect Lady*. Produced by Laurence Schwab, it had music by George Gershwin and lyrics by B. D. De Sylva. There was one ballet for the leading lady, Constance Binney (a screen star making her debut in musical comedy), created by Fokine. The story concerns the rivalry of a mercenary showgirl beauty and her young country cousin for the affections of an engineer with a patent that will make him a millionaire. Act II contained a "Flirtation Ballet" to the song "Virginia" that was danced by Miss Binney.

Although *Variety* deemed the show a "secondary choice," most critics liked it, generally praising Fokine's choreography and Miss Binney's execution of it, taking into consideration her lack of experience in the classical ballet. The *Telegram* (22 April 1924), commenting on "the quality known as class," which was evident throughout, noted that when the star found a step too intricate, she covered the fault "by calling to your attention her adorable smile." When the musical toured the Midwest the *Columbus Evening Dispatch,* while praising Miss Binney, observed that she hardly measured up to the Fokine ballet solo. This musical is not included on any list of Fokine's works.

Fokine also enjoyed a little-known connection with the Neighborhood Playhouse, downtown on Grand Street. Established in 1915, the Neighborhood Playhouse was one of the oldest experimental theater groups in the United States. In 1924 it began producing an annual revue, the *Grand St. Follies,* which wittily burlesqued the Broadway season and was aimed at a sophisticated, theater-going New York audience. The 1928 version moved to the Booth Theatre on Broadway. Among the principals were Albert Carroll, Sophia Delza, Dorothy Sands, Blake Scott, Paula Trueman, and James Cagney. Mr. Cagney also arranged the dances for the show, except for the twelfth scene, entitled "The Ship's Entertainment," which featured a South Sea Island Dance performed by Blake Scott and created by Fokine.

Sophia Delza and Paula Trueman have no memory of Fokine's contribution to this revue, which is not remarkable since they were not in the scene on which he worked. The caption on a photograph of Blake Scott and Vera Fokina that appeared in *Dance Magazine* in September 1927 may give the clue as to how Fokine became involved with the *Grand St. Follies*. The photograph identifies "J. Blake Scott" and Mme Fokina in the Prologue to *Faust* (which the Fokine Ballet had danced in Philadelphia in February of that year) and mentions that they had danced together in *Medusa* at Lewisohn Stadium the previous summer. (The program for the Stadium lists "Jack Scott" dancing the role of Poseidon in this Fokine ballet.) Scott was a pupil of Fokine's and it was probably through his intervention that the Russian choreographer was brought in to create the number for the *Grand St. Follies*.

The aura that surrounded the Fokine name influenced producers of popular entertainment even in the 1930s. Whether Fokine's dances were an integral part of these productions or were inserted merely to glamorize them is unclear. In the summer of 1936 the Shuberts presented the San Carlo Opera Company, under the direction of Fortune Gallo, in revivals of two musicals, *Florodora* and *Blossom Time*, at the amphitheater of the new Municipal Stadium at Randalls Island. A third show, *The Student Prince*, was announced but never produced. The souvenir program for *Florodora* (the show that included the famous sextet singing "Tell Me, Pretty Maiden") devoted a full page to Fokine with a photograph and a write-up that was concerned mostly with his Russian background. Fokine's contribution really had nothing to do with the show itself, but was a special number inserted into Act I (it was number seven of eleven), which was listed in the program as "Michel Fokine presents Paul Haakon in the Fokine Ballet with Nina Whitney." There were twenty-nine dancers in the corps de ballet, but there is no record of what they performed.

Blossom Time, based on the life and melodies of the composer Franz Shubert, with music adapted by Sigmund Romberg, opened at Randall's Island on 29 August 1936. Fokine was credited with staging the ballets, which featured Winona Bimboni, Igor Meller, Selma Sharron, and Clarice Sitomer. The *Times* (6 September 1936) showed a photograph of Bimboni that identified her as the principal dancer in *Blossom Time*. A puzzlement is the discovery that Gallo had presented *Blossom Time* in July of that year at the Jones Beach Stadium with some of the same cast, although the ballets were staged by Gertrude Hoffmann. One can only speculate that the Shuberts felt that, even in 1936, Fokine was a stronger attraction.

The Fokines and American "Society"

From the day of their first arrival in the United States until their respective deaths, Michel Fokine's name and photograph, and that of his wife, appeared often on the society pages of New York City newspapers as well as those in other cities. Several national magazines featured them as well. They were also frequently patrons of and performers at various galas, balls, and other events designed to help charities, for all of which Fokine choreographed.

The American people had an inferiority complex about their country's indigenous talents and were quick to praise any foreign artist. American society, which with a few exceptions generally meant those with money, not only perpetuated this myth but associated high society with high (i.e., foreign) art and were anxious to have their daughters mix with the artists. In the case of Michel Fokine it is probable that both sides benefited from the course of events. Those belonging to society felt that the Fokines, as exponents of Russian ballet, represented the highest form of European culture. The Fokines, in addition to free publicity, gained a source of new pupils and potential audiences and backers. The tradition of giving ballet performances for charity was also part of their Russian background, and Fokine's first works had been presented under such circumstances in Russia.

As early as January 1921, the Fokines participated in Philadelphia's Academy of Music Anniversary Ball, where Mme Fokina performed *The Dying Swan* (in which she was to appear many times) and three other dances created for her by her husband, one of which was an interpretation of a Turkish dance.[22] In February 1923 they performed *Le Rêve de la Marquise* at the costume ball of the Newspaper Women's Club in the presence of Governor and Mrs. Alfred E. Smith. Fokine also worked for Mr. and Mrs. John Aspegren of Aspen Hall, Newport, Rhode Island, who had him create a ballet, *La Fontaine Animée,* for their end-of-season dance. A photograph in an unnamed and undated clipping from a society magazine shows what looks like a two-tiered fountain, with four young women cavorting underneath and one on top, all draped in diaphanous cloth.

The Fokines also took part in several fundraisers for various causes in

Russia during the 1920s, and they seem to have been part of the summer colony at Spring Lake, New Jersey. In August 1924 a Russian fete was given at the Ross-Fenton farm near Spring Lake under the direction of the Advisory Committee for Russian Relief in Europe. The Grand Duke and Dutchess Cyril of Russia (and other nobility) were honorary patrons and Vera Fokina performed a solo. But the main feature of the entertainment was the Fokine ballet *Caucasian Sketches,* to music by Ippolitov-Ivanov.[23] The Fokines rehearsed sixteen Spring Lake society girls for two months for this occasion, which Cholly Knickerbocker of the *New York American* (22 July 1924) called "one of the social events of the season." On 20 November 1924, the Fokine dancers entertained at a dinner given by the National Sculpture Society and the Architectural League to honor the sculptor Ivan Mastrovic.

It was with a group that called itself the Monday Opera Supper Club, however, that the Fokines received the most publicity. Founded by Mrs. Harry P. Loomis and Captain George Djamgaroff, the club always met at Sherry's after a performance at the Metropolitan Opera House (which they left early). The club was very active in 1924 and folded in 1925. Mrs. Loomis, who was also president of the Colonial Dames of America, explained that the Monday Opera Supper Club was created to help remedy the "social havoc" that existed in America. It included as members only those who would only support a cause "maintained along the lines of a fastidious taste, which demands the best in art for entertainment, music and setting." She added that since the war, society in Europe looked to America for help in upholding such standards and the club was founded with this mission in mind. One formal reception for the Grand Duchess was followed by a performance of the ballet *The Thunderbird,* danced by Vera Fokina and a number of her troupe, a version of the work originally presented at the Hippodrome.

There is no mention of Fokine himself performing in this production of *The Thunderbird* or in anything else he produced for the Monday Opera Supper Club. His association with the group began on 7 January 1924, when he directed a Ballet Espagnole to music by Albeniz, with costumes designed by Soudeikine. The two dances, a Sevilla and a Sequidella, both listed by Beaumont as new versions of former compositions, were performed by eight dancers, possibly socialites, among them Ilka Chase.

On 14 February the club had a Valentine Ball at Sherry's and Mme Fokina appeared in a gypsy dance. The *Evening Telegram* mentioned that a feature of the entertainment was the ballet *Humoresque* by Fokine, with "Beatrisa Beleriva" and Inga Bredol, both Fokine students.[24] According to the many other newspapers that covered this event, the dancers were assisted by a number of 1923–24 debutantes. On the Monday after Easter Sunday of 1924, the club gave what one newspaper called the "first important dance of the post-Lenten season" where one of the novelties of the entertainment was a children's ballet under the direction of Mme Fokina.

The most ambitious work Fokine produced for the Monday Opera Supper Club was called *The Mountain Queen* and was presented at Sherry's on 24 November 1924, after a performance of *Mephistophele* at the opera. Described as an "Oriental fantasy," its music was attributed to Rimsky-Korsakov and Ippolitov-Ivanov.[25] According to Beaumont, the work combined *The Shemakhanskaya Tsaritsa* to music by the former composer and *Oriental Ballet* (also known as *Caucasian Sketches*) to music by the latter. Vera Fokina took the leading role of the Queen and was assisted by sixteen members of the Fokine Ballet. The costumes, designed by Fokine, were based on those of *Schéhérazade*.

One of the leading characters in the ballet *Le Coq d'Or*, set to the opera by Rimsky-Korsakov, which Fokine originally choreographed in 1914, was the Queen of Shemakhan. It is possible that *The Shemakhanskaya Tsarita* was based in part on this earlier work, and perhaps *The Mountain Queen* was also. For such events Fokine probably took sections of dance material, ideas, and music from many older pieces and reworked them according to the ability of the performers, the nature of the performance area, and the occasion. There is little evidence, however, to prove conclusively that this was his working process.

Incidental Dances in Plays

It was often the practice during the 1920s to include incidental music and dances in dramas, and Michel Fokine was involved in five such productions during this period: *Johannes Kreisler* (1922), *Casanova* (1923), *Hassan* (1924), *The Miracle* (1924), and *The Tenth Commandment* (1926). Four of the five were innovative by American standards. Three of them had been produced in Europe before being brought to the United States, one was the translation of an older, Italian drama, and the fifth, although originally produced in America, was in Yiddish.

The ideas of the European avant-garde, which included dadaists, expressionists, futurists, constructivists, and surrealists, had, by the early 1920s, begun to affect staging, sets, use of space, the relationship between word and movement, and contact with the audience. Many of their concepts had crossed the Atlantic by means of both actual productions and individuals who had seen them. Although Fokine was not part of any of these groups, the terms *revolutionary* and *daring* were still associated with him from his Diaghilev period, and his ideas concerning the unity of a production fit in with many of the new approaches. In fact, Hugo Ball, one of the originators of dadaism, had included him in the list of ideal artists to be associated with the new theater.[26]

Johannes Kreisler opened on 22 December 1922, at the Apollo Theatre on 42d Street. Based on the life and works of E. T. A. Hoffmann, this "fantastic melodrama" about the eccentric kapellmeister had originally been produced in Berlin, where it was considered by many to be a new concept in scenic and musical production. The music, by E. H. Von Reznick, was of interest because it included sections of actual works by Mozart (*Don Giovanni*) and Hoffmann (*Undine*). Sven Gade, who originated the technical effects for the play, also supervised them in America, because the Germans would not allow his inventions out of the country. Fokine choreographed one ballet, Frank Reicher directed, and the actor Jacob Ben-Ami starred in the production, which ran for sixty-five performances.

A scenic spectacle encompassing forty-one scenes in a prologue and three acts, the play is about a composer who is unable to distinguish between dreams and realities. His visions become actualities to him, the ideal transfigures personalities, and his "evil genius" always pursues him. The composer falls in love with Julia, whose parents refuse to let him marry her, and, in the course of his life, she appears to him in the guise of other sympathetic women he meets: the heroine of his opera; a lovely countess; a great prima donna. In one section a rich man is Kreisler's rival for Julia, and he imagines him to be Bluebeard.

Although it is possible that Fokine was involved in various groupings and pantomimes of the fairies and elemental spirits in Act I, the one ballet in this play occurred in scene 6, "Kreisler's Dream of Undine." It is generally referred to as the "Undine Ballet," and it involved twenty-four dancers, led by Dorothy Dinsmore.

One of the advertisements mentioned "Fokine's Gorgeous Ballet," and preopening publicity included newspaper photographs of Fokine, listing his Moscow, Paris, and Broadway accomplishments, but very little is known of the ballet, and no photographs can be located. There is one sketch of a ballet-girl costume, showing an ankle-length skirt, possibly of a tulle-like fabric, and one newspaper article noting that, whereas most of the scenes were vignettes that took place in different stage areas, the ballet used the full stage.[27]

The revolving stage was divided into six segments on two levels, which could be rolled and slid alternatively or simultaneously, all the while brilliantly lighted, creating a kaleidoscope effect. The flashbacks, the painted canvas and black velvet, and the use of Kreisler as narrator reminded many of a moving picture scenario. Kenneth Macgowan termed it a "cinemese entertainment," in which the narrator became "a sort of audible movie caption." Reicher and Fokine, he said, did their utmost as directors of drama and dance, but the elaborate mechanics wrecked the play.[28] The *Times* (25 December 1922) found the evening interesting in spite of the subordination of the story to the scenery, however, and termed the Undine Ballet "charming if slightly irrelevant."

This play seems to have been conceived with the idea of encompassing all the theatrical elements then appearing and reappearing in the German theater. But, instead of total theater, the result was merely scenic theater, and the dance was swallowed up in the process. This was certainly not in keeping with Fokine's call for the quality of all elements involved, and it occurred in spite of the fact that there was a musical motif for each character in the story (as there had been for the earlier ballet *Petrouchka*). Yet, small as the contribution to the play may have been, it remained with Fokine, who later used many of the same dramatic themes in the ballet *Paganini*.

Casanova, which opened at the Empire Theatre on 26 September 1923, starred Lowell Sherman and Katherine Cornell. The Prologue was a "Ballet Pantomime devised and staged by Michel Fokine" entitled *The Return from the Carnival*.

The musical score for the ballet was composed by Deems Taylor, who also contributed the incidental music used throughout the play. This continuity was in keeping with the purpose of the ballet Prologue, which was to set the theme of the play and prepare the audience, or, as one announcement read, "to get the medieval Italian atmosphere well spread over the Empire Theatre."[29]

The advertisement for opening night, which appeared in all the New York newspapers and gave prominent coverage to the Fokine ballet, announced that it would be absolutely impossible to admit latecomers until after the Prologue ended. The critic Percy Hammond in the *New York Tribune* (19 February 1923), was annoyed because everyone rushed to get to the theater by 8:20 to see the dance, which did not begin until 8:45, and he called the result "a minor Fokine ballet."

The Return from the Carnival used seventeen dancers in an elaborate, ten-minute dance depicting the revels of carnival time. In addition to the characters of Columbine and Pulcinella, there was a Guitar Player, a Page, a Fat Man, a Gentleman in Black, a Roman Soldier, four Harlequins, and six Masked Women. Lora Vinci was the First Harlequin, Desha the Third, and Renee Wilde was a Masked Woman. The program lists a "Helen Beckre" as the Fifth Masked Woman. This was actually Helen Becker, a pupil of Fokine's at the time, who, as Helen Tamiris, became a well-known modern dancer and choreographer. Another Masked Woman was played by Valentine Sanina, a beautiful Russian émigrée who had studied briefly with Fokine. As Valentina, she later became an internationally known designer.

Renee Wilde says that the cast for *The Return from the Carnival* was as large as it was because Fokine had to figure out how to use a great number of the students in his school, all of whom were in competition for roles in his ballets. One article mentioned that most of the young women in the ballet cast—several not more than fifteen years of age—were Americans who had studied with Fokine, some for as little as two years.

The adjectives *delightful, decorative,* and *colorful* appear over and over about the ballet, even among those who did not like the play. The *Times* (27 September 1923) called the dance a thing "of exquisite fancy, redolent of sensual love in carnival, rhythmic, with aphrodisiac pain and longing." The *Tribune* called it "rich," the *Herald* "a fine harlequinade," and the *Post* "brilliant but not particularly elucidatory." Only the *New Republic* found it "limp and uninteresting and styleless." Whatever the verdict, Fokine included it among those works to be forgotten.

Before *Casanova* opened, Fokine had to leave for Europe to begin work on a production of *Hassan* in London, and Vera Fokina conducted the final rehearsals for him. This news received some coverage in the press, as did many events in the lives of the Fokines. One feature evolves into a lengthy article on their initial romance (she was a pupil of his) and the symbiotic nature of their marriage. The author then relates how, on one occasion, they were watching a rehearsal from opposite wings, and as they came on stage, each gave identical instructions to the chorus. It was, in fact, Mme Fokina's habit, throughout their lives together, to attend almost every rehearsal he conducted and to sit by his side, and it is therefore quite natural that he entrusted the final rehearsal of *The Return from the Carnival* to her.

It was during this same period that Fokine received two letters from Russia inviting him to return. The year 1923 was the twenty-fifth anniversary of the beginning of his career in dance, and he had been away from his country for five years. One letter was from Ivan Exkuzovitch, the academic director of the Academic Theatres of Petrograd, the other from the Committee of the Theatres. Fokine initially accepted their invitations for a visit on two conditions: that he would remain there for a month only, after which they must allow him to leave, and that no one else would be evicted from a post because of his coming. As a result of the invitations he even postponed going to London, but the plans did not work out on this occasion, nor on any future ones.

In early January 1924 Westbrook Pegler wrote in the *New York Morning Telegraph* that there had been several tremendous spectacle plays in New York since the war, among them *Chu, Chin, Chow, Mecca, Aphrodite,* and *Johannes Kreisler,* each in turn "the greatest of all indoor shows." He added that another was coming to town—*The Miracle.*

It was Morris Gest who finally succeeded in bringing to America the Max Reinhardt production originally presented in London in 1911 and then throughout Germany in 1913. Reinhardt was known and admired all over the world for his classics, spectacles, pantomimes, and films, and to him and many others *The Miracle* marked the pinnacle of his career. The book was by Karl Vollmoeller. The music score, by Engelbert Humperdinck, was revised by Freidrich Schirmer for the New York production, and new scenery and costumes were designed by the young and then unknown Norman Bel Geddes. Fokine was responsible for the incidental dances.

The pageant, with 700 people in the cast, 120 in the choir, and 70 in the orchestra, opened on 15 January 1924, in the Century Theatre, which had been completely converted into a cathedral. The costs, estimated to be close to $600,000, were so great that on opening night Lee Shubert noted that the production would have to run a year before it broke even. With the exception of a six-week summer break, it played in New York until 1 November and then toured the country during the seasons of 1925–26, 1926–27, and 1929–30. It finally sent Morris Gest into bankruptcy, as well as affecting his health, and, ultimately, the career of Fokine and the development of ballet in America.

The Miracle was conceived because Reinhardt wished to produce a pantomime on the theme of the Virgin and a nun. The story is an elaboration of Maeterlinck's two-act play *Sister Beatrice,* the legend of a young novice who betrays her vows and yields to the temptations of the world. Told through nine scenes of pantomime and huge processions, it was, according to most reviews, not entirely clear, but the general feeling of longings, dreams, and the temptations present in the human masses was obvious.

There was a great deal of preopening publicity, in the typically flamboyant Gest manner, concerning both the entire production and the fact that Fokine was creating the incidental dances. As early as August 1923, word went out that Gest had contracted his services. One unidentified newspaper clipping, dated 25 August 1923, stated that "on the occasion of all the previous productions of *The Miracle* it was the ardent desire of Prof. Reinhardt and Dr. Vollmoeller to have Mr. Fokine associated with them in this capacity, but circumstances have always heretofore prevented the realization of this wish and Mr. Gest reports that they are particularly gratified over this arrangement." Fokine's name appeared on the regular program and the souvenir program of the play for the first two weeks of the run—and then never again!

It is very difficult to ascertain what the "incidental dances" in *The Miracle* actually involved, although the synopsis in the program refers to a czardas and even dancing nuns. Most of the reviewers were completely overcome by the bells, organ, and wind machines in the huge cathedral setting, with its nave, stained-glass windows, and many levels, through which the hundreds of players endlessly passed. Although several mentioned Fokine, little was said about his accomplishments. *Variety* (24 January 1924) commented that "the Fokine dance in the forest was lost. One got a very splendid effect from the shadows, but it's much too charming not to have a little more light." The *Times* (16 January 1924) dismissed it with a line about "a dance of elves in a wood."

Renee Wilde and Lora Vinci, who danced in the production, recall that there were twelve Fokine dancers involved, that they often rehearsed until 4:00 A.M. in a loft on 60th Street that had only one stove for heat, and that it was a totally miserable experience. They were all given two weeks notice on opening night. Wilde says that they were never quite sure what they were—either elves or nymphs—and that they wore masks they hated because they had trouble seeing. Reinhardt and Gest insisted that the dancers participate in the mob scenes. But they soon learned to hide, because Gest had brought in immigrants from Ellis Island as extras, and the girls were constantly getting pinched. Wilde feels that they were fired because Reinhardt did not want Fokine's name mentioned, preferring to garner all the attention for himself as controller of all the elements in the spectacle. Whether the actual dances were eliminated or other dancers brought in is unknown, but Fokine's name was removed from all literature.

John Corbin, in a *New York Times* feature article (27 January 1924) on Reinhardt and *The Miracle*, made some comments that reflect on Wilde's conjecture and might also apply, at times, to Fokine:

There is a paradox in the career of Max Reinhardt. He has produced more dramas of the first order—classics if you will—than any other man in the history of the theatre, and has produced them more successfully. And he is devoting the maturity of his genius, the years of his greatest power in the theatre, to pantomime and popular spectacle. Resolve that paradox and you have the secret of his genius—and of his limitations.

Although the dances of *The Miracle* were apparently less than successful, Fokine once again used them at a later date. In Vera Fokina's solo concert in Carnegie Hall, 17 February 1926, she danced a new ballet based on the story of a nun to Schuman's *Etude Symphonique*. The story, as reported in a few newspapers, closely resembled that of *The Miracle*.[30]

Hassan opened at the Knickerbocker Theatre on 22 September 1924. This verse play by the young English poet and author James Elroy Flecker, with incidental music by Frederick Delius, had first been produced in London a year earlier under the guidance of Basil Dean, one of England's foremost stage directors. In the American production, presented by A. L. Erlanger, Fokine re-created the dances he had choreographed for the London version.

Flecker, who died of tuberculosis without seeing his play on the stage, had spent several years as a consul in Asia Minor, and the five acts and nine scenes of *Hassan* are written in rather exotic poetry that creates an atmosphere of mysticism and sadism. It is really a double Arabian Nights story, concerned with the purgatorial experiences of an "Everyman" and the nature of worldly love. One tale involves Hassan, a philosophical confectioner of Bagdad, who, after being deceived in love by Yasmin, accidentally becomes involved in an adventure with the capricious Caliph, whose life he saves. Elevated to the position of friend of the court, he meets the court poet Ishak.

The other tale tells the story of the love between Parvaneh, who has been kidnapped and sold as a slave to the Caliph's harem, and Rafi, King of the Beggars. At one point Hassan and the Caliph find themselves prisoners in the "House without Walls," which is actually the secret hideout of the Beggar King. In another scene the Caliph sits in judgment on the two lovers and gives them the choice of banishment for Rafi while Parvaneh becomes his wife, or twenty-four hours of love together and then death by torture for both. It is when they choose the latter that Hassan and Ishak renounce worldly life and depart on their pilgrimage.

The production required a large and skilled cast and elaborate stage settings. At one point three theaters were needed for rehearsals; one for the forty principals, another for the chorus of thirty-two, and a third for the ballet, which included fourteen women and ten men. There was also an orchestra of thirty-five. The advance sale set a new record at the box office of the Knickerbocker, in part because it was yet another Oriental spectacle and in part because of the success of the London production. The reputation of the author, composer, and choreographer also helped to establish an aura of expectancy.

Although it had been praised in London for its poetic atmosphere, and the specially commissioned music of Delius had received a great deal of attention, as did the ballets of Fokine, *Hassan* was a failure in New York and closed in less than two weeks. The critics were disappointed by what they considered a dull play, and generally agreed with the *Drama* that the scenery and costumes smothered the poetry of the lines. Stark Young in the *New York Times* felt that the production lacked the dream and charm of the writing, that it had neither fantasy nor reality, and complained of too much "pseudo-Orientalism."

Basil Dean discusses the play at length in his autobiography. He had acquired the rights to it prior to World War I, had been advising Flecker about revisions at the time of the poet's death, had negotiated with his widow, and had asked Delius to write the music long before he acquired backers. Desiring "total theatre," he searched for the best, and while in New York in 1922 persuaded Charles Dillingham, the American theatrical entrepreneur, to introduce him to Fokine. Dillingham "told the great maître de ballet fabulous tales about the play, which he had not read, and about the ballet music, which he had not heard," and Fokine accepted— a tribute to Dillingham's talents as a teller of tall tales!

Dean attributed the failure of the American production to the fact that, in a negotiation that was not under his control, the American rights— along with costumes, scenery, etc.—were sold to A. L. Erlanger. Dean did not feel the production could fit into any New York theater unless carefully rehearsed and that its success lay in his own ability to weld all the elements into some degree of artistic unity, without which it would be merely an "ill-adjusted spectacle." Erlanger agreed verbally to wait until Dean could be in America to begin rehearsals, but the play opened the night before the English director's arrival. Erlanger directed the play himself and, according to Dean, eliminated what he could not understand from the script, cut down or left out scenery that would not fit, and attended rehearsals carrying a football referee's whistle. Dean, who had the greatest admiration for Fokine's work in London, does not discuss it in the context of the American production.

Although the *New York World* (23 September 1924) mentioned seven Fokine ballets "of vivid fascination," it is possible to document only three dances, two of which are actually part of the same ballet. The first dance in *Hassan* appears in Act 2, when the King of the Beggars, who is entertaining the disguised Caliph, claps his hands and calls for music and dancers. The Caliph's statement that "we shall see dancing women worthy of Paradise" and "incomparable houris" does not prepare him for the entrance of a group of lamed and tattered Eastern beggars. Their dance of the halt and maimed was described in the *Telegraph* (23 September 1924) as "an almost gruesome piece of realism," at the end of which they discarded their rags to reveal themselves as virile men dressed in gold. Before this transformation took place the dancing girls entered and performed the ballet "Fair and Dusky Beauties," in which half of them were fair skinned and the other half dark. The play directs them to "surround the Beggars, dancing, and point at them."

There are two extant photographs of this ballet. Both are of the London production, and both show the dancing girls and transformed beggars dancing (or posing) together. In one, the girls are reclining in a circle about one male dancer (possibly Rafi) with one arm raised upward toward him. The other shows two concentric half circles, with the men in profile on one knee in front of the standing women. The arms of the dancers are carefully arranged: the men touch the left shoulder with the left hand, creating a line that extends across the chest and through the raised right arm; the arms of the women are bent in front of the chest, the palms touching, with one elbow raised and one lowered, forming a diagonal line across the front of the body. There were a great many people on stage during this dance, which built to a chaotic climax—really another bacchanale—described as "a perfect blaze of color and movement."[31] One critic referred to the women as "pretty, half bare houris of the better class, who rolled the carnal clouds under one's head with respectable voluptuousness."[32]

The second ballet, which centered around the Procession of Protracted Death, occurred in the third act, when the lovers were led to their tortuous death. The script of the play describes the various characters in the procession, as well as their props, but says nothing specific about a dance. John Mason Brown, discussing the London production in the *London Transcript* (20 October 1923), said that this ballet was impressive "with its ghastly figures sharply silhouetted against the sky and accompanied by Delius's sombre music."

Fokine's dances for the Broadway version of *Hassan* were, as far as can be ascertained, very close to those for the London production, taking into consideration different dancers and a different space. This seems so in spite of the *New York Telegram* critic who, after condemning everything else in the play, wrote, "Those who saw *Hassan* abroad tell us that our Mr. Fokine's dance arrangements are infinitely more thrilling. Let us retire into the security of that pleasant detail." He was not alone in singling out the ballets or the technical performance of the dancers for praise in an otherwise negative review. There were many, however, who did not like the dances, particularly those in the second act, which earned such epithets as "confused," "commonplace," and "heavy."

To date, the historical record reveals little more of the dances in *Hassan,* although Flecker's play is of interest to scholars of poetry and Delius's music is described as containing some of his best work. Fokine, on the other hand, later listed the dances in *Hassan* among those he would like to forget.

The Tenth Commandment, by Abraham Goldfaden, the father of Yiddish theater, was written in 1880, originally presented in New York City in 1897, and was chosen by Maurice Schwartz, the actor and director, to open the new Yiddish Art Theatre on Second Avenue in 1926. Schwartz adapted, directed, and starred; Boris Aronson designed the sets and costumes; and Michel Fokine was the choreographer for the production, which opened on 17 November 1926.

If Fokine's association with the Yiddish theater seems, at first, odd, it must be remembered that most of the actors associated with it were from Europe—Russia and Poland in particular—where both his work and reputation were still well known. In addition, Artef (the Yiddish acronym for Workers Theatre Group), which began in 1925 as a dramatic studio under the auspices of the Communist daily *Freheit,* had hired Fokine in its first season, 1925–26, to give sixteen classes in "Plastique and Dance."[33] He was also known to many members of and devotees to the Yiddish theater from his work in *Johannes Kreisler,* for the star of that play, Jacob Ben-Ami, was a Yiddish actor.

The play, in sixteen scenes, which Brooks Atkinson in the *New York Times* (18 November 1926) termed "a fantasy set to music," is a tale of the struggle of good and evil for the mastery of the human soul—a part of the theology of Orthodox Judaism. In the story, Peretz, the buffoon, is married to Fruma, a pious woman, and Ludwig, the aesthete, is married to the voluptuous and haughty Mathilda. A bad angel—the devil—mixes up the couples, who end up "switching." But, through the intervention of the good angel, neither alliance is consummated, and everything finally gets put back in proper order. The scenes go between the two couples' house and heaven and hell. In addition to Schwartz, the cast featured Lazar Freed, Joseph Buloff, and Celia Adler. The 1926 version was updated by making the good and bad angels symbols of democracy and fascism.

What impressed most theatergoers about *The Tenth Commandment* was its vast energy and dynamic quality. John Mason Brown spoke of the wild excesses, the "sheer joy of theatricality," and the "rare gusto" with which Maurice Schwartz handled the crowds.[34] There were gay and tender moments, devils writhing under green lights, and a heavily populated Hades and Paradise. The often eerie lighting, the grotesque masks, the chants, tableaux, comic bits, and Boris Aronson's endless costumes and multi-leveled sets all helped to create an extraordinary theater experience.

Aronson's costumes, broad and fantastic, matched the exaggerated makeup. One of his sets looked like a castle composed of the oddest possible shapes, each creating a different level. Another, an obviously painted interior, featured crooked windows, a real table and bench, and a ceiling that jutted out from the black curtain behind it.

Unfortunately, almost nothing can be reconstructed regarding Fokine's choreography for *The Tenth Commandment*. The observation that "several excellent ballets were executed under the able direction of Michel Fokine" offers as little insight as Abe Cahan's comment in the *Jewish Daily Forward* that they showed a good deal of talent, but got lost "in the general mishmash" of the play.[35] The program itself is of little help. One may guess that he created something for the seven goblins, the four "Ladies of the Kosher Dance," the German Officers and Ladies at the Ball, and the crowds in both heaven and hell.

Belle Didjah Ehrenreich, who was later a pupil of Fokine's, and saw the play, recalls simply that the production was different and amusing, that the dancers had silver glitter on their costumes when they were in heaven, and that the ballets were lost amid all the lights, sets, costumes, masks, music, and people.

It was *The Tenth Commandment,* with its constructivist sets, that gave the Russian Boris Aronson his real entrée into the international theater world. The many levels and steps, the masks, the crowd scenes, the exaggerated costumes and makeup, and the often multisensory atmosphere of this performance all bear the influence of the various ideas and experiments then influencing the theater in Europe, and brought to America by European-trained artists.

Fokine was never interested in the rapidly developing scientific and in-

Boris Aronson's set for hell in *The Tenth Commandment*. *Courtesy Billy Rose Theatre Collection, The New York Public Library at Lincoln Center, Astor, Lenox, and Tilden Foundations.*

dustrial technology that had begun to affect the entire world—artistic, social, and industrial—prior to World War I, and he was really uninterested in its postwar development. Had he been aware of the Dance Manifesto of the Italian futurists, which included a dance of the machine gun, it would have been abhorrent to him. He found German modern dance ugly, and several years prior to coming to the United States he wrote that, because he was opposed to the mechanical in dance (meaning eurythmics), he was opposed to constructivism and its entrance into the world of art in general.[36] How he defined this movement is not clear. The fact that he was not particularly interested in defining, investigating, or trying to understand any of the new movements leaves him solidly in an older, traditional mold. Diaghilev, on the other hand, showed his awareness of these trends as early as *Jeux* (1913) and obviously in *Parade* (1917).

Fokine worked twice with the director Vsevold Meyerhold—the charity performance of *Le Carnaval*, where the latter took the part of Pierrot, and a production of Gluck's opera *Orpheus* in 1911, which was under the overall supervision of Meyerhold. Beaumont reports that Fokine staged the underworld scene in Act 2 of the opera using hundreds of bodies—dancers, singers, actors, supers—to create agonized masses, and that he worked so closely with Meyerhold on other scenes that the final program read "Opera produced by V. Meyerhold and M. Fokine." Their collaboration, however, seems to have resulted in a unified production rather than an unusual or daring one.

There is no evidence that Fokine ever exchanged ideas or worked with any of the other artistic revolutionaries of the early twentieth century. If he had he would probably have found himself in an alien world, as he seemed to with Stravinsky's later music. He was as much a creator of theater as of dance, but he was not the radical many of the avant-gardists of the theater thought him to be. Because of his innovations in dance they attributed to him more extreme ideas than he, in fact, possessed.

Nor was he a complete stranger to the concept of entertainment for the larger public, as opposed to performances that took place under aristocratic patronage. Bronislava Nijinska's memoirs chronicle her father's participation in the summer theater performances of dance, drama, and music that involved ballet dancers in everything from circuses to variety bills to Offenbach's opera bouffas. On occasion they included entertainers from American minstrels and the English music halls. Even before 1909 a few Russian dancers had appeared in the English variety halls, and after the success of the Ballets Russes Karsavina and others danced at the Coliseum in London.

Fokine was almost certainly aware of all this and very possibly even saw some of the summer entertainment. In his memoirs he recalls vividly the comedies and farces in which his brother Vladimir performed and tells of his brother Alexander's highly successful Theatre Miniature. This form of entertainment, which achieved great success in Russia just prior to World War I, was, in effect, a variety bill, which included one-act plays, usually comedies, and seven or eight other acts offering singers, comedians, acrobats, magicians, and dancers. Alexander Fokine's Troitsky Theatre Miniature featured his wife, the ballerina Alexandra Fedorova Fokine.

In attempting to relate this new American phase of Michel Fokine's career to his previous experience several observations may be made. The bacchanale, as almost a form, allowed him to use all the precepts he advocated for the "new" ballet and had put into practice between 1909 and

1914, and he used it over and over. There is the inevitable comparison, in terms of themes and movements, between the ballets on Broadway and in the various other productions and plays and many of those in the Ballets Russes. Fokine appears to have learned much about the publicity value of spectacle, which occasionally shocks, and was either willing to use it himself or to work with others who would. Thus we have Michel Fokine beginning his American career ten years after the start of his association with Diaghilev, using much of the same material to express the same ideas, on dancers with entirely different backgrounds, to an audience much less sophisticated but equally enthusiastic.

Chapter Four

Classical Ballet: The Fokines and Their Company (1919–1938)

From the Metropolitan Opera House to the Keith Albee Circuit

ALTHOUGH MORRIS GEST BROUGHT Michel Fokine to the United States primarily as a choreographer, he also presented both the Fokines as performers before the year 1919 was over. America had never seen Fokine as a dancer; it knew of him, rather, as a choreographer, but the press, from the time of his arrival, began to mention his reputation and that of Mme Fokina as dancers.

Vera Fokina, like her husband a graduate of the Conservatory of the Maryinsky Theatre in Petrograd, where he was her teacher, had been a member of the Diaghilev Company, although not a primary dancer. It seems to be the consensus among those interviewed that, as a technician, she was not particularly outstanding, and that her success in the United States was due to her husband's ability to coach her and create for her in such a way that her positive attributes were emphasized. She has been described as elegant, imperious, demanding, beautiful, jealous, charming, and accustomed to getting her way. She was her husband's constant companion. Sol Hurok referred to them as Tristan and Isolde.

To a certain segment of the American public Michel Fokine and Vera Fokina personified the ideal of art and beauty. As archetypal representatives of the classical ballet, a form associated with the aristocracy of European society, they stood for "culture." Their initial appearances were as concert artists. They hoped to maintain this elevated status but were not always able to, because of the nature of American entertainment in the 1920s, which was marked by a continuing interest in vaudeville and spectacles and a growing interest in movies.

Michel Fokine in *Russian Dances. Courtesy Phyllis Fokine Archive.*

Michel and Vera Fokine made their first appearance as performers in the United States on 30 December 1919, at the Metropolitan Opera House in New York City. Tickets for the sold-out event were $7.00, making them second in scale only to the *Aphrodite* premiere.

The program consisted of both Fokines in *Le Spectre de la Rose,* Mme Fokina in *The Dying Swan, Salome* (Glazounov), *Chant d'Automne* (Tchaikovsky), and *Gypsy Dance* (Nachez) and Fokine alone in *Bacchus* (Tcherepnin) and *Panaderos* (Glazounov). They concluded together with a group of dances to eight Russian folk songs by Anatol Liadov in the form of a symphonic suite, which included "Meloncholy," "I Dance with a Mosquito," and "Lullaby."[1]

The preopening press coverage reminded the public that several of the dances had originally been created by Fokine for such dancers as Pavlova and Nijinsky, and a number of reviewers inevitably made a comparison with former interpreters. The *Times* stated that no dancer in the decade had ever drawn a greater audience, because the name of Fokine "had been known wherever the Russians appeared in this country." They said, however, that neither her technique nor his leaps were of the virtuosity remembered by those who saw *Spectre* and *Dying Swan* in Paris. The *Musical America* reviewer, invoking memories of the gorgeous Russian ballet, wrote that from the "heralded creator of those brilliant choreographic pictures an evening of rare brilliancy was expected, yet his program pales in comparison with the work of his disciples." To this same reviewer, *Spectre* was unsatisfying, *Dying Swan* rivaled but did not surpass Pavlova's version, *Salome* consisted of little dancing but rather, "the irksome task of unfastening and throwing off seven veils," and Mme Fokina's toe work was not as light as it might have been. The *New York Sun* essentially agreed, pointing out that the Fokines were not in their prime, and concluding, "All honor, then, to the instigator, the organizer, the master of ballets—but as to the dancers themselves, they are approaching the age of disappointment."

Others, however, thought Fokine virile and Vera Fokina light and graceful. Even the negative critics felt that the character and folk dances, with their moods and humors of the Russian peasant, belonged to the highest of arts. The *Nation* (31 January 1920), referring to a statement by Fokine that his dances and dancers were "so many Fokines," expressed the opinion that it was probably via these other performers that he would best be remembered in America, "for he demands such a fabulous sum for his own performances that they will doubtless be few in number." The reviewer concluded that the Fokines showed the greatest achievement in their peasant dances:

Lullaby, with Fokine in his blond wig, drowsing on a bench, his head drooping between his knees, while his wife, also in peasant costume, walked up and down trying to rock the baby to sleep in her arms, was as realistic as a chapter by Tolstoi.

Regardless of the critics, the audience responded to the Fokines with applause, flowers, and adoration, and when they appeared at the New York Hippodrome on Sunday, 18 January 1920, in what was originally announced as their last appearance, the seven thousand seats were sold out two weeks in advance. They repeated *Salome* and *The Dying Swan* but changed musical accompaniment (Arnold Volpe was their musical director and conductor), and their new producer was Sol Hurok. They were so successful that Hurok booked them for a second appearance at the Metropolitan Opera House on 10 February, as well as for a tour that included Boston, Philadelphia, Washington, D. C., Baltimore, and Richmond.

In his autobiography Hurok, recalling Fokine as a stickler for detail, says that the program for the Metropolitan Opera House had been carefully worked out to include, among other things, both the Fokines doing the waltz from *Les Sylphides* and the mazurka from *Coppélia*, some solos for him, and *The Dying Swan*, plus a solo to Beethoven's *Moonlight Sonata* for her. Hurok was beginning to feel content about the performance when he received the news that Fokine had injured himself during rehearsal and would be unable to perform for at least six weeks. A hasty conference between Hurok and the Fokines resulted in a revised program for Vera Fokina that contained seven numbers, including three Chopin preludes that Fokine grouped under the title *Poland—Three Moods: Happiness, Revolt, Sadness.*[2] Hurok immediately mounted an extensive public-relations campaign that heralded Vera Fokina as a prima ballerina of the Russian ballet, and the public responded with yet another full house. The press noted Mme Fokina's virtuosity and endurance with the *Times* observing a debt to Isadora Duncan in the dance to Beethoven's *Moonlight Sonata*.

The tour that Hurok had planned went on, with Mme Fokina repeating her solo performance. The only change was that *Salome* was added and the Beethoven piece taken out. On tour, as well as in New York City, Fokine's "illness" was attributed to influenza. Since the public could not

Vera Fokina in *Lullaby. Courtesy Phyllis Fokine Archive.*

see him hobbling about backstage, giving orders to everyone in a variety
of languages, and, according to Hurok, often creating chaos, they never
knew the real reason for his inability to perform.[*]

The Fokines were back in New York in the Spring, with a performance
at the Metropolitan Opera on 1 May, and their final performance under
Hurok's management (until 1927) on 29 May at Charles Dillingham's
Hippodrome. By then Fokine was again able to dance and the Fokines
performed the Harlequin and Columbine variation from *Carnaval* and a
work called *Amoun and Berenis*. This last, to music by Anton Arensky,
was actually no more than a collection of scenes, some danced and some
played by the orchestra, from *Cléopâtre*.

The Fokines resumed touring in October 1920, shortly after *Mecca*
opened, giving more than one hundred performances in an extensive tour
east of the Mississippi, under the management of Richard G. Herndon.
The first stop was the Metropolitan Opera House in Philadelphia on 20
October. Here the advertising and press coverage was considerable, with
emphasis on the fact that it was Fokine's first appearance in the city. He
was billed as the creator of the Russian Ballet and it was announced that
the Fokines would award a silver trophy to the most talented dance student at a competition to be held on stage during one of the intermissions.

The lengthy program was divided into three parts. In Part 1, both Fokines performed the Harlequin and Columbine duet from *Carnaval* and
Vera Fokina did *The Dying Swan* plus a Passepied to music by Delibes.
Part 2 contained Michel Fokine's solos *Bacchus* and *Panaderos,* the latter
being a Spanish dance with a Russian name, and Vera Fokina's *Bacchanale* (Glazounov), in which she wore a filmy red dress and danced amid a
scattering of red roses. Part 3 opened with both performers dancing a
Mazurka to music by Delibes and ended with them performing the five
Russian folk dances to Liadov's music. Fokina added an encore to Dvorak's "Humoresque" in Part 1.

This format was followed throughout the Fokine's tour under Herndon, with the duets and Michel Fokine's dances remaining constant and
Vera Fokina sometimes performing *Salome* or *Tzigane* (Nachez), a gypsy
dance to a violin solo, instead of the Passepied or *Bacchanale.*

Critical response in Philadelphia was quite good, with the large audience, characterized in one headline as "brilliant," sometimes receiving as
much notice as the dancers. The program was deemed both interesting
and charming, Fokine's athletic skill and muscular strength were noted,
and of all Mme Fokina's dances, *The Dying Swan* was judged the most
popular. On the other hand, the conducting of what was evidently a

poorly rehearsed orchestra (Michel Fokine could be heard prompting them at times) was observed by many. Not all the reviews were positive, and one writer felt that the dancers who followed Fokine surpassed him in technique, grace, feeling, and virility, and that Fokina's appearance was matronly.

The Fokines continued on, going next to Syracuse, and then to Pittsburgh, where they received an ovation for their dancing. (Interestingly, they were followed in Philadelphia by Anna Pavlova and Alexander Volinine, who performed at the Academy of Music on 26 October.) In Wheeling, West Virginia, where Michel Fokine and Vera Fokina danced at the Court Theatre on 28 October, the "high art" of their "emotional technique" completely captivated a "fashionable and appreciative audience." An incomplete typewritten schedule for this tour, as well as the Fokine's press books, indicate that they were in Dayton, Grand Rapids, Saginaw, Ann Arbor, Battle Creek, Peoria, and Chicago—first appearing in the latter city on 8 November and returning for a second engagement with a new program on 28 November, both at the Auditorium Theatre. December found them in Baltimore, Atlantic City, and Washington, D.C., and on 19 January 1921, they appeared at Symphony Hall in Boston with the Boston Symphony Orchestra, in a program that included *Salome*.

In general the tour received very positive press reaction, with more than one writer commenting on the "poetry" of their motion. The *Pittsburgh Dispatch* observed that "if Michel Fokine claims to have been the creator of Dying Swan . . . he had certainly been plagiarized here before his immigration from Russia."

It is almost impossible at this time to reconstruct the relationship that existed between the Fokines and Richard Herndon—or, for that matter, with any of their other numerous managers and producers. There seems, however, to have been a great deal of temperament and several law suits. In an article in *Variety,* dated January 1921, for example, it was reported that Richard Herndon had served an attachment of $4,803.75 on costumes and other effects of the Fokines at the close of their performance in Symphony Hall in Boston on 19 January. Herndon, who was then managing someone else, said that it was the balance due on a bill he had contracted on behalf of the Fokines prior to their opening in Philadelphia the previous October. Fokine denied this charge and added that their appearance in Chicago had been cut short because Herndon did not give them a $3,000 advance he had promised.

It is not clear exactly who arranged this performance with the Boston Symphony Orchestra, at which the program was the same as that which the Fokines had been touring. But the performance was not well received in the press. H. T. Parker in the *Boston Evening Transcript* said that Fokine was past his prime and that Vera Fokina could not be compared with Pavlova. He added that even in the Diaghilev troupe, she had not been a first or even a secondary dancer and that "Fokine set her in a limbo of her own and, rare teacher that he is, has trained her."

In spite of the controversy, on 1 March 1921, Michel and Vera Fokine again appeared at the Metropolitan Opera House in New York. The highlight of this program, which contained *The Dying Swan* and excerpts from *Les Sylphides,* was a new one-act ballet, *Le Rêve de la Marquise,* to music by Mozart. Set in the eighteenth century, it is the story of a Marquise who, left alone to take a bath in a park pool after a tiring dance with the Marquis, falls asleep and dreams that the statue of a faun (who looks like the Marquis) comes alive and passionately pursues her. She jumps into the water and the faun jumps in after her. Vera Fokina was the Marquise and Michel Fokine played both the Marquis and the Faun Awakened.The ballet was later seen at an annual show of Actors Equity.

In one newspaper article, which appeared just prior to the opening of *Le Rêve,* Fokine was quoted as saying that he abominated such American dances as the shimmy and fox trot and that he intended to develop and enrich the technique of dancing and to eliminate tricks and acrobatics. How much time he actually had to pursue this objective during 1922 is questionable, since in February he, Mme Fokina, and a group of dancers and musicians embarked upon what is labeled "Klines Tour" in the Fokine press clippings book.[3]

The tour began in Boston on 5 February, where critics found fault with the poorly rehearsed musical trio that accompanied the Fokines in place of the usual orchestra. The company performed in Poli's Theatre in Washington, D.C., where the *Washington Times* ran an article stating that they were planning to tour the Pacific coast.[4] They then went into Virginia, where, in Roanoke, tickets went on sale at the local jewelry store.

The program in Richmond included Fokine doing *Bacchus,* Fokina dancing *The Dying Swan* and *Salome,* and both doing three Russian folk dances. Also included were *Thunderbird,* the "Dance of the Three Dolls" from *Petrouchka,* and Mlle Talma in the *Bacchanale.* The cast of *Thunderbird* in Richmond was listed in the newspapers as made up of Mlles Ivanova, Waite, Korolova, Talma, and Fokina, which seems to indicate that they performed a cut-down version of the ballet they had presented at the New York Hippodrome in 1921. The excerpt from *Petrouchka* was danced by Mlles Ivanova and Waite and M. Antonoff. The latter was Vitale Fokine, who danced using his mother's maiden name. In Norfolk,

Fokina was featured in *Tzigane* and Fokine in *Panaderos,* and both performed some excerpts from *Le Rêve de la Marquise*. They returned to Washington for a second performance, this time at the Belasco Theatre, where attendance was large and the press praised their virtuosity and found them original and charming.

The Fokines and their small troupe performed once again in Boston, at Symphony Hall, in April 1923, in a program that included *Tzigane* and what one critic called "the famous and overworked *Dying Swan*."[5] In spite of his negative comments on the Fokines themselves, H. T. Parker noted their "quick spirited pupils" and added, "Give Mr. Fokine time and opportunity and we shall yet have an American ballet, Russian crossed."

The Fokine dancers seem to have given no concerts in 1923, although there was talk of a production of the ballet *Judith,* probably based on the dances which Fokine had choreographed in 1912 in the opera of the same name at the Maryinsky Theatre in St. Petersburg. In October 1923, *The Official Metropolitan Guide* reported that this ballet was being planned with Mme Fokina in the starring role. The *New York Evening Telegram* said that the ballet would use ninety dancers and that Michel Fokine would be Holofernes. The matter is confused by a double-page spread in the *London Tatler* dated 8 August 1923, showing photographs of Vera Fokina, purportedly in *Judith,* "which played in New York and created something of a sensation."[6] There is, however, no further mention of this ballet, or any evidence that the plan had ever actually materialized. It is possible that it was put aside because of the debut of the Fokine American Ballet Company on 26 February 1924, at the Metropolitan Opera House in New York City.

This debut, proclaimed as the start of a new era in American dance and in the career of Michel Fokine, had been prophesied almost from the day the Fokines arrived in the United States in 1919. At that time, Fokine announced that he had come to this country in part to study American dance, and that he hoped to be able to produce a national American dance. He noted that he did not consider the Buck and Wing, the Double Shuffle, or the Virginia Reel to be typically American. The caption under a photograph of the Fokines in the *Illustrated Daily News* quoted him as saying that the shimmy "and other exaggerated dances that border on the vulgar have no place in art."

A year later he had modified this outlook somewhat and while on tour in Ohio comments:

Even your shimmy is an art. It is as much so as the peasant dances from which we in Russia have developed our ballet.

There is gradually shaping in my mind an American ballet which will express
the view of your national life in terms of your own body movement. My ambition
is to create an American ballet. I will do it.[7]

The preopening publicity about the Fokine American Ballet stressed the
use of an all-American corps de ballet. Fokine had been training it for
three years in the hope of bringing to fruition his dream of creating a
distinctly American ballet, organized very much like the Imperial School
in Russia. He was reported as feeling that America was ready to encourage native artists and that, because Europe was disrupted and torn, the
time was ripe for the creation of an American ballet. As for the dancers
themselves, Fokine said that they had an advantage over their European
counterparts because from childhood Americans are inspired with an intense love of sports and the outdoors, resulting in great physical strength.

Society, too, was interested in seeing the sixty dancers trained by Fokine, and many members of the Monday Opera Supper Club bought
boxes. A percentage of the profits from the performance went to the Advisory Committee for Russian Relief in Europe. The *New York Times*
carefully summed up the anticipated production when it said that "because of remembered Russian ballet for more than a decade credited to
Michel Fokine, there is interest on the public's part as well as that of artists and musicians."

The sixty dancers who performed with the company were all students
of the Fokines, many of whom had danced with them before, including
Beatrice Belreva, Inga Bredohl, Alice Wynne, Renee Wilde, Lora Vinci,
and Nelly Savage. There were eighteen men in the group, among them
Jack Scott and Vitale Fokine, who continued to use his mother's maiden
name, Antonoff, whenever he performed.

The program for the debut of the company, which on the official Metropolitan Opera House program was labeled "Michel Fokine, Vera Fokina and Their American Ballet," consisted of *The Dying Swan, Le Rêve
de la Marquise, Antique Frieze, Olé Toro, Les Elfes,* and *Medusa.* The
first two were familiar repertory pieces, and *Antique Frieze,* a dance for
three girls to music by Glazounov, was probably the same piece performed in 1923 at a costume ball for the American Committee for the
Relief of Russian Children under the title *Danse Greque.*

Olé Toro used Rimsky-Korsakov's music "Capriccio Espagnole" and
had been performed previously by the Fokine dancers under the same title
as the score. The ballet takes place in the 1860s in a Spanish tavern after
a bullfight. The victorious toreador is attracted to the gypsy dancer in the
cabaret, thus provoking the jealousy of her young lover. The boys and

girls present at the tavern pretend that the lover is a mad bull and they stage a mock bullfight. This was basically a light, even comic ballet, with Vera Fokina as the gypsy dancer, Inesilla, and Fokine as the toreador.

Les Elfes, which used Mendelssohn's "Overture to A Midsummer Night's Dream" and the Andante and Allegro from his "Violin Concerto (Op. 64)," (the same music he used for his earlier *A Midsummer Night's Dream*), was one of the two ballets premiered by the new company. There is no program note or storyline for this work. Section "A" to the Overture contained five parts: a duet, three trios, and a dance for nine. Section "B" was performed by the company to excerpts from the Concerto. The Fokines did not appear in this piece. Photographs show the dancers, whom one reviewer called "green clad sprites," in short costumes that expose the entire leg and seem to be decorated with cloth leaves. The women wear wings, which make them look like wood sprites. Fokine later staged this work for the Ballet Russe de Monte Carlo, and it was performed in New York City in a memorial concert to the choreographer after his death.[8]

The second ballet premiere on the program of the new company was *Medusa,* choreographed to Tchaikovsky's "Symphonie Pathétique." Forty minutes in length, it utilized a large cast headed by the four main characters, Medusa, Perseus, Poseidon, and Pallas. The story, set in Greece, follows the ancient Greek legend in which Poseidon, the sea god, falls in love with the beautiful Medusa and induces her to violate the sanctity of the Temple of the goddess Pallas. The goddess punishes Medusa by turning her into a snake-haired monster, whose glance turns all things to stone. Perseus finally hypnotizes Medusa by using his shield as a mirror, and slays her by cutting off her head.

Vera Fokina was Medusa; Michel Fokine, Perseus; Nelly Savage, Pallas; and Jack Scott, Poseidon. The thirty others in the cast played mourning brides, Greek maidens, warriors, and—dressed in blues and greens—waves on which Medusa floated. Katherine Sergava recalls that there were parts of the stage at the Met that could be raised and lowered, and Fokine used these as part of his choreography. The young dancers, who were, for the most part, inexperienced, were terrified that the machinery would not work.

Almost all of the reviews of this performance were mixed. Although some of the ballets—as well as the intermissions—were deemed too long, it was generally felt that the production was well staged and that the young American dancers had proved themselves the equal of their Russian counterparts. One writer went so far as to liken the Fokines to planets around which the student dancers moved as satellites.

As far as the individual ballets were concerned, the performances of

Michel Fokine in *Medusa. Courtesy Phyllis Fokine Archive.*

both Fokines were found flawless—particularly her graceful Swan and his pantomime. *Elfes,* although deemed playful and delightful in its simplicity, showed signs of needing more rehearsal in order to perfect the ensemble dancing, in spite of the "earnestness and ardor" of the young dancers. *Medusa,* the longest and most advertised ballet, was considered a more mature work, probably because Fokine and Fokina carried the leading roles. Theodore Stearns in the *New York City Telegraph* said Fokina as a Greek maiden was like a poet's dream. When Fokine slew her, Stearns wrote, the entire company accompanied his rhythmic motions. But he observed "a bouncing rubber ball" in front of the ancient Greek temple, and "three Greek maidens with rolled stockings on,—Athenian flappers probably." Since this was not mentioned elsewhere, it is possible that it was inserted just to make interesting copy, especially since Fokine was known for his attention to small details.

A writer named Byrne MacFadden in *Dance Lovers Magazine* gave them an excellent review, although he faulted the ensemble work in *Elfes* and found *Medusa* too long. MacFadden also lamented the fact that the newspaper critics reviewing the Fokines knew nothing about dance. He concluded by stating that Fokine had given us an American ballet and had "founded a new art we may call our own."

MacFadden's statement agrees with those made by Fokine at the time, especially one made in March 1924, when he claimed that he could accomplish in two years what the Imperial School in Russia did in four.[9] Those who worked with him agree, however, that Fokine never had a truly permanent ballet company. Rather, he would merely assemble the dancers from his school, many of whom were very young, whenever he had a performance or a series of performances. At such times, he would often audition for soloists and male dancers. This method of operation seems to have been dictated not only by the relatively small potential audience for classical ballet, but by the lack of any seriously committed backers. Fokine himself, writing in *Dance Magazine* in November 1928, said:

I organized a troupe out of my American pupils and presented a performance . . . in 1924. I called the troupe my American Ballet. In 1927, I gave in the Lewisohn Stadium three recitals and the same number in the Century Theatre with this American Ballet. I think that I can state that during these days and also when I repeated the recitals in other cities the American Ballet did exist, but of course this was not the creation of a permanent ballet, which is lacking, and, about which I speak here.

As he noted, the Fokine American Ballet did not appear again in concert until 1927. From April through October 1925 the Fokines toured Europe—mostly Scandinavia—and on 27 February 1926, Vera Fokina gave a solo recital at Carnegie Hall in a program choreographed and arranged by Fokine. Accompanied by an orchestra conducted by Josiah Zuro, she danced *The Dying Swan, Tzigane,* The Russian folk dances, part of the Queen's dance from Act 2 of *Le Coq d'Or* (1914), called "Shamakenskaya Czarina," *Phoenix* (which appears to be one of the solos from *Thunderbird), Song of India,* and *Etude Symphonique.* The last-named ballet, about a nun who dreams of the gaieties of life, was quite similar to *The Miracle,* a fact noted by several reviewers. Mme Fokina had to overcome several obstacles in this performance: an enormous stage, lack of footlights, an inadequate orchestra, and the absence of supporting artists. In general her dramatic characterization was praised, though her lack of suppleness as a dancer was deplored.

Sol Hurok managed the Fokines and their company once again for a few months in 1927. Three performances at Lewisohn Stadium during the summer were followed by several at the Century Theatre on Central Park West, an evening on Sunday, 23 October, and a matinee and evening on Sunday, 30 October. The first program contained *Elfes, Oriental Dances, Voices of Spring,* and a Harlequin and Columbine Duet from *Carnaval,* danced by Paul Haakon and Tania Koshkina. Mme Fokina did the solo *Phoenix,* and both Fokines danced in selections from *Le Rêve de la Marquise,* the Mazurka to Delibes's music, and what appears to have been the complete *Cléopâtre.* According to one newspaper, Vera Fokina also performed *The Dying Swan,* which might have been an encore since it was not listed on the program. Among the forty dancers were Patricia Bowman, Betty Eisner, Pauline Koner, Paul Haakon, and Vitale Antonoff.

Les Sylphides was announced for two performances on 30 October, but the program was exactly the same as that of the previous week, with Max Hoffmann conducting the orchestra. Both performances were for the benefit of the Jewish Community House of Bensonhurst, Brooklyn. When the Fokines, Hurok, and Herman Fuchs, the manager of the Century Theatre, were brought to court for violating a section of the penal law dealing with Sunday entertainment (Fokina was stripped of some of her veils in *Cléopâtre*) the defense contended that it was a charity benefit and the case was dismissed.

Hurok toured the Fokine Company to the Masonic Auditorium in Detroit on 10 and 11 November, the Mosque Theatre in Pittsburgh on 24 November, and to Cleveland on 14 January 1928. There are indications that they may have performed elsewhere as well, but no verification. Hurok says that "prominent professional dancers" were added to the roster of pupils for this tour, probably meaning the Danish-born Paul Haakon and Russian-trained Tania Koshkina.

Available press coverage again reveals as much preopening publicity as critical reviews, with emphasis on the young American dancers. In New York the *Tribune* considered *Cléopâtre* a failure due to the poor execution and "raggedness" on the part of the ensemble. Nicholas Murray, reviewing the performances in the January issue of *Dance Magazine,* agreed, and expressed the hope that in the future Fokine's genius would create something that had America's vital force as its motive and not the conventions of Louis XVI. The program remained the same on tour, and in Detroit the critics, although full of praise and admiration, noted that neither of the Fokines was young and that the youthful troupe was for the most part unpracticed.

Performances by the Fokines and the Fokine Ballet on the concert stage were virtually nonexistent for the next few years. In 1929 the Fokines were in Europe and Hollywood and in 1931 Fokine worked for several months at the Teatro Colón in Buenos Aires. In December 1932 he gave a program of dance sketches on two afternoons for the Exposition of Women's Arts and Industries at the Commodore Hotel in New York City. Both Fokines gave their last dance performance on 23 January 1933, at the Eaton Auditorium in Toronto, at which time Fokine was fifty-three years old and Vera Fokina forty-five. Vitale Fokine points out that it was in this same year that the Ballets Russes de Monte Carlo came to America with several Fokine ballets in their repertory, and provided a new stimulus to ballet in this country.[10]

In June 1933 Michel Fokine staged *Coppélia* with members of the Chicago Civic Opera Ballet at the Blackstone Theatre in Chicago as part of the Century of Progress Exhibit in that city. This was the first full-length American production of this 1870 ballet choreographed by St.-Léon to music by Delibes. Fokine had danced in it at the Imperial Theatre in Petrograd, and, according to the *New York Times,* if it was a success there would be other productions staged by Fokine throughout the summer, probably *Schéhérazade.* This project seems not to have materialized. Ironically, at the same time and in the same city, a company led by Ruth Page and Blake Scott presented a program that included the Polovtsian Dances from *Prince Igor* "after Fokine."

Except for a few scattered performances under the direction of Vitale Fokine that occurred as late as 1940, the concept of a full-fledged American Ballet Company is one that Michel Fokine seems to have abandoned by the mid-1930s. America in the 1920s and early 1930s was not ready for such an institution—particularly without considerable private financial support. These years did witness the development of American modern dance through the work of Denishawn, Graham, Humphrey, Weidman, and others. With the exception of Denishawn, however, their companies were small, and their performances infrequent and unprofitable. All of them required an additional source of revenue. Ruth St. Denis and Ted Shawn, who were more realistic than the others and possessed more business acumen, made frequent tours on the various vaudeville circuits. Martha Graham danced with the *Greenwich Village Follies*, and Doris Humphrey, Charles Weidman, and, later, Hanya Holm, Helen Tamaris, George Balanchine, and others earned a living from Broadway shows and other types of popular performance.

On the Motion Picture Circuit

A form of entertainment aimed at amusing ordinary Americans does not, at first, seem to be the logical place for displaying an art form developed in Imperial Russia. Yet Fokine's ballets frequently dealt with epic and fantastic subject matter, as did much popular entertainment of the day. This very distance from reality, plus the fact that they were easily comprehended, made them excellent material for the vaudeville and motion picture cum vaudeville circuits. From there, it was only natural that they would become part of the large outdoor spectacles that were so popular in America at the time. Thus, while their aim was the concert stage, the Fokines performed more frequently and made much more money in the popular theater.

The second performance in America by Michel Fokine and Vera Fokina took place in 1920 at the Hippodrome in New York City, a theater ordinarily associated with spectacles and vaudeville. On that occasion their dancing was the only event on the evening's program. The ballet *Thunderbird* was part of a revue at this same theater in 1921. In April 1926 Mme Fokina headed a group of dancers, making what was termed her "vaudeville debut" in a varied bill at the Hippodrome, on which she and the soprano Anna Case were the headliners on a program that included a juggler, a gymnast, and the Albertina Rasch Girls. There is no record of what was on the ballet program, which was arranged by Fokine, although there is a newspaper photograph of Mme Fokina in the nun's habit she wore in the ballet *Etude Symphonique*.

An even more unusual place for performances by the Fokine Ballet was the Club Mirador on West 51st Street in New York City, where they opened on 15 February 1926, for a limited engagement of twenty-four evenings. The club was jammed on opening night, which Clifton Webb and Ethel Barrymore attended, in what one newspaper called a "new era" for nightclubs—the beginning of the "Carnegie Hall tradition." Although an advertisement announced the premiere evening as offering the first of a "series" by Fokine, there is no indication that they ever danced anything but *A Venetian Carnival,* to music by Deems Taylor and Johnny Johnson, and *Caucasian Sketches,* with music by Ipolitov-Ivanov.[12]

The reviewers judged the program a success, especially the scenic and lighting effects. One columnist, observed that it was novel to see Fokine's name in lights over a nightclub, added "not please, let it be clear, that it is declasse, for if more Fokine ideas were used . . . Broadway would have fewer troubles."[13] According to *Variety,* Fokine was responsible for supplying the performers and costumes, in addition to the choreography and staging for this engagement, and received a salary of $4,000 a week. Considering his own costs, and comparing the sum to the salary he received from Morris Gest, this could hardly be considered progress.

The 1920s witnessed both the development of the motion picture as an artistic medium and its continued growth as a form of popular entertainment. Films were originally presented as acts on a vaudeville bill, a concept that continued in a sense even after theaters for motion pictures were built. Fokine started his association with movie theaters on 15 October 1922, when his student company began an eight-week engagement at the Mark Strand Theatre in New York, giving ballets and divertissements before the featured moving picture.

For their debut the company presented *Les Sylphides*—although whether they performed the complete work or only sections is unknown. During the week of 22 October, the three works on the bill were *Humoresque* (Dvorak), *Polka* (Strauss), and *Bacchanale* (Glazounov). The week beginning 29 October, from which a program remains, brought *Russian Toys* and a *Waltz* to the music of Johann Strauss. These were performed four times a day.

The world premiere of the ballet *The Adventures of Harlequin,* to music by Beethoven, took place on 12 November 1922. All that can be discovered about this ballet is that it was based on the standard characters of the commedia dell'arte, and was so popular that it was held over for a second week. In the cast were Vitale Antonoff, as both Harlequin and the Doctor, Maria Chabelska as Columbine, Maria Korolova as Pierrette, and Mlles Hunter and Childe as maids. "M. Wilde" was listed as Pierrot, "M. Vinci" as the Captain, and "M. Desha, M. Lee and M. Bauer" as Policemen. Judging by the casting for the other ballets, all of these were women. Lillian Moore suggests that the M. Bourman, playing Pantalon, was probably Anatole Bourman, an alumnus of the Imperial School.[14] The company performed this ballet three times a day.

The ballet *Fantasie Chinois* (Rebikov)—along with the film *East Is West,* starring Constance Talmadge—was next at the Strand, and *Danse Classique* (Glazounov) followed.[15] During the week of 10 December the company repeated *Humoresque* and *Polka. Dance Review*'s critic called the latter, in which Mlle Chabelska and M. Antonoff danced, a charming evocation of children playing, but he found *Humoresque* very poorly danced. It is interesting to note that by this time there were only two dances on the program, whereas during the week of 22 October there had been three. This could be attributed either to the length of the film, the other acts on the program, or perhaps exhaustion on the part of the young and inexperienced dancers. The last week of the engagement saw a return of the popular *Russian Toys.*

During this period Fokine wrote to his brother Alexander in Russia, noting that his work in New York was diverse and difficult, that he had injured himself four times, and that he had never in his life had to be so persistent. "Every week I put on a new ballet in the Strand Theatre, but of course, circumstances are not as accommodating as those in Russia. . . . Life in America is very hard. All the technical and cultural wonders, but how little intellectual and spiritual life there is." He went on to say that life was expensive, that he was fourty-four, an age when a dancer had to work and not rest, and that his last production was praised a great deal.[16]

Another movie theater with which the Fokine name is associated is the Stanley Theatre in Philadelphia. Completed in 1921, it seated four thousand people in chairs covered in red silk, all of which reputedly offered an unobstructed view of the stage and screen. Vera Fokina first appeared at the Stanley the week of 1 January 1923, performing two solos, *The Dying Swan* and *Tzigane.* In April 1924 she returned with a group of dancers to do *Shemanskaya Tsaritsa,* and in May 1926 she performed *The Mountain Queen* with the group and *Phoenix* as a solo. But it was only in 1927, in Fokine's *Faust* ballet, to music to Moussorgsky and Grieg, that he created a work specifically for the Stanley Theatre.

The preopening publicity for this ballet, as for all other Fokine dances presented in Philadelphia, was devoted to a recapitulation of his ideas and reforms, a brief history of his career, and the role of Vera Fokina as his "pupil and aesthetic counterpart." It was also promised that *Faust* would be unconventional and spectacular.

Little is known about the dance, which, in addition to Mme Fokina, utilized a corps of about fifteen dancers. Pauline Koner, who was a youthful member of the troupe, recalls that this was a two-week engagement, during which they did three shows a day. She and the corps played devils. Her outstanding recollection is that the flames and smoke on stage were made by ammonia of some sort, and that one day the pipes broke and they all were almost asphyxiated. She feels that Fokine was very frustrated and depressed by then, aware that he had slipped from the high position he had held during the Diaghilev era.

The Fokine Dancers started to perform on the Keith-Albee vaudeville circuit in 1924. An item in the *Buffalo Express* in November of that year talks about the film *North of 36* and concludes: "An extra feature is the appearance of the Fokine Dancers, including Desha, the Bubble dancer . . . in a series of beautifully costumed dances."

In December 1924 it was announced that a new dance presentation, *The Immortal Pierrot,* choreographed by Fokine and featuring Michio Ito and eight of Fokine's selected pupils, would open soon on the Keith Circuit. Michio Ito was an internationally known Japanese dancer, but there is no mention of either Fokine or *The Immortal Pierrot* in Ito's biography.[17] This ballet in three scenes, to music by Beethoven, had a libretto, costumes, and scenery by Michel Fokine and Willy Pogany, was sponsored by Martha Lorber, and opened on 16 February 1925, at the 81st Street Theatre in New York City. According to *Billboard,* the eight dancers included Vitale Antonoff, Beatrice Belreva, Inga Bredahl, Alice Wynne, and Desha. The ballet was to break in on the Albee circuit, a tour that had also been announced earlier by the *Morning Telegraph.* There is no record, however, that this tour actually took place, and both Fokines were in Europe from March through October of 1925. During the spring of 1926, Vera Fokina and the Fokine Ballet supposedly toured the big Keith-Albee houses, but the only appearance that can be verified is one at the Albee Theatre in Brooklyn the week of 3 May, when they performed *The Mountain Queen* and *Phoenix.*[18]

It was with these same two ballets that they began their tour of the Loew's theaters during the week beginning 31 May 1926, in Boston. Also on this bill were two singers named Downey and Owens, an accordionist, a harmonica player, a band that alternated between jazz and operatic selections, and the film *Early to Wed,* with Zasu Pitts. H. T. Parker of the *Boston Evening Transcript* labeled *The Mountain Queen* a "quasi-oriental spectacle." He noted that four performances a day were too many for

Newspaper advertisement for the Fokine Ballet at a movie
theater in Pittsburgh.

any dancer, and that the heavy schedule obviously had its effect on the Fokine Company. Calling their expedition into film houses a "happy novelty," he concluded, "If film audiences will have vaudeville turns to spin out their programs, then a ballet surely comports best with the medium of the screen."

The last motion-picture tour of Fokine dancers performing Fokine ballets took place in 1934, when, at the end of August, after their appearance at Lewisohn Stadium, they danced for a week at the Capitol Theatre in New York. Vera Fokina was no longer dancing with them. The program consisted of *Les Sylphides, Bolero* (Ravel), and *Prince Igor.* The *New York Times* matter-of-factly but incorrectly reported this as the company's "first appearance in a motion-picture theatre."

Annabelle Lyon says that they remained a second week at the Capitol, performing *Schéhérazade* and *Carnaval.* She was the leading dancer because Albertina Vitak, who was the ballerina at the Stadium, had left before the start of the engagement. Vitale Fokine records this as a four-week booking. George Chaffee, one of the leading male dancers in the company, left at the end of the first week because he found the four-performances-a-day schedule unbearable and Lyon recalls that the company started an abortive tour of movie theaters across the country, which closed after only two weeks. An advertisement from the *Pittsburgh Post Gazette* dated 12 October 1934, however, proclaims an appearance by the Fokine Ballet at the Penn Theatre, where the film was *Outcast Lady,* with Constance Bennett. This indicates that the tour, in fact, lasted more than two weeks.

Vitale Fokine reports that the company went to Detroit and Washington, D.C., as well, and criticizes the fact that in Cleveland the theater manager inserted a comedian between the ballets. In Detroit, he said the workers were appreciative, and the dancers came to feel that the masses were ready for a more serious art form. In Washington, D.C., however, the company was jeered—an act he deems "hooliganism"—and the "dream of presenting ballet to the masses was abandoned."[19] The remainder of the tour was canceled at this point and the company never again appeared in motion-picture theaters. Fokine left shortly thereafter to work in Europe.

Outdoor Entertainment

Sol Hurok claims full credit for introducing ballet to Lewisohn Stadium on West 137th Street, New York, where he presented the Fokines and the

Fokine American Ballet in August 1927. They would appear there again in 1934, 1935, and 1939. The Stadium was a large amphitheater where, for a minimal entrance fee, up to fifteen thousand people could sit on the poured concrete steps to see different programs, usually of classical music. The program for the three evenings in 1927 (17, 18, and 19 August) was the same: *Elfes, The Dying Swan, Medusa,* a suite of dances from *Le Rêve de la Marquise, Oriental Dances, Panaderos,* and all five of the Russian Songs.

Fokine danced in *Medusa, Le Rêve de la Marquise,* and *Panaderos,* but not in the Russian Songs. This long and ambitious program, accompanied by an orchestra conducted by Arnold Volpe, played to a full house for each performance. Among the company members were Patricia Bowman, Jack Scott, and Tania Koshkina.

In the program notes, entitled "Creating the Russian Ballet," the following statement appeared:

From now on, Mr. Fokine plans to remain in New York, devoting most of his time to creating an artistic American Ballet. Many of his pupils are now dancing in big productions in different theatres, but he wishes to unite them all into one group, to become the foundation of a theatre which would be just as great in its artistic importance as was the famous new Russian Ballet created by Michel Fokine.

When the Fokine company next appeared in Lewisohn Stadium in 1934, seven years had elapsed, during which time there had been practically no performances at all, except for the last months of 1927 and two concerts in Hollywood in 1929. Although he had continued teaching, Fokine had created little in the United States, with the exception of the ballets for *Rosalie* and *The Grand Street Follies of 1928.* He was, however, very active for five months in 1931 at the Teatro Colón in Buenos Aires, Argentina, and had also been working in Europe.

Vita Fokine reported that, in preparation for this second appearance at Lewisohn Stadium, his parents "hastily gathered all available dancers and pupils and began to rehearse."[20] Among the performers they assembled were Albertina Vitak, Leon Barte, Dorothy Hallberg, Annabelle Lyon, Winona Bimboni, Alice Wynne, Thalia Mara, Harold Haskin, Eugene Loring, Betty Eisner, Miriam Weiskopf, and George Chaffee.

The program for the first two performances, on 6 and 7 August, consisted of *Schéhérazade,* with Mlle Vitak and M. Barte dancing the leads, and *Les Sylphides,* featuring Mlles Lyon, Vitak, and Hallberg and M. Chaffee. Although *Schéhérazade* had been seen in America several times previously, this production, with scenery and costumes after Bakst, was the first in this country under Fokine's direction. On opening night two thousand people were turned away, hundreds stood in the back of the amphitheater, some sat on the ground, and others on scaffolding that had been erected for repairs. The headline in the *New York Times* the day after the second performance read, "Police Called as 10,000 Try Vainly to See Fokine Ballet at the Stadium."

With the exception of the *Herald Tribune,* the press was as enthusiastic as the audience. *News-Week* reported that Fokine was still teaching and working on the art that he had raised to such a high level. Samuel Chotzinoff of the *Post* wrote a humorous column saying that his pass got him into a press seat, but that he could see nothing because the stadium resembled the Roman Coliseum in the days of the gladiators, filled as it was with intellectual devotees of Mr. Fokine's Russian Ballet, "who stood on tiptoe, huddled together like sheep at the approach of a storm."

John Martin, the most influential dance critic of the era, was happy that these performances ended the seven years of Fokine's virtual inactivity in America. Martin blamed American artistic taste for neglecting Fokine and pronounced the two ballets unmistakable evidence of the choreographer's genius, even though he felt that they could have been performed better. To Martin, *Schéhérazade* came off as a masterpiece—not an antique—and *Les Sylphides,* with its abstract composition and fine musicianship, even better. He further castigated American audiences by adding that "the balletomane of taste does not exist in any great numbers in America, where a 'toe routine' is likely to be valued largely for its multiple turns and adagio for the sensationalism of its tricks."

The second program, on 13 and 14 August, repeated *Les Sylphides* and added *Prince Igor* and *Bolero.* Fokine had recently created and staged *Bolero* to Ravel's music, for Ida Rubinstein's company in Paris.[21] This ballet, a plotless response to the images of the music, was danced on a raised platform on the stage. It began with one woman draped in white and surrounded by brightly dressed men and women. She was joined by a youth in black and then the entire company danced to the rhythmic music.[22] Lewisohn Stadium was again packed for the performances and the reviews were excellent, causing one critic to predict that the following summer dance entertainments would loom large in the Stadium schedule. True to this prediction, it was announced in June 1935 that Fokine would present four different programs of ballet at Lewisohn Stadium during the first four weeks of July, with Paul Haakon as a leading dancer. Each program was to be given twice.

The first Fokine program, on 1 and 2 July, contained *Adventures of*

Les Sylphides on the stage of Lewisohn Stadium. Dorothy Denton, George Chaffee, and Michel Fokine. *Courtesy Phyllis Fokine Archive.*

Harlequin, Le Spectre de la Rose, danced by Paul Haakon and Dorothy Hall, and *Prince Igor.* In the company, which the *Times* said would number sixty but actually was under fifty, were many of the dancers from the previous year. New performers included Ann Wolfson, who later danced as Anne Wilson; Nora Koreff, better known as Nora Kaye; Virginia Comer; and George Church, who went on to dance in the original "Slaughter on Tenth Avenue." Alexander Smallens was the conductor for the entire series.

Adventures of Harlequin, with music by Beethoven, was not really receiving its first performance in New York. It was an expanded and revised version of the work Fokine had presented at the Strand Theatre in 1922 and had rechoreographed in Buenos Aires in 1931. On this program Vitale Fokine—now using the Fokine name—was Harlequin; Edna Veralle was the First Lady; Harold Haskin, the Captain; Eugene Loring, Pantalone; and George Kiddon, Pierrot. There were also thirty-five others in the cast of what the program called "a choreographic comedy." John Martin did not like this ballet, which he felt leaned on action and pantomime rather than dance, and he called the evening a disappointment on both sides of the footlights, with an unenthusiastic audience of only six thousand.

The second program on 8 and 9 July featured *Schéhérazade, Les Elfes,* and *The Sorcerer's Apprentice.* The last ballet, to Paul Dukas's orchestral score, based on Goethe's ballad "Zauberlehring," was originally presented in St. Petersburg in 1916, and had been restaged in 1931 at the Teatro Colón in Buenos Aires. It is the story of a magician's pupil, who, to test his own powers, sends a broom to draw water from a well. The water keeps rising and almost drowns the pupil, who cannot remember the incantation to stop it, and he is finally saved by the appearance of the magician. Eugene Loring was the apprentice; Vladimir Valentinoff, the sorcerer; and Paul Haakon, the broom. Twenty-six women in the company represented water, and eight men algae.

Because of the threat of rain, only 3,500 people saw the first night of this second program, which John Martin deemed far superior to the first. He observed that nothing could obscure the excellence of *Schéhérazade* as a dance composition, and he praised Paul Haakon as the broom that came to life. In another column on 14 July he noted the publication of Cyril Beaumont's book *Michel Fokine and His Ballets,* adding that it was most appropriate "since this is to all intents and purposes Fokine month in New York," enabling audiences to see twelve of the choreographer's compositions staged under his own direction. He remarked, however, that the company did not do Fokine's work justice.

The third program, on 15 and 16 July, contained *Cléopâtre, Les Sylphides,* and *Russian Toys.* Paul Haakon danced the male lead in all three ballets. Pitts Sanborn in the *World Telegram* praised *Russian Toys* as successful and enjoyable, and several other critics singled it out for praise as well.

The last of the two evening presentations took place on 22 and 23 July, with *Carnaval, Bolero,* and the *Venusberg Scene* from Wagner's opera *Tannhäuser.* The latter, a bacchanale, was originally choreographed and presented in 1910 for a charity performance in St. Petersburg, with Nijinsky as one of the fauns. This was the first time it had been staged in New York.[23] Miriam Weiskopf, who danced in the corps, recalls a series of Greek friezes, danced in bare feet in a very relaxed manner. One newspaper called it the high point of the program, praising its movement, color, precision, and meaning. *Time* magazine gave extensive coverage to twenty-two-year-old Paul Haakon, comparing him to Nijinsky. It was pointed out, however, that he was the exception among the Fokine dancers, who had impressed critics as no more than mediocre, and that he had been brought in to bolster a faltering season.

John Martin also regretted the financial plight of the stadium. While people had been turned away from Fokine concerts a year earlier (1934), now the seats were only half sold for the current season. He attributed this both to bad weather and to the increased number of performances scheduled. His main point, however, was that a lack of responsiveness to the ballet had always characterized the American public, with whom an antipathy to the so-called "aristocratic arts" was inherent. Box-office success had always, he felt, depended upon glamorous names, and the success of the Fokine company the previous year had been due to its novelty and its lack of recent exposure. Martin also observed that the ballets presented were of historical interest, but that orgies and bacchanales had already found their way into Hollywood and were not in tune with the times.

Martin's reasoning makes some sense, particularly in light of his generally strong advocacy of modern dance; but it conflicts with what he had written on 12 August 1934, only a year earlier. The tremendous response to the company at that time had suggested to him that Fokine had a substantial audience awaiting him:

Moreover, it is a popular audience and this is again a bright element in the occasion. American opera houses have chosen to set themselves apart from other opera houses by their indifference to the ballet. . . . There is no cause for worry, however, if the great potential popular audience can be reached, and this can certainly be done if several important conditions are observed.

Martin's conditions included low admission prices, artistic choreographers, and an end to the worship of chic, which so strongly characterized the latter days of the Diaghilev ballet and its successors. The Lewisohn Stadium performances seem to have met these requirements perfectly.

The Fokine company was seen in several popular theaters over the next few years, although they did not dance at Lewisohn Stadium again until 1939. Michel Fokine was, by then, working steadily in Europe, and Vitale Fokine had taken over as director of the company, which was reassembled whenever a series of engagements was offered. Patricia Bowman and Paul Haakon were the featured dancers.[24] The first program, postponed twice because of rain, finally went on 1 July with seventeen thousand people in attendance. On the bill were *Les Sylphides, Schéhérazade,* and *The Sorcerer's Apprentice.* John Martin felt that the company gave a highly creditable account of itself, considering that it had not worked together consecutively. He found *Les Sylphides* gay, debonair, and "distinctly American," lacking in atmosphere but not in entertainment value.

On the 27 and 28 July schedule were *Le Spectre de la Rose, Schéhérazade, Prince Igor,* and *Tennis,* a solo for Bowman discussed below. The second night of this program took place 30 July and drew an audience of 4,500, despite uncertain weather. The company appeared again on Monday, 21 August, in *Les Sylphides, Le Spectre de la Rose, The Sorcerer's Apprentice,* and *Tennis,* with Alexander Smallens conducting the orchestra.

The appearances by the Fokine Ballet at the Municipal Stadium on Randalls Island and in the outdoor theater on Zach's Bay at Jones Beach, Long Island, were arranged by Fortune Gallo, director of the San Carlo Opera Company, and an impresario who, at one time, was associated with the American tours of Anna Pavlova. The stadium at Jones Beach was new when the Fokine Ballet, an ensemble of seventy-five dancers under the supervision of Vitale Fokine, performed there on 3, 4, and 5 July 1936, the second weekend of its operation. There was a different program each evening, accompanied by a symphony orchestra under the direction of Max Hoffmann. The first night an audience of six thousand saw *Les Sylphides, Russian Toys,* and *Prince Igor. Elfes* was danced by Dorothy Hall, Thelma Himmel, and Grace Walsh, suggesting that this dance was only a divertissement from the larger piece. There was also *Blue Danube,* a solo, and the Glazounov *Bacchanale,* danced by the ensemble. Patricia Bowman performed the solo, as well as *The Dying Swan,* and was featured in *Les Sylphides.* The two remaining programs, which were different, included *The Sorcerer's Apprentice,* selections from *Adventures of Harlequin,* Miss Bowman in *The Dying Swan,* and a ballet by Vitale Fokine called *Artist's Dream* (Strauss). Also included were *Persian Angel* and *Tennis,* two solos that Michel Fokine had created for Patricia Bowman, which she danced for the first time in the series.

Persian Angel, to music by Moussorgsky and Glinka, is the story of an angel who tires of life as a celestial being and wants passion and love. She takes off her crown and wings; her embroidered Persian costume is changed to red chiffon, and she becomes a human being who ends up consumed by passion and dances herself to death.[25] Fokine designed the costume, and Patricia Bowman performed this dance at Radio City Music

Hall and in vaudeville and theaters all over the country, as well as at Jones Beach. Bowman's mother thought this piece too classical, and felt that her daughter needed another one to show off her versatility, which is how *Tennis* was created.[26]

This ballet, only four minutes long, used music from the last act of "Coppélia," by Delibes. In it, Miss Bowman wore a short tennis tunic and a visor, and played four sets of tennis, during which she galloped and ran, served, and picked up the ball. She recalls that, before choreographing it, Fokine spent several Sundays on Riverside Drive, watching the tennis players. John Martin enjoyed the humor of *Tennis*—not only the actual tennis movements, but the way in which Fokine played with the music. Calling it one of Fokine's "rare excursions into colloquialism," Martin felt it an "extremely successful trifle that fit the dancers like a glove."

The following year, 1937, the Fokine Ballet appeared on three Sunday evenings, when the operetta was not performed at Jones Beach. On 4 July, before an audience of over ten thousand, with four thousand others turned away, the company danced *Les Sylphides* and *Schéhérazade,* and Patricia Bowman danced *Tennis, Blue Danube,* and *None But the Lonely Heart* (Tchaikovsky). Michel Fokine was in Europe and Vitale Fokine directed the performances. On 11 July, with an audience held down to four thousand because of bad weather, they repeated *Les Sylphides,* but also danced *Russian Toys* and *Prince Igor,* and Patricia Bowman did *Persian Angel. Les Sylphides* was performed for a third time on 18 July, and *Prince Igor* and *Russian Toys* were also on the program.

There is a record of only one performance by the Fokine Ballet at Jones Beach in 1938, this one also directed by Vitale Fokine, on 3 July with an audience of 7,500 in attendance. The company was again led by Patricia Bowman, courtesy of the Mordkin Ballet, and André Eglevsky (listed in the program as "Andrew") was also featured. Max Hoffman conducted, and the ballets were *Carnaval, Tennis, Russian Toys, Blue Danube,* and *Les Sylphides.*

Fortune Gallo's San Carlo Opera Company presented many musicals in the Municipal Stadium on Randalls Island, just off the Triborough Bridge in New York City, in conjunction with the Shuberts. In 1936 both Gallo and the Fokine Ballet were associated with *Florodora* and *Blossom Time,* and by the following summer it is obvious that the Fokine ballet had been carefully scheduled to appear both at Jones Beach and at Randalls Island in the same repertoire. Geographically these two stadiums were far enough apart so that they attracted different audiences, and since both were subsidized (Jones Beach by the state and Randalls Island by the

Patricia Bowman in *Persian Angel* (program cover).

city) the price of admission was kept quite low, as it was also at Lewisohn Stadium.

The practice at Randalls Island was to present the dance company in one ballet during an intermission of a musical—a practice that seems to be a remnant of vaudeville and the programs at motion picture theaters. Virginia Comer Spencer, who performed with the Fokine Ballet during this period as a lead in *Prince Igor,* says that the dancers were all in the chorus of whatever musical was being presented, as well as in the ballets. She cannot remember how they were paid, but an equity audition was required for every dancer in the musical. It was, however, just a formality, since they were always accepted.

During the 1937 season at Randalls Island, the Fokine Ballet, under the direction of Vitale Fokine, performed the following works during the intermission of the musicals shown in parentheses: *Schéhérazade (The Firefly); Prince Igor (The Student Prince); Les Sylphides (Gay Divorcee); Sorcerer's Apprentice (Of Thee I Sing); Russian Toys (Anything Goes).* The dancers were usually cast in the same roles at Jones Beach.

In 1938 *Showboat* was featured at Randalls Island. Robert Coleman in the *Daily Mirror* reported that Robert Alton was the dance arranger and added that "there is an interpolated ballet conceived by Fokine." The program reads, "Fokine Ballet" in large letters, but nowhere does it indicate what work was danced. Vitale Fokine remained as director. André Eglevsky and Christine Kriens were featured, and the other dancers included Muriel Bentley, Olga Suarez, Helene Ecklund, Igor Meller, and John Taras. Patricia Bowman's name is noticeable by its absence from all Randalls Island programs.

In *Memoirs* Fokine talks of his travels one summer (probably 1902 or 1903) in Switzerland and his encounter with Russian political émigrés, who introduced him to the works of Kropotkin, Bakunin, Bebel, and Lasalle. He says, "My attempts to make the ballet accessible to large masses . . . were inspired not only by the views of Leo Tolstoy but also by everything I read in these books." Since this was not written until 1937, it is impossible to ascertain what really came first, the philosophy or the actuality, but America certainly gave Michel Fokine the opportunity to bring classical ballet to the masses.

Chapter Five

Back to Europe

BECAUSE MICHEL FOKINE WAS WORKING at such a diverse and exhausting pace, rushing from project to project, he did not have the time to work extensively in Europe during the 1920s. It is also possible that he preferred to concentrate his efforts in America at that point.

He did go to London, where, in addition to his work on the original production of *Hassan* in 1923, he created the dances for *A Midsummer Night's Dream*, directed by Basil Dean, in December 1925. The program simply credits Fokine with the ballets and lists the three major dancers. This production used the same music (Mendelssohn-Bartholdy) as the 1906 ballet for the Imperial School, which was based on Shakespeare, but what else was repeated is unknown.

Fokine went to Stockholm in 1925 and rehearsed the ballets he had previously staged there.[1] The Fokines also toured as guest performers in Denmark, Sweden, Latvia, Estonia, and Finland for several months in the spring of 1925. Among the ballets they presented was *Fra Mina*, to Schumann's "Symphonic Etudes," which was first performed in Berlin. Based on "The Saintly Satyr" by Anatole France, it does not appear again on their programs, and it was included on Fokine's list of ballets to be forgotten. In 1929 he staged *Prince Igor* in Paris and Latvia, and *Les Sylphides* in the latter. The year 1931 really marks the height of Michel Fokine's disillusionment with America, and it is no surprise that although the 1930s was a decade of renewed creativity on his part, his energies were directed outside of the country.

Shortly after returning from California, he received an invitation from the Teatro Colón in Buenos Aires. This well-equipped opera house, with a stage that could accommodate over six hundred performers, was regarded as one of the great theaters of the West. Owned by the Argentine government, it was known for having one of the most outspoken and knowledgeable audiences in the world, quite familiar with the Diaghilev Ballets Russes. The theater had its own ballet company, which was often supplemented with guest dancers. Here Fokine staged *Prince Igor, Carnaval*, a new *Sorcerer's Apprentice* (probably the same version Paul Haakon danced), *Spectre de la Rose, Les Sylphides, Schéhérazade,* and a new version of the 1922 *Adventures of Harlequin* that was twenty-five minutes long and used one hundred performers.

In *Memoirs* he recalls that the dancers, with their laughing eyes and Spanish temperaments, became stiff and mechanized as soon as they performed a ballet sequence, the result of demands made by former Russian ballet masters. Igor Schwezoff says that this was a minor problem compared with the often hostile atmosphere in Buenos Aires. Fokine arrived in a rather strained state, very demanding and exacting, to find a number of dancers he did not wish to use—most especially Olga Spessivtzeva. The company, in turn, resented the fact that Fokine insisted on examining each dancer individually and they disliked Mme Fokina, who was present constantly and whose every suggestion her husband followed immediately.

Schwezoff remembers that when Fokine arrived, he lined up all the dancers and, conducting the audition in French, gave them sequences from *Carnaval* and *Prince Igor*. The ballet master eventually brought Schwezoff out from the back row and asked him to demonstrate the steps, and they worked together for nine months, with Schwezoff dancing many leading roles.

He recalls one quarrel he and Fokine had at a rehearsal that was conducted before the "elite" of Buenos Aires. Fokine was very nervous and accused Schwezoff of changing the choreography—specifically, which corner of the stage was used for a particular exit or entrance. Schwezoff became angry and left the rehearsal. That night Fokine, in relating his problems to Schwezoff, began to cry!

Fokine's acquaintance with Olga Spessivtzeva, the beautiful, shy, frail, superb technician, went back to the Imperial School, where he had been one of her teachers. In *Memoirs* he relates an incident when, as a joke, she gave incorrect technical information to Akim Volinsky, who later used it to denounce Fokine. She had danced in his ballet *Francesca da Rimini* in St. Petersburg in 1915 and in *Spectre de la Rose* and *Les Sylphides* on the Ballets Russes tour of the United States in 1916. Anton Dolin, in his book *The Sleeping Beauty,* says that Spessivtzeva was dancing in Buenos

Aires with an English partner, Keith Lester, and that initially Fokine was cold and distant toward her. He approved of her dancing of the waltz in *Les Sylphides,* however, and became more friendly when her portrayal of the Firebird, to which he added new lifts, received excellent reviews.

Dolin reports that trouble began with rehearsals of *Carnaval.* Fokine thought that Lester was too big for the role and insisted that Vitale dance it. According to Dolin, the management withdrew the ballet after two performances.[2] He says that Fokine revived *Spectre de la Rose* but departed after two days of rehearsal, leaving Spessivtzeva to coach Lester, and was most pleased with the results when he returned. Fokine and Spessivtzeva must have parted on somewhat amicable terms, since he staged two ballets for her performance at the Théâtre National de l'Opéra Comique in Paris in 1935, *Psyche* (Franck) and *Mephisto Valse* (Liszt).

During the 1930s Fokine's former pupil Ida Rubinstein presented four of his ballets at the Opera House in Paris: *Semiramis* (Honegger), *Diane* (Ibert), *La Valse* (Ravel), and *Bolero* (Ravel). Historically, the specially commissioned music for the last work, which was originally choreographed for Rubinstein by Nijinska in 1928 and rechoreographed by Fokine, has far outshone the choreography. In addition, Fokine worked at La Scala in Milan, creating the dances in the opera *Samson et Delilah* (Saint-Saëns) and the ballet *The Love of Three Oranges* (Simoni and Sonzogno), both in 1936.

But the event that brought Michel Fokine, the creative force of the early Ballets Russes de Monte Carlo, back into the European mainstream was a request from René Blum to be the artistic director of his new company, Les Ballets de Monte Carlo. Blum, a Frenchman who had worked with the opera ballet in Monte Carlo and was granted the right to use the name, had, in partnership with Col. Wassili de Basil, kept alive the repertory of the Diaghilev company after Diaghilev's death in 1929, as well as keeping the dancers employed. The Blum/de Basil Ballets Russes toured America in 1933, 1934, and 1935, bringing *Les Sylphides, Petroushka, Schéhérazade, Spectre de la Rose, Thamar, Carnaval,* and *Firebird*—with no royalties paid to Fokine, and little press credit given to him as choreographer.

But when Blum and de Basil parted (some claim Blum was eased out) and Blum decided to form his own company, it was Fokine to whom he turned.[3] André Eglevsky, who had earlier left the Blum/de Basil company, recalls arriving in Paris after another tour, learning that Blum and Fokine were auditioning dancers, and dashing over, to be accepted.

The Blum company, which lasted for two seasons in 1936 and 1937, included, in addition to Eglevsky, such dancers as Vera Nemchinova, Natalie Krassovska, Leon Woicikowsky, Anatole Vilzak, and Maria Ruanova. Fokine restaged and rehearsed many of his old works for the company: *Les Sylphides, Petroushka, Carnaval, Spectre de la Rose, Schéhérazade, Prince Igor, Les Elfes, Igrouchki* (the ballet he had made for Gilda Gray as *Russian Toys*), and *Jota Aragonesa*. He also created three new ballets: *L'Epreuve d'Amour, Don Juan,* and *Les Elements*.

When Fokine arrived in London in May 1936 and began to work with the company for their debut at the Alhambra Theatre, he received wide press coverage even before the season opened. Across the Atlantic, John Martin, writing in the *New York Times* on 24 May applauded Blum's decision to have Fokine rehearse his own ballets, noting how many companies had presented them by relying on someone else's memory. Martin went on to state that it was good to have one of the greatest masters in ballet history again actively at work, since in America, although Fokine was treated with respect, it was always with the attitude that he was a contemporary of Shakespeare. The season in general received positive press coverage, with the revivals, especially the dancing of the corps, praised as excellent under Fokine's hand, demonstrating that no apologia was needed for bringing him back.[4]

The first new work Fokine created for Blum was *L'Epreuve d'Amour,* produced at the Theatre de Monte Carlo on 4 April 1936, and first seen in London on 15 May 1936. Categorized as a form of "chinoiserie"—the eighteenth-century European version of Chinese figures on porcelains and screens—the ballet was said to have been inspired by the discovery at Graz of an unknown score by Mozart. To date, however, no musicologist has credited the work to Mozart and it is now believed to be the score to a divertissement, "The Recruit," with music by various composers, first performed in Vienna in 1838.[5] The libretto, by Fokine and the painter André Derain, who also designed the decor, was suggested by the score. It is probable that Derain first designed some of the costumes, which in turn helped inspire him and Fokine in devising the libretto.

The story, in three scenes, centers on four main characters: a Mandarin, his daughter Chung-Yang, her lover, and an Ambassador from a Western country. The first scene opens on a Chinese landscape with a group of monkeys and the pompous Mandarin, who dismisses with his stick both the monkeys and a butterfly who darts about him. The Chinese maidens enter with the lover, whose duet with Chung-Yang is interrupted by the returning Mandarin, who also dismisses him with his stick. The next scene shows the arrival of the Western Ambassador, who sets up a tent, gives out gifts, and does a spectacular dance. The young girl is left behind by her father and when the Ambassador creeps out of his tent in an attempt to seduce her, he is attacked by a dragon (the lover). The Ambassador is left poor after the lover's friends rob him, and the Mandarin consents to Chung-Yang's marriage to her beloved when he discovers the Ambassador is no longer rich. When the latter's goods are returned, the Mandarin reverses his decision, but the Ambassador refuses to be loved for his money, the lovers are carried to their wedding, and the Mandarin is left alone with the monkeys, the butterfly, and his empty visions of wealth.

Vera Nemchinova danced Chung-Yang, André Eglevsky, the lover, Anatole Oboukhov, the Ambassador, Helene Kirsova, the Butterfly, and Jan Yazvinsky, the Mandarin. Nicholas Beriozoff, who also danced in the ballet, staged it at Indiana University in 1980. A press release quotes him describing the delicate Chinese style movements, noting that without Fokine to provide the inspiration, it was difficult to stage the work in later years. This may account for the reviews it received in New York in 1938, when Denham's Ballet Russe de Monte Carlo performed it, and the reaction was that it was a weak and routine stage chinoiserie.

Eglevsky, however, recalls it as a lovely ballet, where Fokine used his own abilities as both a classic and a character dancer to create movement, and every step was performed "double," always finishing in a turned-out plié in second, which, tongue-in-cheek, was supposed to represent the "Chinese" element. Nemchinova, who still refers to this work as "my ballet," says that Fokine completed it in one week, surprised that she learned the role so quickly, and invited his friends to see it on the fifth day. She recalls Helene Kirsova's outstanding performance as the butterfly and Fokine demonstrating every step of this role for her. Nemchinova performed a phrase that involved a jump that landed on one knee. Her aunt, who traveled with her, had fashioned a knee pad for the "landing," and Nemchinova, seeing Derain at rehearsals, became apprehensive about the costume he would design for her. She was very happy when she learned that she was to wear full pants under her skirt. Another memory is of a long-winded after-curtain tribute by René Blum in South Africa that left his dancers limp with heat exhaustion.

A silent rehearsal film made by the Denham Company does give occasional glimpses of what most of the London critics regarded as a fresh, witty farce and a charming fantasy. (The Sunday *Times*, however, found it childish, the music at cross purposes with the Chinese figures.) In the film, the maidens and the butterfly perform their many fast parallel runs

en pointe, and the maidens often stop and politely give each other a dart-
ing kiss. Their later tiny hand claps for the Ambassador's virtuosity are
also obviously satirical. The Mandarin's walk is flat-footed, with the heel
hitting first, and his lower back is curved forward, causing his buttocks to
stick out. His strong poses (sometimes with clenched fists) and the maidens' often simpering ones, give the feeling of an old-fashioned melodrama. The two lovers have one pas de deux in which one or both of them
are in profile to the audience: sometimes he is on the floor while she is
standing or kneeling. There are many slow turns where their curved torsos move together in half circles, or one or the other turns under the arch
made by their intertwined arms.

    This ballet was a favorite with audiences, and Derain's decor was con-
sidered his masterpiece for the stage. The *Dancing Times* termed the set,
with its sparse architectural motifs of a few red pagoda roofs and blue
mountain peaks, one of the best the age could produce. The different tex-
tured costumes were also praised, although the *New English Weekly* observed that the corps de ballet displayed a flavor more Japanese than
Chinese, especially in hairstyles.

    A. V. Coton, writing later in a *Prejudice for Ballet*, calls *L'Epreuve d'A-
mour* a comic work filled with lyrical and farcical movements, which had
the success it deserved. He points out that the near-human antics of the
monkeys at the opening and closing of the work and the flittings of the
butterfly create an obvious comparison between human and animal characteristics throughout. The rage of the Mandarin and the anger of both
the Ambassador and the lover at different times contrast with the sweet-
ness of the maidens and the innocence of Chung-Yang. Cyril Beaumont
praises the beautiful groupings, the manner in which the movements
combine with the music, every step and gesture emerging naturally from
the development of the action, and the contrast of the flowing movements
of the Chinese with the stilted ones of the foreigners, in this carefully con-
structed and refined ballet.

    The second work that Fokine created for Blum that first season was
Don Juan, based on Molière's play *Don Juan ou Le Festin de Pierre*,
which was adapted from the sixteenth-century Spanish playwright Tirso
de Molina. In 1761 Gluck wrote the score for a ballet based on Molière's
play, choreographed by Gasparo Angiolini and presented in Vienna the
same year. Gluck's music, far in advance of its time, emphasized the dramatic elements in the plot and offered programmatic sections of Spanish
flavor. The last section, The Dance of the Furies, was later expanded and
became the opera *Orfeo and Eurydice*.

The idea for a new *Don Juan* ballet was suggested to René Blum by the conductor Roger Desormière. Blum asked Eric Allatini, his musical director, to find the original score, which was finally located in Germany. The libretto by Fokine adhered closely to Molière's plot. The three scenes were performed on a two-level set, one level on the stage itself and another up four broad steps and hidden behind a curtain. In the first scene, musicians are seated on the steps as the curtains are drawn aside to reveal the Commander's house. Sganarelle, Don Juan's servant, encourages them to play while the Don sneaks into the house where Donna Elvira is waiting. When the couple emerges, they encounter the Commander, who challenges Don Juan to a duel and is killed. After cowled figures in black draw the curtains on a mourning Elvira, a jester dances a spirited solo. Except for the jester's dance, this section of the ballet is basically a mimed drama.

When the curtains open on scene 2, they reveal Don Juan as the host of a party, heavily attended by his former mistresses. The guests dance, the Don performs alone, and shortly after they sit down to the banquet table there is a knocking, and the Commander's ghost appears. The Don invites him to have a drink, the guests are calmed, and the entertainment begins. A veiled woman (Elvira) is brought in, and Don Juan introduces her and forces her to join his guests. The Commander appears twice more, the last time inviting the Don to visit his tomb.

Scene 3 takes place in the cemetery amidst cypress trees and under the gaze of a large equestrian statue of the dead man, which nods its head in a return of the Don's greeting. The Commander conjures up Don Juan's dead mistresses, at whom the Don laughs mockingly. Finally, Don Juan is caught in the stony grip of the statue, and a horde of furies descend upon him, tossing him back and forth and leaving him lifeless upon the ground.

The ballet was first shown at the Alhambra Theatre in London on 25 June 1936, two weeks later than planned, because the costumes, designed by Mariano Andreaú, were destroyed by fire and had to be remade. In the original cast were Anatole Vilzak as Don Juan, Jeannett Lauret as Donna Elvira, Jan Yazvinsky as the Commander, Louis Lebercher as Sganarella, and André Eglevsky as the Jester.

Grace Roberts, in *The Borzoi Book of Ballets*, points out that *Don Juan* and *L'Epreuve d' Amour* both suffered from neglect and gross miscasting when brought to the United States in 1938 by the Denham Ballet Russe de Monte Carlo, and suggests that both are worthy of revival. The silent film of *Don Juan* made by Denham's company gives hints of the intrinsic interest of this work. In it, scene 1 comes across as a quick series of mime tableaux, noteworthy for the use of the entire body. The dance

André Eglevsky as the Jester in *Don Juan. Courtesy Dance Collection, The New York Public Library at Lincoln Center, Astor, Lenox, and Tilden Foundations.*

of the Jester appears to have been cut short, although one can recognize standard ballet steps such as cabrioles, pirouettes, and pirouettes à la seconde. (It is possible that some of this was added by the performer.)

In scene 2 the dancing begins with the male guests performing quick athletic movements involving fast foot work and pirouette turns without a preparation. The female guests reveal flowing arms, several movements led by and leading into the hip, and other gestures reminiscent of Spanish classical dance. Don Juan's vigorous solo finishes with multiple turns ending on the knee.

There are also three dances performed for the entertainment of the guests: the Jester's dance, for four men and a leader, a dance for three bacchantes, and a solo Gypsy dance. The jesters move with maximum speed, and their steps include a spectacular leap in the air with the leg completely bent under and a final leap into a sitting position. The bacchantes all carry tambourines, which they handle like balls. Their movements cover various levels and include a backbend performed with the weight on one knee. It is difficult to distinguish the Gypsy dance from any other of this genre. Don Juan's mime in this scene is limited to arm and facial gestures and suggests soap opera. The dancer playing Sganarelle, his servant, is more successful in embodying his character with the feeling of the commedia dell'arte.

In the last scene, it is The Dance of the Furies that dominates. Here, approximately twenty-four dancers move on the six steps and the stage, revealing numerous asymmetrical and/or curved body movements, which are performed on different levels in circular patterns, and with increasing speed and intensity. At several points, a female fury is raised and passed from one to the other, and at the end, Don Juan is frantically tossed from one group to another.

The critics were mixed in their reaction to *Don Juan*, although unanimous in their praise of Vilzak's dramatically created Don and the dance of the Jesters, led by Eglevsky. On one hand, The Dance of the Furies was called one of the best things in modern ballet, and on the other, complaints abounded against both a rambling scenario more appropriate for Shakespearean drama than ballet, and insipid music. Both scenario and music were judged to obscure the choreography.

Eglevsky adored *Don Juan*, although he feels it was as much theater as ballet, and without Fokine to rehearse and inspire the pantomimic gestures the essence of the ballet was lost. He remembers that the cast walked and walked for weeks until they acquired the aristocratic gait the choreographer wanted. He says that Fokine was very proud of Don Juan's variation at the banquet because it was based on a book about the Spanish court. Eglevsky's own role of the chief jester was a technically stunning one that he did not enjoy because it was very difficult and he was always afraid of damaging his legs, a fear that annoyed the ballet master.

Fokine mounted two more ballets for Blum: *Les Elfes*, created for his own company in 1924 and discussed in chapter 4, and a work called *Les Elements*. John Martin regarded the elves as a more impish race of creatures than the sylphides to which they were often compared. A. V. Coton, writing about the Blum version, describes it cuttingly as twenty-five minutes of pink-clad dancers, doing movements against a pink background, to pink music. He feels that it represented a mass display of torso lines more suitable to the Hollywood Bowl or Lewisohn Stadium. Accusing both Fokine and Massine of allowing their work in America to be influenced by luscious scoring, circus standards of illumination, and huge choruses, he deplores their use on the ballet stage, where he feels they have no place.

Les Elements, to the Second Suite of J. S. Bach, consists of a number of dances corresponding to the rondo, the sarabande, the bourree, the polonaise, and the minuet. The premiere was given at the Coliseum in London on 26 June 1937, and was later performed by Col. de Basil's company. Fokine's choreography may have been an attempt to create a work like those of the ballet masters of Bach's day, involving Zephyr, the god of wind, and his consort Flora. There are vapor, rain, flowers, a volcano, ocean waves—the eternal cycle of nature, mixed in with gods and spirits.

A silent black-and-white rehearsal film of this ballet, danced in soft slippers, shows a baroque setting including candelabra, several pillars entwined with leaves, and five or six steps leading up to the pillars. Photographs indicate that the dancers had small heels on their shoes and that there was a painted backdrop of clouds and leaves. The ballet begins with several figures lying on the downstage floor—in all probability flowers. There is a considerable amount of running on and off stage, although the dispersion and reappearance of groups and individuals appear effortless. The occasional sinking into and rising up from the floor are crystallized in one section where the male and female dancers are obviously waves, and a figure carrying a trident emerges from them. The last section begins with eight women seated in two rows on the floor, legs crossed and arms down and slightly sideward—a position quite similar to that often seen in the Graham technique. They are joined by eight men and four women who weave in and out while those on the floor begin swaying their torsos and adding round circular arm movements.

The *London Observer* in an article dated 27 June 1937, and signed by "H. H." found *Les Elements* a distinguished work, danced delightfully, and suggesting the contrapuntal nature of the music, although the movements did, at times, outweigh the music. The costumes, with some of the men in skirts and buskins, evidently ranged from the neoclassic to bizarre. Charles Dickson, who later danced a volcano in the ballet, says that it was tricky rhythmically and that somehow Fokine never quite succeeded in accomplishing his aim. Sol Hurok rejected this work when he toured the de Basil Ballet Russe in the United States.

The second season René Blum's company returned to Monte Carlo they ran out of money, disbanding in late 1937. Meanwhile Col. de Basil's Ballet Russe, with Leonide Massine playing a strong role, was having internal problems, centering on the conflict between Massine and de Basil. Sono Osato, in *Distant Dances*, says that Massine contacted Blum and others as early as spring 1937 to suggest starting still another company, and went after the backing himself, although he assured de Basil that he would fulfill his contract. The result was that Serge Denham and Julius Fleishman formed Universal Art, Inc., and bought Les Ballets de Monte Carlo from Blum, entitling them to use the Monte Carlo name and giving them the rights to all the ballets in Blum's repertoire, incuding those of Michel Fokine. Massine, of course, was the artistic director of the new company, which was based in New York. During the late summer and fall of 1937 many dancers who had been with de Basil followed Massine into the Denham company and former Blum dancers (many of whom had been in the Blum/de Basil company) went to either one or the other.

Fokine worked with de Basil unofficially in 1937 (during part of the year Massine was still there), polishing some of his old ballets and setting *Coq d'Or*.[6] He formally joined the organization in the spring of 1938. This seems to have been a compromise move for Fokine in at least two ways: he had already initiated a lawsuit against de Basil for presenting his ballets without permission or royalty payments; and he probably chose not to remain with the Blum organization as it passed into new hands (even though Blum was technically retained as codirector) because he had no desire to share the artistic leadership with Massine.

Michel Fokine, more than anyone else, was caught in a difficult situation when the Blum company folded. Col. de Basil, who may not have been as creative a thinker as Diaghilev, but certainly possessed some of the latter's capacities for manipulating individuals, undoubtedly realized that it was to his own benefit to hire Fokine. He gave the stranded ballet master a base of operation, at the same time preempting Fokine's legal suit against him, and simultaneously created increased competition for the departed Massine. In *The One and Only: The Ballet Russe de Monte Carlo,* Jack Anderson points out the irony of the situation: Massine now headed a company whose repertoire was dominated by Fokine ballets and Fokine headed one filled with Massine's notable works! And once again Fokine found himself in the midst of a power play over which he had no control.

The ballets that Fokine restaged for de Basil—*Prince Igor, Firebird, Petrouchka, Schéhérazade, Les Sylphides, Spectre de la Rose, Thamar,* and *Papillons*—were well received, but it was with his new strictly dance version of *Coq d'Or* that he scored a popular and critical "hit." For this new piece, Fokine slightly reworked the story, still based, however, on the libretto of the poet Vladimir Belsky, who in turn had used Pushkin's poem. With the help of the composer Tcherepnin and the conductor Antal Dorati, Fokine cut the score, eliminating some of the vocal parts and giving others to the orchestra.[7] The story line still revolved about an Astrologer bringing the Golden Cockerel to King Dodon, who promises him anything for this gift; the discovery by Dodon of the Queen of Shemakhan; her return with him to his kingdom; the Astrologer's desire for her; her disappearance; and Dodon's death by a pecking bird.

In *Memoirs,* Fokine points out that the new balletic version and the old opera/dance version differed in their realization: in the ballet, the story was told almost exclusively through dancing, allowing him to intensify the movements of the body. In addition, he was able to transform the Golden Cockerel from a prop to a living character to be danced. He also introduced a prologue inspired by Belsky's libretto, in which the Astrologer first captures the Cockerel and then, by a magic spell, is able to conquer the Daughter of the Air, Shemakhan. He put the Queen and the Cockerel en pointe, and at the end he had the Astrologer, in a sinister green light, walk on the stage past the others, who remained frozen in their positions. Fokine states, "While I by no means disavow the opera-ballet version . . . and while I always listen with great pleasure to the music of *Coq d'Or* staged as opera . . . I still favor my last, purely ballet version."

In this cast, which was rehearsed in London, Irina Baronova was the Queen; Tatiana Riabouchinska, the Cockerel; and Marc Platoff, Dodon. Fokine thought them all excellent: "It was as if every dancer found the best way of expressing his talent." Riabouchinska, he felt, was born for her role; Platoff, the American, astonished him as a very Russian Dodon; and Baronova amazed him by the rapidity with which she learned her role. He did, however, object to the fact that Baronova began to change and simplify her part and he could never forget the image of Karsavina, who danced the Queen so meaningfully in the 1914 version. In addition to the main roles, Fokine utilized the entire corps of the company, which, according to the *St. Louis Post Dispatch,* numbered sixty-five. In an interview in the *Boston Herald* he stated that it took him sixteen days to create this work.

The silent film of this ballet is in color, and although sections seem to have been left out, the often witty satire comes through. At one point, when the King's advisors come to blows, the slapstick quality of the movement brings to mind an Abbott and Costello comedy. When the King "mounts" his horse, the "animal" is a wooden cutout on its hind legs, several times his size, and the use of a ladder is required to get up. The Queen's dance of seduction is very Oriental in feeling and beautiful in the flow of the movement; then suddenly Dodon is trying to dance with her, and hopping on one foot. Fokine's handling of groups is kinetically exciting, even as palely transmitted on the film.

The costumes by Gontcharova are striking: the members of Dodon's court wear brilliant Russian peasant dress; the Queen is in long braids and a clinging, sinuous dress that Osato says was really pink chiffon pajamas and a gold lamé girdle; the Cockerel is in a yellow leotard with large wings of gold; and Dodon, in gaudy colors, sports a huge stomach, a false nose, and a large wig. Gontcharova's sets, which, according to reports, were always greeted with spontaneous applause, as reproduced in photographs give the feeling of archaic Russian peasantry, with fantastic flowers and castles created in brilliant orange, lemon, gold, rose, maroon, blue, and green.

Sona Osato, who was a member of the Queen's retinue, remembers Fokine's passion as he demonstrated each role, coaching the dancers to be sinuous by slanting the pelvis and neck. She also recalls that her costume of silk skirts over tight-fitting pants was so heavy that once she started spinning she could not stop. She says that Baronova, through her use of her body alone, was able to transform herself into an enchantress, that Riabouchinska had speed, lightness, stamina, and spontaneity, and that Platoff attacked his role with a verve that amazed Fokine.

Recalling this *Coq d'Or* today, Marc Platt (Platoff was his stage name) says the company held Fokine in awe: for them, he still embodied the tradition of dance. In his presence no one made jokes and all understood their humble position in relation to his. He would arrive at the hired hall in London wearing a suit and carrying a small piece of paper, never larger than six by eight inches, on which were his notes.

Platt, who was a demi-caractère and character dancer, remembers vividly one late afternoon, when, in his role as Dodon, he rehearsed a series of turns and then fell down on his back. He was quite exhausted by this time, and, out of pure silliness, added two or three soft arm movements. Fokine immediately started screaming incoherently, stopping about five minutes later when Mme Fokina murmured to him and patted him on the head. Platt, embarrassed and bewildered, went over to Gregoriev and, upon asking what happened, was told it was his improvisation with the arms. He immediately went to Fokine and apologized, saying he was young and fairly new to dance, and Fokine was the last man in the world he wished to offend. They were good friends thereafter.

Assessing *Coq d'Or*, today, Platt feels that the emotional and theatrical qualities in the ballet required superb artists and careful direction, but that it would still be considered a classic, unlike *Don Juan*, which, from an audience viewpoint, he considers a dated and "hammy" piece. Betty Low, a Canadian dancer and actress who performed with the company at this time using the name Ludmilla Lvova, describes the ballet as "beautiful, brilliant and a glorious pageant."

The ballet was a great success in London, where its premiere on 23 September 1937, coincided with the coronation celebrations for King Edward VIII. The following month the company brought it to New York, where it became the highlight of their United States repertoire.

Whereas some English critics faulted the cutting of Rimsky-Korsakov's opera music to fit the ballet (a charge eloquently defended by Fokine, who pointed out that the composer himself had created a purely musical suite from the opera), American reviewers, among them the music critic for the *New York Times*, Olin Downs, expressed absolute joy over this new version. He defended Fokine's legitimate right to make it as pleasant to the eye as to the ear. Several others pointed out that one could go back and criticize Rimsky-Korsakov for using Pushkin's poems. Jerome Bohm of the *Herald Tribune* regarded this latest metamorphosis of the music the most effective, and applauded Fokine's deft wedding of fantasy and satire. Irving Kolodin of the *Sun* found it heartwarming to see the choreographer applauded on both sides of the footlights.

But it was John Martin, writing in the *New York Times* on 3 October 1937, who was most eloquent: stating that in presenting *Coq d'Or* the de Basil Ballet Russe had made itself eligible for a distinguished service medal, and citing Fokine's magnificent collaborators, he called it an "expansive, lusty, colossal, humorous piece of work, so warmly alive and ingratiating that it is quite unnecessary for its enjoyment to bother with the fact that it also happens to be a masterpiece of theatrical craftsmanship as well as of choreographic design." He noted the wit, the comments on human foibles, the scenes that built rhythmically and with fine detail, yet no superfluity, the characters, especially Dodon, built with love and humanness, and the truly beautiful scenes in the Queen's tent.

Other critics on the tour route praised Fokine's mass movements; the unity, which caused all elements to interweave; and the whirlpool of color in this most elaborate of spectacles. There were some, however, who, though they found it entertaining, thought it overrated as a novelty. Coton's feeling was that both *Coq d'Or* and *Don Juan* were overloaded mime pageants, and he preferred the music of the *Coq d'Or*.

The next ballet Fokine created for de Basil was the full-length *Cendrillon*. Based on the Cinderella fairy tale, set to a commissioned score by Frederic D'Erlanger, with a pre-Renaissance decor by Gontcharova, it was first performed in London 19 July 1938. From the outset, this work was promoted as being for children and usually scheduled at matinees only, a fact regretted by John Martin when it was seen in New York in November 1940. He found its unpretentious naïvité, charming dances, and freshly dramatized situations most enjoyable and advised anyone who loved the fairy tale to see Tatiana Riabouchinska as Cinderella and Paul Petroff as the Prince.

Osato recalls rehearsing *Cendrillon* in Berlin in the spring of 1938, when Hitler was in full power and Goebbels came to all the ballet performances. Fokine became furious when the theater manager informed him that he would have to stop rehearsals because it was Hitler's birthday, and he refused to obey the request. There was also a question of whether or not *Schéhérazade* could be performed, because Bakst was a Jew, and the half-Jewish David Lichine lived in constant terror. Later, Fokine refused an invitation to meet with Goebbels but seems to have suffered no consequences, possibly due to the German's respect for him.

The film excerpts from *Cendrillon* evince a style similar to that of *Coq d'Or*, with color, pageantry, and comedy. In addition, there is a cat en pointe, who, among other things, unties Cinderella's shoe at the ball. The sisters, played by men, are broad farcical roles involving exaggerated balances. Everything else in the film is so truncated that a clear concept of the work is not possible.

It was almost a year before Fokine presented his final ballet for the de Basil company.[8] *Paganini* was the result of two years of collaboration between Fokine and his old acquaintance composer Serge Rachmaninoff.

The story of this psychological ballet, based on the talented virtuoso whose life was surrounded by myth and scandal, unfolds in three scenes.

Scene 1 shows Paganini in public on a concert platform, with an audience, through whose eyes he is seen. The devil appears in a goat mask, and dark figures seem to pluck at the strings of his violin. Gossip, Scandal, and Envy weave through the spectators (they actually came through the audience), and ghosts and phantoms leap about as the light fades.

The second scene, which shows Paganini in a social setting, takes place in a mountain landscape above Florence. Here youths and maidens dance, and we focus on a beautiful girl in a pink dress dancing with her lover. A gaunt figure (Paganini) enters carrying a guitar and begins to play music, to which the Florentine Beauty dances as if possessed, finally swooning in exhaustion at his feet.

Scene 3, depicting his solitude, finds Paganini, old and ill, in his large dark study, with its single candle-lit table. He picks up his violin and begins to improvise, comforted and inspired by the Divine Genius. Then he has a nightmare in which his tormentors appear, led by Satan and all looking exactly like Paganini. When the spirits of Envy, Guile, and others appear, he beats them off with his bow. Finally, as death approaches, Divine Genius reappears with a group of Spirits and leads Paganini's soul up the staircase to heaven.

The letters between Fokine and Rachmaninoff begin in 1935 when Fokine writes that he is trying to grant the composer's wish and create a libretto for which Rachmaninoff can write the music. In August 1937, Fokine writes about his continuing difficulty in finding a suitable subject, saying he needs a spark to set him off and that "often it is music. . . . For it is music that teaches me ballet and I investigate my thoughts about dance listening to substantial discussions about music."[9] Finally, on 29 August, Rachmaninoff writes to Fokine, suggesting a ballet based on the legend of Paganini, "selling his soul to a dark spirit for perfection in art." Fokine's answers that he is busy working on *Coq d'Or* but wants to know where he can learn more about the Paganini legend.

When Fokine is in New Zealand in February 1939, he writes that he is working on the ballet and that the second scene, where the "delicate dance" of the maidens is in strong contrast to the devils of the first scene, is too short, and he requests permission for a repetition of the music. Rachmaninoff's letter of 3 April gives his permission to repeat the twelfth variation exactly as written, adding that it would be better to make up a new variation, but "my season is not yet finished, and Hitler is strictly watching that no one in Europe gets any peace." He also discusses the repeat of the eighteenth variation at the end of the score, suggesting that it be played a half tone higher than the original, thereby creating more tension.

Rachmaninoff, injured in a fall, then writes that he will be unable to come to the London opening. He had noted beforehand that the role of ballet composer, new to him, certainly had its problems and unpleasant moments. Fokine assures him that the cast is excellent, the production going well, and that Antal Dorati has told him the new pianist will be good. He adds that "every time it seems that a show won't come out successfully . . . the ballet master yells in desperation." After the opening, he reports that it was magnificent and flawless and that the music critics approved of the "special" ending, failing to notice that it was a repetition of music heard seven minutes earlier.

Rachmaninoff writes on 4 July that, in addition to Fokine's detailed report and the reviews sent, he has received a letter from his children and one from the theater. All are filled with praise, but point out two problematic moments: the very end, where there is so much bustling and movement that it interferes with Paganini's playing and the "white ladies," who seem to weaken the impression in the third scene. He feels the pianist was probably nervous and will improve with time.

In the original cast of *Paganini*, Dimitri Rostov danced the virtuoso; Irina Baronova, Divine Genius; Tatiana Riabouchinska, the Florentine Beauty; Yurek Lazowski, Scandal; Alberto Alonso, Gossip; and Tamara Grigorieva, Guile. The decor by Serge Soudekeine was effective, if not outstanding. Paganini's costume consisted of black tails, Scandal was in red, the Spirits of Envy in green. Gossip had four faces. The Florentine boys and girls were dressed in blues and purples. Grace Roberts remarks that the headdresses of the Divine Spirits looked like those of celestial Red Cross workers, and suggests that the romantic tutu might have been more appropriate, but, aside from this cavil, judged the work a masterpiece.

The few excerpts from this ballet on a black-and-white silent film made in 1946 show only the scene with the Florentine Beauty. The other maidens, wearing long dresses with empire waists, display flexible backs and soft, asymmetrical arms. The group movements are flowing in quality. The Beauty, wearing pointe shoes, performs a lovely solo that at first is softly romantic and employs an expressively arched back. The speed of movement then increases, as does the use of the floor, as she appears to be possessed by demons. One is reminded somewhat of Giselle.

Sono Osato, who was one of the maidens, writes that during her hypnotic solo the body of the Florentine Beauty was in constant motion. In scene 3, she recalls Baronova, as Divine Genius, wearing a diaphanous floor-length white costume and leading a chain of Spirits who performed slow, sustained arabesques around Paganini. Osato says that although her own sentiments about this ballet may sound trite today, Fokine made

Genevieve Moulin and Vladimir Dokoudovsky in *Paganini*. *Courtesy Dance Collection, The New York Public Library at Lincoln Center, Astor, Lenox, and Tilden Foundations.*

every step one of conviction. Yurek Lazowski, who enjoyed his role of Scandal, says that although the part of Paganini was mainly mime, there was a great deal of dancing in this work.

Betty Low remembers rehearsing *Paganini* while the company was on a tour of Australia and New Zealand. She was a maiden in scene 2 and a spirit in scene 3. She relates the story of opening night in New Zealand when the management discovered that the Fokines, who had gone for a walk after the dress rehearsal, could not be found anywhere. A desperate call to the police revealed that they were in jail. As the story emerged after Grigoriev bailed them out, they had gotten lost and asked a policeman (in their very poor English) for directions back to the theater. As he pointed out the correct street, he inadvertently hit Mme Fokina. Fokine immediately punched him.

Low says at this stage in their lives neither of the Fokines made any attempt to speak English, that they sneered at everyone and everything, and that Fokine was bitter and never showed a sense of humor during rehearsals. She vividly remembers the opening night of *Paganini* in London. She had a terribly infected little toe and, showing it to the ballet master, said she would dance in pointe shoes for the performance (she swears the spirits bourréed for eternity) but requested permission to dance the dress rehearsal in soft slippers. Fokine said "No," and Grigoriev took her to a doctor who gave her an injection to kill the pain before the performance.

Paganini was very successful in London, where it played to sold-out houses at Covent Garden. Most critics considered the work a perfect collaboration between the composer and the choreographer. One reviewer observed that Fokine was obviously familiar with Heine's "Florentine Nights," and pointed out that, somehow, the use of old pantomime props and ancient stage devices was nonetheless theatrically effective. Antal Dorati, who conducted the orchestra, still considers this work a very fine one.

The ballet opened in New York on 8 November and Irving Kolodin, writing in the *New York Sun* the following day, called Fokine's realization of the essence of Paganini in terms of dance "superlative," the blending of choreographic and theatrical elements "masterful," and the whole piece thoroughly worthy of Fokine's name. John Martin, too, felt it was a masterpiece, although more choreographic theater than ballet, and especially praised the opening scene, still terming it "deeply beautiful" after seeing many performances.

There was some criticism of the obscure philosophical ideas, and several deplored the obsolete notion of having angels with wings leading a soul up a staircase. Cyril Beaumont cites moments of great beauty as well as of weakness. For him the figure of Paganini was successful, but Scandal, Gossip, and Envy did not suggest their attributes in terms of movement. He finds the dance of the Florentine Beauty well composed, but the contrast of its classical technique and en pointe dancing jarring after the less traditional dances that preceded it. He thinks the final scene is too formal and heavy with sentiment.[10] The critical and popular success of *Paganini* spurred Rachmaninoff and Fokine on to plan another collaboration, but it never materialized.

During the years 1936–39 the old ballets that Fokine restaged and/or rehearsed for both Blum and de Basil were revitalized and regained much of their former stature under his guidance. Contrary to his own statement in *Memoirs*, he did change many of the old repertory standards, such as *Les Sylphides*. In fact, he was notorious for changing at least one little thing each time he staged a ballet. To this day, there is discussion between Ballet Russe dancers of different eras and those who learned the works in either Russia or the Diaghilev Company as to which is the "real" Fokine version.

The Denham Ballet Russe de Monte Carlo brought Fokine's ballets to all parts of the United States from 1938 until its demise in 1963, and they remained the favorites on all programs. The dancers and regisseurs seem to have made every attempt to maintain these ballets as they thought Fokine wished them to be, although the critics sometimes found them dated.

Fokine never received any compensation or royalties, since rights had been purchased from René Blum. In light of this and the widespread plagiarism of his work by assorted friends and colleagues, a certain degree of aloofness on his part is understandable. Fortunately for Fokine, in 1939, having proven his continuing ability to create, he was soon involved in still another venture.

Chapter Six

Ballet Theatre (1939–1942)

RICHARD PLEASANT, THE EXECUTIVE DIRECTOR of Ballet Theatre, a new company in the process of being organized, invited Michel Fokine to become one of its choreographers. He was to have the responsibility of recreating and rehearsing his own ballets. Fokine initially declined the invitation since he had a contract to serve as ballet master for the Royal Swedish Ballet, but when the war in Europe seemed imminent, he changed his mind. Ballet Theatre represented a brand-new concept in ballet in general, as well as a new organization in the world of American classical ballet. It incorporated part of what had been the Mordkin Ballet, and was sustained largely by the financial backing of Lucia Chase, a leading dancer with and backer of the Mordkin group.[1] Its organizers knew that classical ballet in twentieth-century America had never been a success because it lacked the two attributes of its European counterpart: wealthy patrons and a strong ballet master or chief choreographer.[2]

Mikhail Mordkin and Anna Pavlova had originally appeared in America in 1910; the Diaghilev Company made its second American tour in 1916–17, backed by Otto Kahn; Pavlova made her last tour here in 1925–26, many years before her death; Adolph Bolm, the former Diaghilev star, had made some attempts at a company in Chicago in the years 1924–27; the Ballet Russe de Monte Carlo (de Basil) came in 1933, 1934, and 1935; the Mordkin Ballet gave a few performances in the years 1937–39; the story of the Fokine Ballet has been noted. All of these were—if not always financial disasters—far from successful. The Ballet Russe de Monte Carlo (or, rather, one of the numerous companies using that name), which was financed in 1936 by Julius Fleishmann, was to survive until 1963, but it was not an American company. The American

Ballet, backed and directed by Lincoln Kirstein with additional backing from Edward M. M. Warburg, and George Balanchine as its choreographer, had made its first appearance in 1935. But it was to fold and reopen several times under different names until it emerged in 1948 as New York City Ballet.

Ballet Theatre announced that it would be an American company whose ideal was to produce ballet as theater. It was to be a community, with no star system, and no one individual or taste was to dominate. The idea was to present both the great classics of the past and contemporary ballets that would become the classics of the future. Richard Pleasant wrote, many years later, that his purpose in forming Ballet Theatre was "to offer up to the gods a heady draught distilled from many elements." America, he said, needed great copies before it could build its own originals, and Fokine was one of those who brought them, thus freeing everyone else to begin creating.[3]

The choreographers, besides Fokine and Mordkin, were Adolph Bolm, Agnes de Mille, Anton Dolin, José Fernandez, Andrée Howard, Eugene Loring, Bronislava Nijinska, Yurek Shabelevski, and Antony Tudor. There were a few, notably Balanchine, who would not participate. Among the twenty principal dancers and twelve soloists, seven had worked with the Fokine company: Patricia Bowman, Viola Essen, Annabelle Lyon, Eugene Loring, Leon Varkas, Nora Kaye, and Harold Haskin. In the corps were Anne Wilson, Muriel Bentley, Orest Sergievsky, Dorothy Hall, and Maria Karnilova, all of whom had had some association with Fokine. Alexander Smallens was the chief conductor.

Mikhail Mordkin was disturbed to find that he was not to be the artistic director and choreographer-in-chief of this new company, which had incorporated his own. He was probably even more upset when he learned that there were to be four "wings": the Classical, under Dolin; the English, under Tudor; the American, under Loring; and the Fokine, under Fokine. Charles Payne, in his book about Ballet Theatre, says of Mordkin, "he had only to review the experiences of Michel Fokine, a friend from his old Imperial Ballet days, to make him wary."[4]

Fokine, whose own career had been so drastically changed because Diaghilev had brought in another choreographer, was not permitted to change the structure of Ballet Theatre. But he made sure that his contract with this organization read: "In no case shall it appear that Mr. Fokine works under the direction of any other choreographer." Before he signed it, he insisted that the phrase "or any other person" be added. This contract, signed on 27 September 1939, made him the first official choreographer of Ballet Theatre. It also stated that Fokine's name had to be mentioned in all advertising, posters, and programs, that it could never be smaller than that of any other choreographer, and that at the head of any list of the choreographers it must read, "All Fokine ballets revived under the personal direction of Michel Fokine."

During the first season Fokine staged *Les Sylphides* and *Carnaval*. On opening night, 11 January 1940, at the Center Theatre, *Les Sylphides* opened the program—as it did for the next fifteen years. Also seen this first night was *The Great American Goof,* with choreography by Eugene Loring, a libretto by William Saroyan, scenery (projected on screens) and costumes by Boris Aronson, and music by the young American composer Henry Brant. There was also a revival of Mordkin's ballet *Voices of Spring* (Strauss). The next three weeks introduced restaged versions of *Giselle, Swan Lake,* and *La Fille Mal Gardée,* plus Tudor's *Lilac Garden, Dark Elegies,* and *Judgment of Paris,* de Mille's *Black Ritual,* and Bolm's *Peter and the Wolf,* as part of a repertory of twenty-one dances that ranged from traditional to contemporary and used such designers as Lucinda Ballard, Nicholas de Molas, Lee Simonson, Nadia Benois, and Serge Soudeikine. The season was a success from both a critical and audience point of view. By the day of the last performance, standing room was all gone and spectators were turned away. Charles Payne points out, however, that the engagement lost money at the box office and that many of the orchestra seats were given away.

From the first evening's performance everyone agreed that it was probably the most important venture ever to take place in American dance, a unique combination of excellent choreographers, dancers, and designers. John Martin's opening-night review said that New York had acquired, for the first time, a cosmopolitan ballet company, "comparable in its field to the opera house and the art gallery." In the *Christian Science Monitor,* Margaret Lloyd, noting all the preopening publicity and rumors, called the realization of these plans an "astonishing phenomenon" and a "historic occasion." Although some felt the American dancers, especially the men, were not as good as their European counterparts, there were almost no negative comments about the company.

Les Sylphides, with new scenery by Augustus Vincent Tack and costumes by Lucinda Ballard, was carefully rehearsed by Fokine.[5] The leading dancers were William Dollar, Lucia Chase, Nina Stroganova, and Karen Conrad. The last, a hasty replacement for Nana Gollner, who left the company at that point, astonished everyone on opening night, including Fokine, with her amazing leaps.[6]

John Martin wrote that the piece, with its excellent ensemble, had opened the evening in "the best of all possible manners." Walter Terry in the *New York Herald Tribune* called it a "beautiful breath-taking work staged by the master himself." Peter Lindamood said it was "a triumph" that revealed its "momentous significance of the romantic revolution in choreography." From another point of view, Rosalyn Krokover in *Musical Courier* felt that there had seldom been so delightful a presentation of so hackneyed a work. Albertina Vitak, a former Fokine dancer, reported in the *American Dance* that it was a fine technical display, but she found the ballet's soul and many of the Fokine lines missing.

The second Fokine classic to be introduced into Ballet Theatre's initial season was *Carnaval*. Although there is much fun in the amorous episodes that take place during a masked ball, the character of Pierrot (a role originally danced by Fokine himself) is always a tragic one. Adolph Bolm received unanimous praise for his portrayal of Pierrot, and Patricia Bowman was acclaimed as Columbine. Vitak said, "Did I recently write that Fokine's *Carnaval* showed its age? Not as danced by this company." The opinion, in general, was that all the sparkle and life in the work had been brought back by Fokine's staging.

At the conclusion of Ballet Theatre's first three weeks, it was headlined by *Newsweek* as "Sparkling Project Scores Hit." To most, its significance was that it had established a native American ballet, what John Martin called "a foundation for a truly popular center for the ballet, reconciling the best tradition of the past with a recognition of the intellectual and emotional necessities of today in America, without reliance upon esthetic snobbery." As Richard Pleasant later wrote to Anton Dolin about *Les Sylphides* and *Carnaval*, it was the spirit, not the mere existence of Ballet Theatre, that made these productions different from others. The big question was about the direction the many-faceted company would take—or as Walter Terry asked, "What lies ahead?"

There were plans for reorganization as a permanent company, and hopes of obtaining a permanent home. The irony about this new enterprise and the reactions to it is that, although most of the dancers were American, only two of the twenty-one ballets were by Americans (Loring's *Great American Goof* and de Mille's *Black Ritual*). The only completely American aspect of the company was its financial backing—and possibly the fact that it was such a mixture of styles, traditions, and people, what Donald Saddler referred to as a "university of the dance."[7]

Before discussing the next few seasons of Ballet Theatre, in which Michel Fokine participated, it is necessary to examine his relationship to the dancers and others in this new company, which, over forty years later, is still presenting his ballets. Lucia Chase says that the company was "full of Fokine" in that early period, in terms of what he brought out of them as dancers. To them, he was *the* choreographer; his name was still magic, and they stood in awe of him as the grand old master. Richard Pleasant asked both Mordkin and Fokine to audition the original corps, but Chase recalls that Fokine alone did most of the auditioning. He and Mordkin were the two oldest people actively involved in the daily operations of the company.

Mordkin had ample reason to compete with Fokine, and Leon Danielian feels that what had always been a rivalry was intensified on Mordkin's part. But Chase says that the superstitious and idiosyncratic Mordkin had great respect for Fokine and, in fact, clicked his heels and saluted whenever the latter appeared. This attitude, however, was not taken by the largely American corps, unversed and ignorant of the discipline inherent in Russian Imperial ballet training. When Fokine walked into a studio at Ballet Theatre and said, "Good morning," the dancers, who were sitting on the floor stretching, did not get up. Yurek Lazowski says that Fokine was not happy with the overall lack of respect accorded him. He was usually reserved, quiet, and demanding, but the company was not terrified of him as it was of Mordkin. They all knew he could be temperamental, but the lowering of the eyebrows signaled an approaching storm, and that was usually enough. Antal Dorati says that he never observed any especially close friendship between Fokine and any one person, but that Fokine was generally very much respected and his relationship with all was pleasant.[8] He evidently did not have complete control over the casting of his works, but seems to have managed to exist with that situation. He must have had some input, however, because Nora Kaye says that, even though she was in the corps, he gave her little solo roles because he knew her.[9]

Richard Pleasant arranged for a second "season" for the company in 1941, and they gave several programs at Lewisohn Stadium, where *Les Sylphides* (probably the work most frequently seen there) and *Carnaval* were included. The attendance figures were not as high as they might have been, and when the company went on to Chicago, the critics raved but the house was empty. A four-week engagement at the Majestic Theatre in New York in February and March 1941 produced the same results.

Because of these problems, the Board of Directors of Ballet Theatre fired Pleasant and, in May 1941, hired German Sevastianov, the Russian husband of the Russian ballerina Irina Baronova, as the new managing director. Fokine had worked with him in the de Basil company. Sol Hurok was signed as their booking agent. The two newcomers evidently found the company in a state of anarchy, with the Russians not very active at all, and no really strong leadership. They immediately took control. Hurok's contract stipulated that he would pay the company a weekly salary and would take the dubious box-office receipts for himself. But in return he demanded "approval" of all dancers hired and all ballets presented. Thus, from a purely business point of view, he had to make his product salable, and the result was the "Russianization" of Ballet Theatre, reflecting the popular opinion that only Russians could create ballets and that as many as possible should dance in them.

Hurok advertised "The Greatest in Russian Ballet by the Ballet Theatre," and many new dancers, either Russian or with Russian names, were hired. The fact that the new regime at Ballet Theatre seemed to have no faith in American choreographers—feeling that American taste was molded by Europe and that in ballet only Russians would sell—benefited Michel Fokine greatly. His name remained first in the listing of choreographers and it was agreed that he would revive *La Spectre de la Rose* and choreograph two new ballets, *Romeo and Juliet* and *Bluebeard*. He later restaged *Petrouchka* and created two more works, *The Russian Soldier* and *Helen of Troy*.

Le Spectre de la Rose was first performed in December 1941 by Annabelle Lyon and Ian Gibson, a Canadian, who continued to be its main interpreters until Gibson left the company in the fall of 1942. The critics did not comment on the choreography of this pas de deux, but Lyon as the young girl, and Gibson as the specter, were universally praised.[10]

Romeo and Juliet, with music by Prokofiev, was announced by Hurok in the souvenir program he sent out publicizing Ballet Theatre's first continental tour. The program probably went out during the summer of 1941, since the *Dancing Times* of London, in its October issue, reported a letter from Sevastianov, dated 15 August, in which *Bluebeard* and *Romeo and Juliet* "in two acts" were mentioned as forthcoming in the new season. For whatever reason (probably lack of time and money), *Romeo and Juliet* was never created by Fokine. Ballet Theatre did, however, premiere Antony Tudor's version, to Delius's music, in 1943.

Bluebeard, the first ballet by Fokine to be choreographed specifically for Ballet Theatre, received its world premiere on 27 October 1941, at the Palacio de Bellas Artes in Mexico City, and its American premiere on 12 November 1941, at the Forty-fourth Street Theatre in New York City. The music, by Offenbach, was arranged by Antal Dorati; the libretto, after the opéra bouffe of the same name by Henry Meilhac and Ludovic Halévy, was by Fokine, and the decor was by Marcel Vertès. This ballet was specifically commissioned by the new management, which wanted a comic closing work for what has been referred to as its "Ham and Egg" program. Hurok hired many new dancers, and devised a basic touring program of three one-act ballets, presenting it in fifty-one cities in the United States and Canada. The three ballets were *Pas de Quatre*, choreographed by Dolin, *Princess Aurora*, revised by Dolin, and *Bluebeard*.

Fokine changed the libretto of Offenbach's *Barbe Bleu* just enough to create as many roles as possible for the new Russian stars and soloists. Dorati arranged the music and added some from other Offenbach scores, although his contract with Ballet Theatre stated that he was also "to work out said libretto," which suggests that he and Fokine worked on it together.[11]

The program description of *Bluebeard* reads:

The ballet takes place in the mythical domaine of King Bobiche at the beginning of the 16th century. It concerns the sad experience of King Bobiche, who having exiled his infant daughter, Princess Hermilia, grows into an unhappy old man, infuriated by the infidelities of his Queen, Clementine, and plagued by the Philanderings of Baron Bluebeard, his impetuous vassal.

Bluebeard has four acts, two prologues, and three interludes, one each after the first three acts.

Fokine and Sevastianov met and cast the ballet. In the New York premiere were Antony Tudor as King Bobiche, Boris Runanin as Count Oscar, Anton Dolin as Bluebeard, Simon Semenov as Popolino, an alchemist, Lucia Chase as Queen Clementine, Alicia Markova as Floretta, a shepherdess (really Princess Hermilia), George Skibine as Prince Saphire, and Irina Baronova as Boulotte, a peasant girl. Bluebeard's five wives were danced by Nora Kaye, Maria Karnilova, Rosella Hightower, Miriam Golden, and Jeanette Lauret. There were also numerous soldiers and members of the court, the Queen's lovers, shepherds and shepherdesses, and the Spirits of Glory and Innocence. This was a broad burlesque that parodied everything including ballet—all in a make-believe world that revealed many of the follies of the human condition.

According to Charles Payne, who was then executive manager of Ballet Theatre, Fokine worked out the choreography for the ballet, using himself and his wife. He did not find it necessary to travel to Jacob's Pillow in Massachusetts, where the company was in residence during the summer of 1941, but instead taught it to them in a few days when they returned to New York City.

The farcical score by Offenbach, and the costumes and sets by Vertès, who had made sketches of corpses, criminals, and prostitutes for a sensational magazine in his native Budapest before coming to New York, combined with Fokine's sense of humor and ability to satirize, produced the smash hit of the season. There were love scenes, duels, masques, slapstick comedy, and—most of all—movement, in what one review called "a kind of Shavian tone." From available photographs, reviews, and the recollections of those who were in the ballet, or saw it, it was an excellent example of the unity Fokine had advocated in his basic principles.

Fokine's handling of parody had been shown as early as 1914, in *Le Coq d'Or,* where ladies-in-waiting danced around the King's bed, waving handkerchiefs to ward off flies. Later, his ability to turn his acute observations into humor had been seen in America in such minor works as *The Sorcerer's Apprentice* and *Tennis.* Lincoln Kirstein, in his monograph on Fokine, quotes André Levinson, the expatriate Russian critic, who had earlier spoken of Fokine as a parodist and referred to his "ironic deformation of ballet steps." Lucia Chase remembers his marvelous sense of humor and the fact that he could and would do a takeoff on anyone. He would, for instance, walk behind Antony Tudor and mimic his walk exactly, including the lifting of one elbow.

In Marcel Vertès, Fokine had a set designer who once said that dance inspired most of his drawings. His sets for *Bluebeard* consisted of painted backdrops that made no attempt at realism. They were all obviously painted, with figures often four times larger than the dancers on stage, and used broad, curving strokes to suggest clouds, birds, flowers, a sun, and floating figures of goddesslike women.

The costumes, hats, and wigs were numbered in the hundreds, and were striking in their elaborateness, variety, and color. The women of the court displayed a superabundance of jewels on their flowing, multicolored crepe gowns. Their headpieces resembled square pancakes covered by diaphanous scarves, and their hairdos of coils and braids were often intertwined with ribbons and jewels. Bluebeard, who actually wore a blue beard, had several costumes, one of which was a striped leotard with sleeves puffed to the middle of the arm. On another occasion he wore a leopard hat that curled upward and terminated in a feather. King Bobiche wore a crown that was almost as high as his face was long, and in the last scene he wore boxer shorts over his tights and a garter around one knee. Floretta wore a little angora wool hat as a peasant; when she became a princess her hat resembled a flattened pin cushion topped by a "creature" with a scowling face and eagle's wings. The original costume bill from Karinska, which did not include wigs, boots, or tights, was $6,000, which was reduced by $200 when it was decided to let John Fredericks, the hat couturier, make twenty-one hats.

There is a short segment of color film that gives a sampling of Bluebeard (Anton Dolin) and Boulotte (Irina Baronova), with a glimpse of Floretta (Alicia Alonso) and Popolina (Jerome Robbins). Most of the action takes place downstage right, in front of a drop, and there is some exaggerated mime as well as such classical steps as an arabesque, an attitude, and fouetté turns, all performed in a light, rapid, comic manner.

Bluebeard, in spite of its length of one hour, was so popular with both audiences and critics that it was the only ballet featured on the cover of a flyer advertising Ballet Theatre in March 1942. There was a positive response to the wit, the technique, the vivacious decor and music, and the dance action, which according to Albertina Vitak in *American Dance* "said more by innuendo than could be expressed half as well by mime or out and out clowning." *New York Post* critic Edward O'Gorman said that its intricacies suggested "an alliance between 'Il Trovatore,' 'La Gioconda' and Robert Benchley's version of a Wagner libretto," but added that the dancing and the pantomime revealed it all with clarity. Irving Kolodin in *The New York Sun* noted the comic wit and invention, the richness of human observation couched in criticism of ballet itself: "Fokine has taken traditional clichés of movement, tossed them in the air, and made them behave his way—with devastating burlesque and oblique humor." John Martin, who was one of the few who did not really like the ballet, said it was not first-rate Fokine, but did admit that it had its moments, "for give Fokine a chance for comedy invention and he will cause the veriest misanthrope to chuckle and the rest of us to guffaw."

Edwin Denby, whose voice was also negative, felt that the decor was fussy and boring and that Fokine did not convey the tender lyrical aspects of Offenbach's music. He admitted that this farce was a hit, but "a little in the manner of a collegiate show." The positive side of this last statement can be seen in the headline which read "Ballet Theatre's Bluebeard Makes Dancing Understandable," and in the fact that the ballet was listed in *Vogue*'s "People Are Talking About" column. One writer, Mark Schubert, in *PM's Weekly*, summed up this viewpoint when he noticed that *Bluebeard* was "entertaining the customers in the best Broadway sense of the word." This was obviously Hurok's intention in commissioning the ballet and Fokine, who had been thrust into the position of creating for the larger public before, fulfilled his task.

The world premiere of the next ballet Fokine created for Ballet Theatre

Anton Dolin as Bluebeard and Irina Baronova as Boulotte in *Bluebeard*.
Courtesy Maurice Seymour.

took place shortly after *Bluebeard,* on 23 January 1942, in the Opera House in Boston. *The Russian Soldier* was choreographed to Prokofiev's Symphonic Suite "Lieutenant Kije," a score the composer had written in 1933 for a satiric Russian film of the same name. The story of the ballet is quite simple. A young Russian soldier lies wounded on the battlefield, and as he is dying, visions of his past go through his mind—farm life, harvest, marriage, military academy. The work, which was dedicated "to all valiant warriors," seems to have been a blend of pantomime, pageantry, and folk dances, with scenery and costumes by the Russian Mstislav Douboujinsky. The ballet was performed on two levels, with the flashbacks on the upper level and the dying soldier on the lower one.

Several problems were apparent in this work before it even appeared on the stage. The music, a fairly well-known piece at the time, was written to accompany a film that was set during the Napoleonic wars and told the story of Czar Paul I, who wanted a certain lieutenant killed but could not remember his name. It was a rather black satire on royalty and the military. The score contains several Russian folk tunes, as well as what

Bluebeard. The company in front of one of Marcel Vertès' sets. *Courtesy Maurice Seymour.*

Rosalyn Krokover in *Musical Courier* described as "delicious wit, warmth and mock burlesque pomposity." Fokine, however, heard nothing funny or satiric in the score, but felt, instead, that it represented the soul of the Russian peasant. He might also have been influenced by the fact that he was not against the Imperial regime, which had actually treated him quite well, as opposed to that of the Revolution, which had made life so difficult that he left Russia and settled in the United States.

The second obstacle to be overcome was Sol Hurok, who, anxious to publicize anything Russian, and not above taking advantage of the fact that the United States had just entered World War II, originally dedicated the work to the "valiant soldiers of the Red army" and then rededicated it to the "soldiers fighting on the Eastern Front." Vitale Fokine writes that several months after his father's death, the curtain call was changed to a single spotlighted Russian soldier in a modern uniform. In his opinion, this cheapened the ballet, detracted from it, and was an "obvious display of opportunism."

Yurek Lazowski was the Russian soldier and Donald Saddler was Death, in a cast that also featured a mother, father, brother, bride, and a drum major. Saddler recalls many groups of soldiers and peasants, a famine scene where the girls were stacks of wheat, and a great deal of trepak dancing. He says it was an old-fashioned spectacle, with little outstanding dancing, the kind of thing the Russians would have loved.

Russian Soldier was seen in Chicago and Montreal before it opened in New York on 6 April 1942, and the critics there, as in Boston, had nothing but praise for a timely, human, and poignant ballet. The *Boston Herald*, noting that it was more miming than actual dancing, nevertheless felt it fully worthy of Fokine's conception. The *Montreal Gazette* called it an achievement in dramatic choreography, finer than most of Fokine's recent dramatic creations. In Chicago it received an ovation in spite of the need for a larger stage, and the *Sun* termed it "stark and beautiful."

But the reaction in New York, where it was first seen on an all-Fokine program that included *Les Sylphides* and *Bluebeard,* was much less adulatory. Everyone agreed with John Martin when he said that it was a minor work, in spite of the patriotic dedication. He felt that there was little choreography in it, except for some peasant dances in the wedding scene, and that its sentimental symbolism was trite. Others, like Robert Lawrence in the *New York Herald Tribune,* said that the flashback method was too obvious and that the choreograhy was of the pictorial school, leaving little to the imagination. Edwin Denby, who had never been a Ballet Theatre fan, called it "a darling Radio City spectacle" that was "heartless."

Yurek Lazowski and peasants in *The Russian Soldier. Courtesy Dance Collection, The New York Public Library at Lincoln Center, Astor, Lenox, and Tilden Foundations.*

What upset everyone who was familiar with the music, however, was the divergence between music and ballet. Those who knew Prokofiev's "Lieutenent Kije" score found the music light and charming, with a feeling of humor and mischievousness, and felt that Fokine's interpretation of it was so entirely different that it was actually jarring. Fokine himself did not hear the music as funny. He wrote:

... it was not a satirical impression I carried away with me when I heard the music, but the reflection of a folk song—the multiform emotions of a simple Russian peasant's soul. I heard it in tears and laughter and joy, and playful games and a wedding feast, and struggle and death.

Russian Soldier was neither a success nor a failure and, in any case, Fokine probably had little time to think about it before he was into his next project for Ballet Theatre. On 26 March 1942, German Sevastianov sent Fokine a letter of agreement in which the choreographer granted to Ballet Theatre, in perpetuity, the license to perform the choreography of the ballet *Petrouchka*, without any additional royalty payments. Fokine also agreed to restage, rehearse, and supervise it until 1 November 1942, in New York City. For this he was to receive $100 at the first rehearsal and $1,250 at the last rehearsal. The document further stipulated that rehearsals were to begin on or about 26 March and to continue through April.[12] According to a letter Anton Dolin sent to the *Dancing Times* of London, dated 2 August 1941, Fokine continued rehearsing *Petrouchka* even while the company was spending the summer in Mexico City. A rehearsal schedule for 13 July, printed in the *New York Herald Tribune* on 9 August includes a rehearsal of this work.

Ballet Theatre gave its first American performance of *Petrouchka* on 8 October 1942, with Yurek Lazowski dancing the lead. It was universally praised as the best staging ever seen of this masterpiece. Lazowski says that Fokine made some changes in the ballet, as he did every time he staged it, changes that Lazowski incorporated whenever he staged the work himself in later years. Although American Ballet Theatre claims still to be dancing the version set by Fokine, there is some disagreement.[13]

Michel Fokine's major task for the summer of 1942 was to create another ballet following much the same formula as that of the previous year's hit, *Bluebeard*. *Helen of Troy*, based on Offenbach's *La Belle Hélène*, with the music arranged by Antal Dorati and decor by Marcel Vertès, was to be given its world premiere in Mexico City and to highlight the New York season of Ballet Theatre, which Hurok planned to open in October. Dorati's contract again stipulated that he was "to work out in collaborations with Mr. Michel Fokine, the libretto of said ballet." Hence, this was obviously to be a companion piece to *Bluebeard*, another popular comic ballet, that everyone was counting on to be a success.

Fokine wrote a comment on his approach to this work in which he says that life has undergone very little change in the four thousand years since the Trojan Wars and that fashions and bric-a-brac seem very similar to their ancient counterparts. He feels it unnecessary to give a synopsis of the ballet, sure that audiences will be able to understand the sequence of sad events that lead from the dispute over the Golden Apple to the Trojan wars. On the basis of his observations, he concludes, tongue in cheek:

Homeric Greeks danced in the same manner as our ballet dancers. . . . Surely the dance of our Goddess of Wisdom is the same as the "intellectual" movements we see painted on ancient vases or performed in recital halls by our modern intellectuals. And our fight for the Golden Apple is nothing more nor less than a present-day football game.[14]

In Mexico Fokine began to set this ballet, which, as usual, he had worked out completely prior to rehearsals. According to Anton Dolin, he even danced the actual movements of the first scene. During the first ten days, however, he began to feel ill. He had developed a blood clot on his leg and was in bed for several days. When he resumed rehearsals, he had to sit constantly. Since he was unable to climb stairs, the dancers carried him up to the rehearsal hall in a wheelchair; the final rehearsals were held in the roof garden of his hotel, the Reforma, which had an elevator. He and Mme Fokina then left for New York, where he was hospitalized for pleurisy shortly after his arrival, and died of double pneumonia on 22 August.

Helen of Troy had its premiere on 8 September 1942, at the Palacio de Bellas Artes in Mexico City. In the cast were Donald Saddler as Menelaus, Irina Baronova as Helen, Anton Dolin as Paris, and Ian Gibson as Hermes. Sol Hurok flew to Mexico for the premiere of the ballet. What happened to *Helen of Troy* between the performances in Mexico City and Ballet Theatre's opening in New York a month later is still not entirely clear.

On 11 September the *New York Times* reported the world premiere of this ballet and announced that it was on the list of works to be presented at the Metropolitan Opera House when Ballet Theatre opened its season. On the same day, the *Herald Tribune* contained a similar statement, as did *Cue* in an obituary entitled "Taps for a Master." Later on in the month, the *Times, Post,* and *Women's Wear Daily* repeated the announcement; and an advertisement in several newspapers on 20 September listed the premiere as Wednesday, 28 October. The first indication that the American premiere of Michel Fokine's last work might not take place came in a small article in the *Herald Tribune* on 9 October headlined "Helen of Troy Ballet to Be Revised by Lichine." The date of the first performance, however, was still given as 28 October.

Ballet Theatre had already signed a letter of agreement with David Lichine on 1 October, which stated that he was to devise the choreography for *Helen,* for a fee of $1,000, and that they were to have absolute rights to it.[15] The Lichine version of the ballet finally opened on 29 November 1942, at the Masonic Auditorium in Detroit, with the preopening press describing it as "bright and spicy, like *Bluebeard,* its predecessor in the ballet bouffe." The program listed a prologue and three scenes with a libretto by David Lichine and Antal Dorati, and described the ballet as a "bouffant version of the Greek myth which concerns Paris and the manner in which his flight with Helen of Troy was accomplished." In the new cast were Dimitri Romanoff as Menelaus, Nana Gollner as Helen, André Eglevsky as Paris, and Jerome Robbins as Hermes.

New York finally saw *Helen of Troy* on 4 April 1943, with Vera Zorina as Helen and André Eglevsky and Jerome Robbins in the same roles they had danced in Detroit and on the road. It did not meet with critical acclaim. Irving Kolodin said it was a "routine job" and a "needlessly long and elaborate affair," adding that only the fact that Offenbach wrote the music allowed it to be mentioned in the same breath as *Bluebeard*. Noting that Lichine was now given sole responsibility for the ballet, he wrote, in the *New York Sun*, "It doubtless would have been a different affair had Michel Fokine lived to shape the work as he conceived it." John Martin, observing the gum-chewing Hermes, the opening scene in which Paris is seen tending a flock of sheep, and the travesty on *L'Après-midi d'un Faune*, felt that Lichine had couched the work in the medium of second-rate musical comedy dancing, and that Zorina seemed aloof and lost.

Robert Lawrence (who found that the ballet lacked motivating drive and that Zorina was lacking warmth) hinted at the intervention of a third choreographer. He wrote that Fokine had not lived to put the finishing touches on his version and that Lichine had been called in to start from scratch, and he finished by saying, "Now . . . a third choreographer—officially anonymous but related by marriage to a member of the cast—has lightened some of the loose ends left by Mr. Lichine." The third choreographer, whose version Lawrence found considerably more sparkling than the "echt Lichine version," was George Balanchine. André Eglevsky claims that Balanchine, who was then married to Zorina, actually rechoreographed 80 percent of the ballet.

Even now, from the perspective of several decades, it is difficult to determine the exact state of *Helen of Troy* as Fokine left it, and why Ballet Theatre and Hurok decided not to present his version, but rather, to invest more money in order to revise it. Vitale Fokine claims it needed only a few finishing touches that his father planned to add in New York. German Sevastianov, in a letter to a lawyer representing the Fokine heirs, claimed that he and Dorati had worked out the original scenario, which Fokine did not follow, and that Fokine "sketched in" the second half of the ballet in a great hurry and then left for New York in spite of Sevastianov's protests. He further states that Fokine apologized before leaving because the ballet was not finished and promised to complete it in New York, and that they tried to present the ballet in Mexico. "But one attempt we made was catastrophic and therefore, we had to abandon the idea." He goes on to say that Lichine was hired to save their investment and that Fokine's heirs are not entitled to any money.[16]

Donald Saddler says that the company did a run-through for Fokine in costume, but that there was still a great deal of corps work to be done and changes to be made. Irina Baronova agrees. She says Fokine did not finish it and the company completed the job as best they could. She says also that it was underrehearsed and that it was Lucia Chase who asked Lichine to redo it, adding that Fokine's ballet was a spectacle of great beauty and Lichine's a "slap-sticky" musical comedy.[17] Miss Chase claims not to remember why they did not perform Fokine's version, but does recall that, as his train was pulling out of the station in Mexico City, he did a "bump and grind" to remind her of her part in the ballet.

Yurek Lazowski, who was regisseur at the time, says they did six to ten performances of the ballet—thereby disagreeing with Sevastianov—and that it was quite long. After the run-through, Fokine gave the corrections for everyone to Lazowski and said that he would cut the ballet himself when the company came to New York. Lazowski also recalls the second act, which contained a satire on the Three Muses, with Lucia Chase as Terpsichore. This was a parody of Martha Graham, which even included the use of a drum. He says that this sequence was absolutely hilarious and that part of the reason for Hurok's negative reaction was that he felt that this section and others would offend too many people.

Ian Gibson remembers the ballet as long and is hazy about the number of performances the company did in Mexico. He does, however, recall being scheduled for a rehearsal of the Three Muses in Boston, but Lichine never got to him. He was drafted soon after and left the company. John Taras says that the ballet was very definitely completed and was performed several times in Mexico. It was very long and quite elaborate, with a final costume change just before everyone came on stage for the last time. He thinks that Hurok did not feel it was as good as *Bluebeard* and that he called in Lichine because he wanted another popular success. Anton Dolin, in a note to the *Dancing Times* dated 2 August, said that Fokine had finished the ballet and was leaving for New York the following Wednesday. In another letter, dated 23 August, the day after Fokine's death, he wrote that whether or not the ballet would prove to be one of his greatest works remained to be seen.

Antal Dorati, who was the musical director of Ballet Theatre at the time, arranger of the music, and coauthor of both of the libretti for *Helen,* says the piece, which was about two hours long, was performed in Mexico City about half a dozen times. Its success was considerable, but not overwhelming. He writes:

It was heavy, over-loaded with detail—some of which was absolutely splendid: for instance, the scene when the gods began to throw around the apple which was bestowed by Paris on Aphrodite, and thus the first Rugby game in the world was created. There were many more such gems in the choreography—nevertheless as a whole, it was cumbersome and blocky.[18]

Dorati states that they knew that a number of revisions were in order and that he and Fokine planned them together. After the choreographer's death, the ballet, as it was, was not usable "or so it was thought," and after many debates Lichine was called in. He produced a light, frothy thirty-minute piece entirely different from Fokine's.

What seems to emerge from these varied recollections is that Fokine completed *Helen of Troy* under difficult conditions resulting from poor health, that it was performed several times in Mexico, that it needed some revisions, and that Hurok and Ballet Theatre, desirous of another popular hit and having already invested a great deal of money in decor alone, decided to invest a little more and revise the ballet.

On 8 October 1942, at the Metropolitan Opera House in New York, Ballet Theatre presented an all-Fokine memorial program. On the bill were *Les Sylphides, Bluebeard,* and *Petrouchka.* John Martin spoke briefly. It is difficult to speculate what Ballet Theatre might have become and what Fokine's role might have been in it had he lived. George Beiswanger, writing in *Theatre Arts* in June 1943, said that there would have been no Ballet Theatre if Dolin, Tudor, and Fokine had not given it the bulk of its sustaining repertory. Donald Saddler feels that, had Fokine lived, the company would have done more and more of his works, which could have provided a cornerstone for them. "The company was Mr. Fokine. We felt that was our image. . . . On the classical side, he would be comparable to what Mr. Balanchine is with the New York City Ballet. He was our classical creator."[19]

Richard Pleasant wrote to Anton Dolin that Fokine received from and gave to the company. Lucia Chase says simply that Fokine was a genius and was a part of Ballet Theatre.

Chapter Seven

Fokine as a Teacher and Ballet Master

A Class with Michel Fokine

SHORTLY AFTER DECIDING TO REMAIN in America Fokine started to teach, opening his first studio in 1921 at 226 West 72d Street, New York City. An advertisement on 2 January in the *New York Herald* announced private and class lessons, special children's classes, classes in composition of dances, and classes for dancing instructors. An announcement in the *Clipper* on 2 February said that Fokine would establish a school through arrangement with Morris Gest and that it would be "for the benefit of beginners, those who know, and those who want to know more."

In 1923 the Fokines rented the former Booth House at 4 Riverside Drive, with an option to purchase it. The lease included a large corner plot, which Fokine hoped to turn into an open-air theater like that at the designer Paul Poiret's in Paris. The anticipated opening of this garden was spring 1924, but no further mention of it can be found. Number 4 Riverside Drive was home to the Fokines for over fifteen years, but, more important, it was Michel Fokine's New York studio.

The house has been described by former students as a "small mansion" where the butler often opened the door. There was a wide staircase with a carved balustrade, high ceilings, huge French windows, parquet floors, Louis XVI sconces and chandeliers, plus numerous paintings, many the work of Fokine himself. The students took the small elevator up to the fourth floor, where there were dressing rooms and a "barre room."

Through advertising and word of mouth, Fokine managed to attract a small, steady band of students. Some were referred by other teachers and a good many were brought by parents who were themselves Russian immigrants to whom the name Fokine was especially significant.

Fokine's former pupils, upon whose recollections this report is based, were, for the most part, either children or in their teens most of the time they studied with the great Russian. Although some took class in the 1920s and others in the 1930s, many of them were in class together at some point or remembered seeing the others come to take class. Very few took more than two classes a week. The reason for this was not so much that the habit of taking daily class was not yet part of the American dance discipline, but rather the cost of studying with Fokine. From the day the studio opened until he stopped teaching, a single class cost $5 and a half-hour private lesson $20. In one or two instances a favored pupil was not charged; but, as a rule, Fokine was adamant about the remuneration he felt he deserved. Pauline Koner's parents paid for her first ten lessons and then her father, a lawyer, agreed to do the Fokines' legal work in exchange for his daughter's training. Anne Wilson had to stop taking class for a year, and Annabelle Lyon's father signed an agreement saying she would pay the tuition herself after she came of age and was working. Agnes de Mille recalls that when she said she could not afford his classes, he shrugged his shoulders and said, "That's a great pity. That's how it is." She never did take class with him.[1]

Fokine did not treat boys differently from girls in the classroom, but there were far fewer boys in his classes. Leon Danielian recalls that he and a few other students of Mikhail Mordkin would occasionally take class with Fokine, for which they paid $1 or $1.25 rather than the customary $5, just because they were males. Fokine stressed masculinity and virility only as it was directly related to the particular role being created. André Eglevsky remembers the choreographer telling him that, although he danced *Spectre de la Rose* quite well, he was really too masculine for the part, whereas Nijinsky had been androgynous, and was therefore better.

Classes were held five days a week and on Saturday morning. There were two or three classes offered each weekday. The 7:00 P.M. class was for advanced children and included teenagers. There was a class for older pupils in the morning and the most advanced class was given in the afternoon. Someone recalls that a class for businesswomen was also offered. No one is very clear now about the exact number of classes and hours, and it is most probable that they varied over the years. It is also likely that Mme Fokina taught the very young children. Miriam Weiskopf remembers that Fokine wanted her to study with his wife initially, but Weiskopf refused. Mme Fokina did teach his classes when he was out of town, as did Vitale Fokine when he grew older.

There was some kind of audition for everyone: for some their first class served this purpose; for others it was a more formal situation. Patricia

Bowman remembers that when she finished her audition, Fokine said, "You're a very good technical dancer, but you don't know how to run." Annabelle Lyon came on a scholarship given to her by an organization in Memphis, Tennessee. Her interview was acceptable, but her first class left her in a state of dismay. John Taras came in 1935, when he was sixteen and without any formal training, as a result of an ad in the *Times*. In his first class he was taught *Schéhérazade*.

A ballet class with Fokine lasted one-and-a-half to two hours and began with a barre, which was given in the small studio on the fourth floor. This warm-up took twenty to thirty minutes. It was given occasionally by Fokine himself, but more often (especially when he had a number of pupils) by Mme Fokina or Vitale. Sometimes the more advanced students did their own warm-ups, although the level of a class was not always clear cut. He expected his pupils to come early and work out before the barre and to remain and practice after class. The barre was usually perfunctory and done by rote. When Fokine gave it, it was even quicker than usual. He gave many petits battements after the pliés. His rondes de jambe and grands battements were done without preparations and his abhorrence of ugliness resulted in his insistence that sur le cou de pied be done with a stretched foot. One famous exercise recalled by several former students emphasized his desire for perfect coordination. He would ask for a ronde de jambe en dedans and port de bras en dehors. One variation on this was a figure eight with the arms, to be repeated eight times, while doing sixteen rondes de jambe and turning the head left and right.

But the essence of the Fokine class was to be found in the centre and adage, which were given in the second floor studio. It was here, in the ballroom of the house, with its French windows overlooking the Hudson River, that Michel Fokine, impeccably dressed in an open-necked shirt, trousers and ballet slippers, usually waited for his pupils. He would give his favorite steps, teach sections of repertory (mostly his own, but sometimes Petipa as well), and try out and develop his new choreographic ideas. From this, a very definite approach and style emerged.

There were almost no mirrors in the large studio. Fokine said that he did not believe in teaching with mirrors because it was necessary to train the "third eye" to look inside yourself and visualize what you look like on all sides. The class always felt that it was dancing, not exercising. He would say that he was teaching the Italian technique as he had learned it in Russia, pointing out the changes he had made. He felt that the Russian approach was only two-dimensional and therefore very flat. He preferred

The studio at 4 Riverside Drive with the Fokine Ballet rehearsing *Les Elfes*. *Courtesy Phyllis Fokine Archive.*

glissades, for instance, to the front or croisé. Sometimes he would get very excited when speaking against the Russian methods, but these discussions were wasted on his pupils, who were mostly completely ignorant of them. Fokine deemphasized technique in class in order to create flow and get rid of a stilted style.

His former students agree that it was the fluidity in a Fokine dancer that always made him or her stand out; everyone else looked rigid by comparison. Every step had to be done with a flow that was based on natural movement and involved the entire body, never a part in isolation. He would, for example, give a complex turn series consisting of a pirouette, attitude derrière, attitude devant, and arabesque, all to be performed in one continuous phrase, allowing the body freedom and flexibility in making its own adjustments in order to create the desired fluidity. His instruction to "pull up until you have not weight" was often accompanied by his own demonstration, which was always that of a light, effortless, and technically proficient dancer.

Fokine taught his students to move and cover space. He taught a walk, a run, a wave goodbye (in which the dancer was supposed to feel the wave from the torso), a waltz, a gallop, and a polka, which was even done en pointe. His pas de chat was front or back, not side, and he used his teaching stick as a sort of low bridge under which he would make his pupils move in order to progress backward. This constant spatial emphasis also involved many different and rapidly changing levels, often going to the knee and the floor.

The essence of the Fokine style as taught by the man himself, with its stress on natural body flow, can be further explained in the areas of line and musicality. Fokine taught everything by looking at the line or picture of the entire body, not anatomically, but as forming a complete image. He talked about the harmony of line and the necessity of following through a movement to its ultimate conclusion. To him, dance meant a beautiful line—one that was long and unbroken. This continuous line or shape was a complete body movement, coordinated and harmonious from all sides, which involved a sense of outward flow and inward feeling. Many of his movements were light, with a sense of the torso reaching from the diaphragm. He would not tolerate cautiousness in the use of the torso, demanding that it be experienced in its greatest capacity. The torso was never squared off, but always had a slight twist. This resulted in the asymmetry he favored. The head went with the body and was never still, helping to carry the line to its final point. A student could not begin to do anything until he or she knew where the head was. Fokine loved the head to be in opposition, and he always wanted it to turn and incline in a soft, reaching manner.

The flow of movement that created the line eventually went through the arms and hands. Fokine sometimes demonstrated with his hands and he often talked about their relationship to the rest of the body. Here again he stressed natural flow and used as an example a painter painting a wall: as the arm goes up the brush (hand) is down, and as the arm goes down the brush (hand) is up. He would never allow the palm to be shown to the audience. Orest Sergievsky remembers him saying, "Arms are not pictures on the wall, but horizons."

Lincoln Kirstein, who studied with Fokine, wrote in 1934:

To have studied under Fokine is to have experienced an unforgettable illumination into the sources of gesture, the definition of style, the creation of theatrical effect. His exercises are not dry, back-breaking labour. When he indicates a reaching motion of the arms, he says: "Reach as if you are touching." . . . He discovers for his pupils the basic idea behind motion.[2]

In addition to remembering his extraordinary musicality, his students recall that, to Fokine, music and movement were inseparable. A self-taught musician, he would usually sing as accompaniment in class. Sometimes he would put rolls on the player piano that sat in the alcove of the ballroom. On occasion he would sit at the piano and play a phrase—always a phrase, never a note. When he taught sections of his own ballets in class, he taught them phrase by phrase, never step by step. The dance steps were often in anticipation of the music. He taught that the movement had to breathe with the musical pauses and fill them out; that it had to go beyond the music, but that there was always a connection between the two. Carola Goya suggests that he felt the aesthetic result was produced by incorporating the technical aspect of dance in a musical way. Many students remember the variations to different musical compositions not only as dance training but as a wonderful introduction to the composers.

Those of his students who were with him for any length of time ended by learning most of Fokine's ballets, even the very young pupils. For instance, the Prelude from *Les Sylphides* was taught to improve balance, jumps, and pointe work. He would demonstrate the movements and give an outline of the ballet. He stressed characterization through imagery, and rarely gave specific emotions for a work that was already choreographed. Katherine Sergava recalls, however, that he would sometimes give a spe-

Michel Fokine at the piano in his studio. *Courtesy Phyllis Fokine Archive.*

cific dramatic situation and dissect it into different emotions. One of the stories he used was that of the medieval knight who meets an opponent, slays him in combat, and removes his helmet to discover that the dead adversary is a woman. The scene was divided to evoke happiness at killing an enemy, surprise that it is female, remorse because it is not knightly to kill a woman, an impulsive desire to save her, and, finally, the act of falling in love with her image. Sergava says that Fokine attempted to lead his pupils through the whole scale of emotions, from moment to moment.

Beauty was the major goal of Fokine's teaching, and to many this concept was demonstrated most clearly in his bourrées. They moved sideward, only the back foot moved noticeably, and the feet never opened up. Improvisation was strictly forbidden in class. Even in giving a step, Fokine would stop to think a moment and then show exactly what he wished his students to perform. In his children's classes he did sometimes give choreographic assignments, but these were to be prepared for the next class. Miriam Weiskopf remembers his being exceptionally pleased with one of her endeavors and calling Mme Fokina in to see it. When she could not repeat it the same way a second time, he made a gentle joke about it.

Only two people seem to have studied choreography with Michel Fokine: Ruth Page and Virginie Mauret. Page, a pupil of Adolph Bolm in Chicago, had about six private sessions with Fokine, during which she found him both critical and helpful. She remembers that she had made up some dances using a long, golden wig and a mirror, and that one of the things he told her was not to use the properties. Mauret, who studied technique as well, says he would give her a piece of music and instruct her to use it as a basis for composition, but forbade her to create a step for every note. He used to tease her because she was very little and he wondered why she composed such big dances, such as one using Wagner's music in which she was a phoenix.

Many remember that he talked a great deal and John Taras feels that he learned just from listening. Fokine's classes were an odd combination of traditional, almost puritanical correctness, which included bowing at the beginning and end of class, together with a certain amount of flexibility. For instance, he was against the rigidity of having only one answer to the question, "Is the accent down or up on a jump?" His English was far from perfect, even in later years, but this fastidious and at times imperious man created an aura of aristocracy and uniqueness for all who studied with him. Most of the girls (and their mothers) worshiped the dramatic, creative male with the luminous face and piercing eyes. In his classes dancers did things that were impossible elsewhere. He was strict and became angry when his pupils were not prepared. He wanted things his way because he felt that if a student was worthwhile he could teach that student anything, but only if they followed his instructions. "It was a combination of him and you," says Leda Anchutina. He had a sense of humor, although he could be cutting in his humorous way.

On the negative side, he did not build strength in a dancer or stress pure technique, but he expected his pupils to acquire it somehow and to use it when needed. He avoided fifth position, considered second position plié vulgar, and regarded turnout as anathema. Many students went sneaking off to other teachers to learn some technique, risking Fokine's wrath if they were discovered. During her interview, Pauline Koner stated emphatically that what she had learned from Fokine was a sense of feeling about dance, not technique. Two days later she telephoned to say that she had been thinking about it, and that since she never really studied with anyone else, she must have learned some technique from him after all. Nora Kaye, who studied with him from age seven to fourteen, has called him one of the greatest choreographers who ever lived. Although she went elsewhere for the fundamentals and technique of dance, he taught her how to act and to create a role.

There were a few things that Fokine did demand technically: heels had to be on the floor after a jump; the foot had to be pointed and aligned as soon as it left the floor; in ronde de jambe the toe had to touch the knee. He liked high extensions, but not tricks. Although he did not believe in pointe work in most ballets, the advanced children's class was taught en pointe because he felt that the shoes should be part of the dancer.

The advertisements for the Fokine School over the years reveal much about the change in attitude on the part of both the public and Fokine and his wife. Mme Fokina was not mentioned at all in earlier advertisements. Although she often arrived in the middle of class, elegantly dressed and bejeweled, causing her husband to comport himself for her approval, she taught little at first. She later received equal billing, and evidently taught more. One advertisement, in 1926, said that the studio was not just for professionals and the very gifted, but for everyone, and that one could learn to compose dances and to become an instructor. Another advertisement offered a daily class for practice and exercise at lower rates. Greek dances, plastic and expressive movements, and ladies' physical culture were included in 1931. By 1933 the advertisements were saying, "Modern Russian Ballet—Necessary foundation for all forms of the dance."

For several summers Fokine gave a Normal Course for teachers, which attracted people from all over the United States. In 1927 the Fokine Studio offered two six-week summer courses, 20 June through 1 August and 11 July through 22 August, for a fee of $150 each. Many of these teachers also took private lessons, but the course promised:

Technique of the Classic Ballet
Explanation of the difference between the old and the new ballet
Explanation of the difference between false Greek dances and the Greek dances
    based on authentic plastique
Explanation of Mr. Fokine's exclusive theory of arm, neck, head and body
    movements and special exercises to soften and beautify movement
Explanation of system for developing an entire dance from fundamental
    rhythm
Special Rhythmic Exercises
Routines from Fokine Dances

Thus it may be seen that, without forsaking any of his basic tenets, Michel Fokine had learned the art of advertising in order to bring in pupils and make money.

All of Fokine's former students agree that he instilled a love for dance and a strong sense of feeling before mechanics. His emphasis was on performing a dance, and he refused to kill the quality of a movement for the sake of technique. For him dance had to be beautiful or it was nothing. The consensus is, however, that Fokine probably did not enjoy teaching very much. He really wanted to choreograph and stage his own ballets. If anything, he should have been a coach for professional dancers. He taught to earn a living, and as long as the school kept going his name was kept alive. Recalling that his classes were often built on a choreographic pattern, Anne Wilson feels that this attitude was that he was teaching "the choreographic spirit."

The Choreographer at Rehearsals

Since Fokine probably did not consider himself primarily a teacher, it is not surprising that there are certain similarities between his teaching and his approach as a choreographer and rehearsal director. As a choreographer he followed his own early statement that he disapproved of any choreography that came out of class technique. Many dancers who worked with him, either as students or experienced performers, feel that in his ballets one had to be an artist, and that the ensuing experience was one of great joy. Every movement had meaning and the dancers felt that they grew artistically. Yurek Lazowski feels that Fokine's great genius lay in the fact that when he created a role he actually transferred himself to the part. Lazowski recalls that when Fokine was setting *Helen of Troy* for Ballet Theatre and was trying to explain the role of a fat priest to Simon Semenov, he first performed it himself, explaining exactly how much the priest ate. A few minutes later he performed Helen. In his ability to see and do both of the roles he choreographed he displayed his unique talent.

Fokine's approach to character was a sensitive and reasoned one: a prince did not walk like a peasant; in *Les Sylphides* the dancers did not look at the audience because they were not human; in *Carnaval* the dancers looked as though they loved; and in *Spectre de la Rose*, he would say, "You are not a human being until you touch her." Annabelle Lyon feels that part of his brilliance as a choreographer lay in the exact way he envisioned a character and the manner in which he communicated this to a performer. Donald Saddler, who was the first dancer after Anton Dolin to dance the lead in *Bluebeard*, compares Fokine's characterizations to Molière's, recalling that his method of instruction was one that initially required an exact imitation of Fokine and then allowed Saddler to develop his own subtleties, once he was secure in the role.

Fokine's approach to choreography was logical and precise, and he came to every rehearsal with careful notes and diagrams, everything always completely prepared beforehand, and with a thorough knowledge of the musical score on which the steps were notated. There was no improvising, and not one minute was wasted. For him the logic of a movement or design lay in its dramatic validity and organization—it had to come from somewhere and go somewhere.

But he could also be flexible, realizing that, because of personality and physique, each dancer's approach to a role would be different. He knew how to create roles for a dancer like Ida Rubinstein, who was tall and beautiful but had no technique, and he would make changes in subsequent stagings of his works to suit an individual performer. Anton Dolin once said that Fokine's method of teaching a role allowed the best of an artist to emerge. He thought "not only of what steps and choreographic pattern he wanted, but of allowing the dancer to express himself. Perhaps that is why in his ballets in particular one always remembers the original creators of the parts."[3]

He never told a dancer how many pirouettes to do, but they did have to be done to the music. This use of music was not blind adherence to a beat, in which a movement was performed to every note in the score. This adherence was often seen in his ballets when he was not there to direct them, a tendency he termed "rhythomania," and which Lyons thinks he realized would occur without his presence. Paul Haakon says that Fokine often purposely choreographed in dance phrases that did not mirror the musical ones.

His sense of design and his ability to manipulate performers on a stage were obvious to all. Fokine constantly urged the dancers to think of the design on the floor, using as an example the fact that if one came in on a diagonal one went out differently. The floor plans he wrote for *Les Sylphides* show carefully conceived and intricate designs.[4] Neither his designs nor his characters were ever contrived, but evolved with a clarity that was the result of simplicity. Tatiana Lescova believes that his avoidance of intricate steps may have been a weakness, and adds that most of his ballets were really demi-caractère in nature. Irina Baronova also says that one had to be a good actress in Fokine's ballets: she speaks of creatures nobody sees, hidden in the trees somewhere, waiting to be discovered.

Antal Dorati, the conductor, who worked with Fokine in the 1930s when he was with de Basil's company, and later with Ballet Theatre, writes, "He was aristocratic, could be warm and wonderful, could also be cold, and he was always caring, perhaps not so much for people, but for his art. When I knew him he was definitely the grand old man of the choreographers' world."[5]

As a rehearsal director, Fokine evidently had two sides. One was kind and calm: without saying much, he could push the role out of a dancer; the other was sarcastic and cruel, sometimes manifesting itself in tantrums. He was more severe in rehearsal than in class, a real "workaholic" in the theater. Miriam Weiskopf says that he was rarely temperamental with her group, perhaps because they were young and not well trained; yet Gemze de Lappe feels that he overworked the very young students in rehearsals, completely ignoring the fact that they were children, and frequently becoming irritated with them. Others describe him as dignified and private, stern but kind.

Fokine was also very superstitious and did not believe in smooth dress rehearsals, so that he would sometimes purposely scream about some minor point in order to insure a good performance. Lazowski, who called him "maestro" as long as he knew him, feels that he had a split personality, noting that he was very cruel to many, among them Massine and Graham. All agree that Fokine was moody, seldom gave compliments, and could be quite sarcastic, particularly with those who tried to impose their own interpretations on his ballets. In rehearsal he was a task master, strict and exacting, who expected complete silence and concentration, and showed no favoritism (he made the corps de ballet feel important). He was remarkable at spotting and correcting mistakes. A very strong technician himself (he could do ten or twelve pirouettes), he demanded faultless technique and unflagging stamina from his dancers. As a left-sided performer, he rarely permitted experienced dancers to do anything to the right.[6] He also expected them to understand intuitively the different styles of his various ballets.

Fokine had an extrordinary memory and was quick to remind someone of a correction he had made the previous day. He was very particular about the hand, the turn of the wrist, the eyes—small details and qualities. He would make a dancer perform a particular phrase hundreds of times, comfort her when she cried, and then make her do it again. He knew what he wanted, down to the most insignificant detail, and was determined to get it. He never counted musical beats, and his dancers, if forced to do so, were careful never to let him see them. Among themselves the dancers would often try to determine what it was he wanted—and they generally felt inspired to try for a level of performance previously unknown to them.

Fokine used various methods to achieve this inspiration. Once, while rehearsing the Paganini variation for Harlequin in *Carnaval,* he put chairs all around the stage and made Leon Danielian do his various jumps over them. He then took them away, saying that it would undoubtedly now be easier. A reporter who observed him rehearsing *Hassan* in London wrote that he made the dancers sit on the floor and beat time with their hands, while listening to the music. Although patient in attempting to make his performers feel the atmosphere, he could make such remarks as "Too difficult for you this step? This step is first we teach babies in Russian school."[7]

It is possible that the technical level of the dancers with whom he worked, in comparison to the Russian-trained performers to whom he had become accustomed, frustrated Fokine. And perhaps his frustration was, in part, responsible for some of the famous tantrums and cutting remarks. But in his classes and in his role as a creator there was still the basic personality—strong, proud, stubborn, with a clear, undeviating concept of what was artistically acceptable.

Fokine's Lecture-Demonstrations

Another type of teaching in which Fokine was involved was the lecture-demonstration, which gave him exposure and a platform for his views, while, at the same time, further educating a segment of the public in ballet. One of the first events of this sort took place before an audience of several hundred women teachers from the city schools in January 1921, the same month that the Fokines opened their school in New York City. The Anderson Club met in the auditorium of St. Agatha's Church on 87th Street and West End Avenue, and Fokine, assisted by Virginie Mauret, gave the first in a series of lecture-demonstrations on various subjects, his being on "The Art of Ballet."

A large audience was present and much publicity received in March 1923, when he lectured the New York Drama League at the Earl Carroll Theatre. Assisted by seven pupils Fokine spoke in Russian, with E. C. Ropes of the Putnam Publishing Company acting as his interpreter. Terming the old ballet a "false art," he had his pupils demonstrate some of the "unnatural movements," which traveled only in a sideward direction. They then demonstrated the "natural" movements of the new ballet.[8]

Fokine was still explaining these same reforms in December 1932 when he lectured in the New School series on Contemporary Dance on the difference between the old Russian ballet and the new international ballet.

In a presentation entitled "From the Classic Ballet to the Modern Dance" he attempted to show the principles of the old ballet and the new changes wrought in it by his reforms.

In the years between these two lectures, he and his pupils probably appeared in dozens of such events, although it is doubtful if all were as colorful as the one in 1926 at the Colony Club, where Fokine's pupils "exhibited uncanny skill in doing their steps on the mantelpiece." There is a photograph showing Desha, Martha Lorber, and Alice Wynne posed on the mantel of the famous club on 62d Street and Park Avenue.[9] The event was even covered as far away as Washington, D.C., where the *Washington Times* (5 January 1926) featured three photographs, one of which was captioned "Beauty and Grace," with the pungent addition, "no Charleston here," suggesting that wherever and however he might be found, Michel Fokine was still considered a model of classic ballet.

Chapter Eight

Europe and America: A Summing Up

WHEN HE DECIDED TO SETTLE in the United States, Michel Fokine—the cultured, polished, highly successful, and world-famous Russian, accustomed to honor and respect from audiences, his fellow artists, and the aristocracy with which he frequently socialized—experienced a "culture shock" from which he probably never recovered. It was not just a difference in language, or the youth and vast size of this nation, or the suspicious attitude toward the arts as elite and unnecessary. Rather, he was stunned by the conflict of values and the American method of conducting day-to-day business that was still influenced by the pragmatic mentality of the frontier.

Agents, managers, and lawyers ranked high among those with whom Fokine frequently clashed and they, along with Hollywood and its citizens, personified America's negative traits to this Russian émigré. Martha Graham, so American in her background and rebellious aesthetic concepts, which were unacceptable to him, appeared inflexible and rude. Fokine talked about incorporating the American character into the creation of dance as a national art form, but one wonders if he really understood the myriad attributes that resulted in this character. This query leads to a comparison of Fokine with George Balanchine, who succeeded so well in forging an American ballet.

On 23 March 1923, New York newspapers reported the fact that on 20 March a jury sitting before Justice Walsh in the City Court of New York had awarded Michel Fokine $1,590 in his breach of contract suit against J. J. Shubert. The suit involved Fokine's work on the choreography and direction of a ballet in the musical *Rose of Stamboul*. Fokine claimed that he had received only $500 of his $2,000 fee, when he was unjustly fired in February 1922. Shubert claimed that the dismissal was completely justified.[1]

In a letter written to his brother, Fokine refers to the American penchant for litigation as an "amusing pastime." He mentions that after a three-day trial he won his suit against the Shuberts, owners of 186 theaters. He asks his brother to imagine him in an American court without an interpreter, defending himself and "speaking for hours in the horrible English language." He goes on to say that this is not the first time he has been in court with managers, and gives the example of one who swindled him, appropriated the show's costumes, and disappeared. Fokine writes that he was billed by a lawyer who searched unsuccessfully for the manager, and then had to hire another lawyer to settle the first attorney's bill. He calls the art of the lawsuit "an unavoidable situation of life in America."[2]

Rose of Stamboul, an operetta with a score by Leo Fall and Sigmund Romberg and a book and lyrics by Harold Atteridge, was staged by J. C. Huffman and opened on 7 March 1922, at the Century Theatre in New York. The operetta was originally scheduled to be premiered on 27 February. A press release prepared at the time says that the Messrs. Shubert had arranged for Fokine to conceive and stage a special ballet in which the Lockfords, from the Follies Bergère, Paris, were to be seen.[3] This dance, which took place in the second act, represented an Oriental betrothal ceremony and was called the "Ballet of the Turkish Wedding." On 10 February the columnist Ben F. Holzman in the *New York Evening Mail* reported that a "new" Fokine would reveal himself in this ballet based on authentic Turkish wedding dances. Fokine was reported to have said that the public was familiar with a style of Oriental dancing in which the arms alone were used in various poses, but that his study in Turkey had revealed a great emphasis on the feet. He also added that he had contributed certain interpretative movements that would bind the whole together. Holzman's column adhered closely to a press release sent out by the Shuberts, which also stressed that the ballet revealed a sense of humor and gaiety heretofore unseen in Russian ballet. On 17 February 1922, the *Evening Telegram* reported that the work had been completed and that it involved a chorus of 150, plus a group of Fokine's pupils.

The review of *Rose of Stamboul* that appeared in the *Sun* the day after its opening on 7 March referred to the "spirited and colorful Turkish wedding ballet which is said to have been devised by Michel Fokine, although the program did not give him any credit." The final program read "numbers staged by Allan K. Foster," although the original draft listed Fokine's name.

The reason the Shuberts fired Fokine may be deduced from a few scattered bits of information. They claimed that he had engaged in a thoroughly unprofessional temperamental outburst, and that he had walked out on an incomplete ballet. *Billboard* reported that the incident occurred at a Saturday-night rehearsal and was a result of the chorus girls' laughing at Fokine. The *Morning Telegraph* (17 October 1924) was more specific. According to its version, Fokine turned to one of the chorus and asked, "Are you a terpsichorean?" She replied, "Naw, I'm a Presbyterian," reducing the others to laughter.

There seems to be no question that Fokine did walk out, but whether or not the ballet had actually been completed is unclear. To substantiate Fokine's claim that it was, there is the newspaper article of 17 February announcing its completion, and another one giving Foster credit for the Oriental effect and the handling of mass movements, and repeating the statement about the use of the feet in Turkish dance, which had earlier been attributed to Fokine. The Shubert lawyers, William Klein and Maurice Wormser, insisted, however, that Fokine had left his work incomplete and that the Shuberts had to employ Allan K. Foster to finish it.[4] The Shuberts used the testimony of several chorus girls to substantiate their claim. When Fokine won the suit, the Shubert lawyers immediately filed an appeal to a higher court, and on 31 October 1924, the Appellate Division reversed the original judgment and ruled that J. J. Shubert was justified in canceling the contract.[5]

Of all the managers and entrepreneurs with whom Michel Fokine came into contact in the United States, the most colorful, and in many ways the most instrumental in his new life, was Morris Gest. Gest, whose real name was Moisha (Moses) Gershonovitch, was born in Russia and began his producing career in New York in 1905, after serving as an assistant property man for a group of Yiddish players in Boston. For several years he was associated with Oscar Hammerstein, for whom he recruited European acts. In 1906 he went into partnership with F. Ray Comstock and in 1911 he married David Belasco's daughter, Reina. He had been Gertrude Hoffmann's manager at one time and profited from her success, although he did not make any money when he produced her season of Russian ballet in 1910. He was also responsible for bringing Anna Pavlova and Mikhail Mordkin to the United States in 1910, and again in 1924. He managed Mordkin and a touring company of dancers for two years in the mid-1920s, reintroduced Eleanora Duse to America, and brought over the Chauve Souris, the Moscow Art Theatre, and Max Reinhardt, as well as Michel Fokine.

Gest was a colorful figure who always wore a flowing Windsor tie and a large black hat, had a tendency to make flamboyant statements about his productions (many of which were actually true), and seemed to combine the characteristics of P.T. Barnum with those of a true believer in the arts. His successes were phenomenal and his failures equally so. He once sued Henry Ford for $5,000,000, saying that Ford had libeled him in an article in the *Independent* that attacked his *Aphrodite* and *Mecca* as salacious spectacles.

Gest was invited by Otto H. Kahn to take over the Century Theatre. His first spectacle there, *Chu Chin Chow* (1917), was a financial success, but *Aphrodite* and *Mecca*, in both of which he involved Fokine, were losing propositions. It was probably because of his unique personality that he had been able to convince Fokine to come to America in the first place. Gest's devotion to ballet was undoubtedly genuine and one tends to believe his statement that "I have only one love in the theatre, and that is the Russian Ballet."[6] His passion was not always a very profitable one. When he presented the Fokines at the Metropolitan Opera House on 1 March 1921, his 25 percent share of the profits came to $364.44.

Gest evidently realized that it was necessary to have a school in order to create a national ballet company; and his plan to involve Fokine in such a venture was announced in January 1921. The *Sun* (20 January 1921) under the headline "Fokine to Head a Gest School," announced this venture and went on to say that the curriculum would accommodate everyone from beginner to advanced student, and that Fokine hoped to establish a company from his students. The *Morning Telegraph* (20 January 1921) quoted Fokine as saying that he had decided to remain in America because of Gest's offer, and reminded its readers that he had come to America originally under contract to Gest. A press release had evidently been sent to every newspaper in New York and almost all of them reported the plan for the school, as well as the fact that Fokine was to give recitals in New York, Boston, and other cities. In addition, Fokine was quoted as saying that he was already negotiating with Igor Stravinsky about a new score and with Boris Anisfeldt about settings—all for a work he planned to choreograph for Gest. It was also announced that "next spring, Mr. Gest will accompany Mr. Fokine on a trip to Europe to arrange with composers for special scores, so that by next season, New York may expect to see some really novel ballets, made in America and danced by all-American talent."[7]

The reasons this project never materialized are not presently known. The relationship evidently continued amicably, in spite of the circumstances of *The Miracle* (see chapter 3), and in May 1929 Gest and Fokine signed a letter of agreement, addressed to Gest, in which Fokine said that he would give his exclusive services to Gest for a period of one year, commencing 1 September 1929. He was to assist in conducting a studio under his supervision and name, for which he would receive 50 percent of the net profits, with a guarantee of $25,000. Fokine also agreed to stage and supervise the ballets of Gest's productions or any other production Gest desired, "including movies, vitaphone or similar," at a rate of $1,500 for each production. The letter continued, "I understand that you are to stage among others the following: *Coq D'Or, Cleopatra, Celphide* [*Sylphide*], *Chu Chin Chow, Prince Igor, Firebug* [*Firebird*], *Mecca*." It was further understood that the artists were to be agreed upon mutually, that all publicity, advertising, and management of employees were to be handled by Gest, and that prior to 1 September 1929, Fokine would do no work without Gest's permission in writing. The letter was signed by both men and witnessed.[8]

Unfortunately for Fokine, Gest was still involved in the production of *The Miracle,* which had opened in 1926, vainly trying to make money by touring the play. It was on the road in the fall of 1929, and ended up in Dallas, Texas, in January 1930, because the financiers who had backed it called in their notes, because of the crash of the stock market. Gest filed an involuntary petition of bankruptcy in 1930, probably had a nervous breakdown, and went into seclusion until 1932. He died on 16 May 1942. He suffered from poor health during the last ten years of his life, was never really successful again, never honored the letter of agreement with Fokine, and was never again involved with him. Ironically, it was his brother, Simeon Gest, whom he put in charge of the Mordkin group when it toured in the 1920s, who helped Mikhail Mordkin set up his school and establish the Mordkin Ballet in 1937, thus creating a foundation for Ballet Theatre.

When Fokine signed the letter of agreement with Gest in May 1929, he had already made plans to spend the summer in Hollywood. If one takes seriously the terms of the letter, he went with Gest's blessing and, possibly, with some financial help from Gest. The May issue of the *American Dancer,* a West Coast publication, announced that the Fokines would be soloists in a series of divertissements to be seen in the Hollywood Bowl on 9 August, and would appear there as featured dancers in *Tannhäuser,* choreographed and staged by Fokine, the following week. The choreographer said he would have to assemble a company for the Bacchanale from Act I, scene 1 of Wagner's opera, and the magazine issued a call to all dancers with sufficient background and training to register to audition at the offices of the Hollywood Bowl Association. It will be remembered that he originally staged this at the Maryinsky in 1910.

On 19 May the *Los Angeles Times* reported that Los Angeles was the latest world-famous metropolis to "capitulate" to the art of the Russian ballet and that "Michel Fokine himself is to head the local branch of the modernized Imperial Ballet School of Petrograd." The Hollywood Bowl Association had received a telegram from Fokine, saying that he had made arrangements with Edith Jane, a local dance teacher, to rent her studios in July in order to offer a class for advanced students and establish a local headquarters. In the June issue of the *American Dancer,* the dates of the course were given as 8 July to 2 August and it was stated that the more promising pupils would be used in the Hollywood Bowl concert. The July issue of *Dance Magazine* carried an advertisement for the four-week master class, listing the Fokines' Riverside Drive address for inquiries.

In a feature article written just after he arrived for his first visit west of the Rockies, Fokine was described as a trim man, "whose every gesture, intonation and posture denote the aristocratic." His advent was proclaimed "comparable to the coming of the spirituelle Elenora Duse to America for a belated premiere in the sunset moments of her great career." Noting that he had been too busy teaching in New York to come before, he was quoted as saying that it was the lure of the master class that had convinced him and Mme Fokina to accept the engagement.[9]

There was evidently a large class, because, when the Bacchanale (also referred to as the *Venusberg Ballet*) was performed at the Hollywood Bowl, there were fourteen nymphs, nine bacchantes, and sixteen fauns. Among the nine male fauns, the program listed M. Haakon. Vera Fokina was the First Bacchante, but Fokine did not dance in the Bacchanale. He had danced the previous week, when he and Mme Fokina appeared together. On this first program, both Fokines gave excerpts from *Le Rêve de la Marquise* and danced the Mazurka from *Coppélia*, Fokina danced *Phoenix*, and Fokine, *Panaderos*.

In spite of the fact that the program notes on the soloists referred to their appearances as "an epoch making event in the artistic annals of the West," neither of the evenings received favorable reviews. Rather, they disappointed the critics. The *Los Angeles Express* (10 August 1929) stated that the Bowl was no place for solo or duet dances because the performers tended to "evaporate like drops of water in hot sand." The *Express* critic thought the Fokines' dancing charming in a way, but far below expectations. He found the repetitiveness of the excerpts from *Le Rêve de la Marquise* wearying, and pronounced both Fokine's and Fokina's solos lacking in individuality. The *Los Angeles Times* (10 August 1929) praised the musical selections on the program, especially the Ballet from the film score of *Paris Bound*, by Arthur Alexander, but also said that the performers were a disappointment. In the *Times*, too, it was pointed out that the intricacies of *Le Rêve de la Marquise* required a more intimate concert hall; in addition, the reviewer did not like Fokine's interpretation of the Mozart music, and she found the bathing scene to contain "not a little vulgarity, which left the audience quite cold."

The Bacchanale from *Tannhäuser* was generally thought to be interesting because of its colorful costume effects, but hastily prepared and poorly danced. Most critics expected it to be a sensual, riotous ballet. Instead, they found its nymphs and fauns tame and indifferent to the music, and agreed with the *Times* that it was a poor idea to attempt to concertize a Wagner opera. Perhaps the harshest criticism of the entire venture came from the *American Dancer*, which found Mme Fokina artificial, deemed Fokine's dancing unnecessary, and said that the physical defects of the Bowl should have been taken into consideration by such veteran performers.

The precise order of what happened next is unclear. Vitale Fokine says that since Gest had been unable to fulfill the obligations of his contract, the Fokines had decided to close their New York studio and move to California because Fokine had been approached by several film studios to choreograph ballets. When they arrived, however, they waited nine months for his first contract. Fokine himself wrote that he felt "absolutely sure that in the cinema, it was possible to achieve even greater results than on the stage," because of all the technical possibilities. But he found the studios interested only in light, commercial dancing.

On 27 October 1929, the *Los Angeles Times* reported that Fokine would be returning to the Pacific coast to give a four-week master class at the Edith Jane School of Dancing, to commence the following day. This was possibly a test situation before he returned to New York and permanently closed his school there. Olga Maynard says that Gest had made arrangements with a film magnate who wished to record the repertoire of the Diaghilev era, but then changed his mind. The school was to train the dancers for the film, but it was decided that it was too serious a subject to be entertaining.[10] It is probable that Gest did have some role in the arrangements and that he had hoped that the film would support the school and, eventually, a company, until both could become established on their

Michel Fokine costumed for *Panaderos* at the Hollywood Bowl. *Courtesy Phyllis Fokine Archive*.

own. But his own problems intensified at the same time, and his bank-ruptcy in August 1930 followed shortly after Fokine's move to Holly-wood. Thus the Russian choreographer was left to face the vagaries of Hollywood without a business and financial manager, and he returned to New York to reopen his old studio early in 1931.

Martha Graham's dance is the antithesis of all that Hollywood stood for in the 1930s, yet her approach to her art is as uniquely American as the California film town. It is possible that the disillusionment and bitter-ness Fokine felt with Hollywood caused him to react so strongly when, shortly after his return to New York, his well-known "confrontation" with her took place.

On 20 February 1931, Graham was the guest speaker at one of a series of lectures on modern dance organized by John Martin and given at the New School of Social Research in New York. Fokine was in the audience, as he had been at some of the previous lectures. At one point, he asked Miss Graham a question regarding the use of the arms. He kept asking additional questions, pressing her to explain her philosophy. This heated exchange went on for a few moments until John Martin said something about "Mr. Fokine," at which point Graham realized to whom she was speaking. A short time afterward there appeared in the New York Rus-sian weekly, *Novoe Russkoe Slovo* (The New Russian Word), an article entitled "A Sad Art," in which Fokine recounted this confrontation and expressed some of his ideas about modern dance.[11]

He described Graham as looking like a "fanatical prophetess" on a platform in the middle of the room, severe, elbows turned out, hands either straight or tightly clenched, explaining that the chest and stomach represent the "center" of her movement. He said that the demonstration dances, on flat feet, consisted of two basic movements—the chest thrust forward or sinking in—movements of grief and hatred, which he saw as ugly in form and spirit. Then someone asked Graham's opinion of ballet and he reported her as saying that it was a form of dance she liked, espe-cially Pavlova's bow, but that when a ballet company performs a Grecian dance it is ugly. He wrote that he was determined to keep quiet, but that Graham, noticing the expression on his face, asked him if he wanted to say something, and he said that he asked a question about natural move-ment. As an illustration, he said that her dancers lifted first the shoulder, then the elbow, and then the whole arm, in order to gesture—which he found unnatural. He demonstrated this series of movements and reported that many laughed, including Graham. He recounted that further questions from him led to her saying that he knew nothing about body movements and that a Greek dance could not be done in fifth position. Martin stopped the exchange by saying that ballet had had three centuries to explain itself and modern dance should be allowed three weeks. Fokine reported Graham as saying, "We shall never understand each other."

Several of those who were present at the New School still remember the incident well. George Chaffee recalls Graham saying, "Next season we are going to do this," and then stretching her arms out to the sides, shoulder level, palms facing forward and hands cupped. He says the atmosphere became so tense that at one point, he laughed out loud. Anne Wilson calls it a "terrible tempest in a very public teapot," and remembers Graham looking very small and Fokine being very angry. She thinks he was angry because she presented her ideas as an absolute, and that probably, had they both moved and not talked, there might have been less of a misunderstanding. Wilson feels that Fokine was talking about gestures and their validity and that Graham was interested in abstract emotion.[12] Agnes de Mille was also in the audience and she says that Fokine badgered Graham with questions and that the whole incident was unbecoming to him. She feels that, although Fokine might have felt that Diaghilev's treatment of him had been shabby, he was a choreographer of "unexampled achievement and glory" and should not have heckled a "young, helpless, naive beginner."[13]

Graham had brought along several dancers to demonstrate for her, including Gertrude Shurr and Dorothy Bird. Shurr says that the dancers all knew that the questioner was Fokine, but that Graham was completely unaware of this as she was fielding questions from the audience, and that she thought that Fokine was just another bothersome person interrupting her. Shurr feels that Graham was going through a period when she was still very antiballet, and had she known she was talking to Fokine, would probably not have been so adamant.

Dorothy Bird recalls that Graham had them do an improvisation using the arm simultaneously with the breath, raising the elbow first and then lowering it from the shoulder, all while walking. She says that at this time Graham was working on breathing and that she believed in deep stylization and real abstraction. Bird remembers Fokine, looking like a Wall Street businessman, stepping out after the demonstration and asking, "Why?" When Graham said that it was the natural movement of the arm, they started to argue and reached a deadlock. Martin, who was sitting behind the dancers, whispered that it was Fokine, and asked Bird to tell Graham; but by the time she crawled out and tried to do so, it was too late. She feels that Graham would not have behaved as she did had she known who it was, and that someone, either Martin or Fokine himself, should have made an introduction.

Vitale Fokine and the editor Anatole Chujoy chose to reprint "A Sad Art" in its entirety in *Memoirs of a Ballet Master,* entitled that chapter "The Fight against Modern Dance," and included other negative comments on modern dance by Fokine. An English writer, Peter Williams, who reviewed the book, called the chapter "a rather unhappy inclusion." He felt that they had simply met at a time when the old world and the new were at loggerheads and eventually both Fokine and Graham would have mellowed and recognized each other.[14]

Was Fokine—the innovator who had rebelled against the hallowed balletic traditions of the Imperial Theatre—really a conservative who opposed any reform that was not his? He was indeed a conservative, yet he probably would not have opposed an idea because he had not conceived of it. Still, he would not veer from the artistic principle that had guided him from the very beginning—that beauty had always been the ideal of humanity.

He argued in "A Sad Art" that Graham's comments were founded in ignorance (his own Greek ballets and bacchanales did not use the ballet turnout). He felt that ballet was quite capable of being modern, and gave as examples the Diaghilev Ballet and Rolf de Maré's Ballet Suédois, which were far more radical than the German modern dancers. He also felt that true expressiveness requires technique, a point he made in an essay entitled "Dillettantism in Dance," where he said that an art form cannot start from the individual self, but must be in touch with all that has gone before. He warned that the propaganda of freedom carries with it mixed blessings, and that it is not only what is expressed, but how. Fokine felt that the "New Ballet" had what the proponents of free dance were looking for—that one can possess a technique and still be expressive.[15]

Although there is no evidence that he was familiar with the work of Doris Humphrey and Charles Weidman, Fokine knew of and admired Loïe Fuller, Ruth St. Denis, and Isadora Duncan, and seemed to understand their viewpoints and reforms. He wrote in 1928 that they had given the art of dance new ideas and possibilities. He felt that Fuller enriched dance, with her use of lights and shadows and the combination of "body motions with flying silks," that St. Denis had contributed an awareness of the East, and that Duncan had reminded the world of the beauty of natural movements.[16] Katherine Sergava, who was also present at the Graham lecture, says what Fokine was really arguing for was this concept of natural movement, and that he was trying to deal with the laws of nature when Graham became very defensive.

Fokine always admired Isadora Duncan because of her belief in natural movement, although he denied the fact that it was her appearance in Russia that influenced his original reforms, even becoming quite angry when this was suggested. He readily admitted, however, that he respected her expressiveness and simplicity, and that they shared many ideas, particularly those involved with rebellion against the unnaturalness of the ballet at the turn of the century and the need for the body to be free. But, as he wrote to John Martin, the similarity stopped there; for Duncan had one costume and one style of movement for all periods and all music, which was completely against his beliefs—although he admired naturalness, it was as the foundation of the art of dance, not as an end in itself.[17] As Lincoln Kirstein has pointed out, Duncan's theories were based on her own personality while Fokine's were supported by the conventions and traditions of classical ballet, in which he remained.[18]

It was perhaps because Fokine really believed in the importance of traditional training, and the concept that dance as an art should express a feeling or emotion, not an individual choreographer's personality, that he was so adamantly opposed to modern dance as he saw it personified in Graham. He could not tolerate the lack of form, the constant ugliness and tension—what he saw as the influence of the German modern dance, which, to him, was a morbid art, leading to the creation of "dark souls and ugly bodies."[19] He did not deny the expressive or dramatic need for grotesque or angular movements, pointing out that he himself had used them in *Petrouchka* and *Firebird* twenty years before they appeared under the label of modern dance, and that Nijinsky, Massine, Nijinska, and Balanchine had used them as well.[20] But he was unable to accept an entire philosophy of dance that, to him, denied beauty and flow in movement as well as the necessity of technique as a tool for expressiveness.

Fokine talked about creating an American dance, nurtured in American soil, from the moment he landed in this country. Although he initially downplayed jazz, musical comedy, and vaudeville, putting them in the category of light entertainment forms rather than an indigenous art, he soon included them among America's assets, along with its energy, vitality, and adaptability. In an article written in 1928, entitled "The American Ballet Today," he argued that ballet developed because the French took the transplanted Italian art, and the Russians the French art. Hence America could take the migrating Russian art and make it American. He listed the things needed to create a ballet in America: a ballet master with knowledge of the art, experience, and creative talent; enthusiasm; dancers from a good school; an executive to relieve the artists of business problems; and financial backing. He goes on to say that there is no American who qualifies as the ballet master, nor is this necessary. He ends by saying that America has given a great deal to dance, but nothing to the ballet, emphasizing that there is a difference between the two: "The dance is like a field flower . . . where the soil is good it grows. It needs no worry, no care. But there are other flowers. These are transplanted from one earth into another, they are cared for, they are watered, they are placed into plant-houses, they are treasured." The second flower, ballet, was for Fokine a product not only of nature, but of knowledge, science, art, love, and care.[21]

Five years after Fokine published the above statements, Lincoln Kirstein wrote an article in the *New England Weekly* in which he said that Fokine was still alive, training the best dancers in the United States, and was still a great choreographer, who has been denied the one position in America befitting his talents—at the Metropolitan Opera House in New York—because of the opera's Italian prejudice against Russian music and dance. Kirstein asked, "Would Fokine seem vieux-jeu now? Could he adapt himself to 'modern' choreography?" He answered, "One hopes not." Kirstein went on to cite the need for a little integration after the "dilution" of the late Diaghilev excesses and the "spasmic hypnosis" of Central European dance. He concluded: "Whatever threatens the world in the way of economic disaster, we need what Michel Fokine alone can give to us in the science of dancing. He was once the victim of an historical accident. He was once, and is becoming again, an historical necessity."[22]

Yet, in the same year that he wrote these lines, 1933, Lincoln Kirstein went to Europe and made an offer to George Balanchine, another Russian-trained dancer, who was Diaghilev's last choreographer, to come to America. Here he and Edward M. M. Warburg, a Harvard classmate, would establish a school for Balanchine that would train dancers for an American ballet company. This is not the place to discuss the subsequent emergence of George Balanchine, the School of American Ballet, which was established in 1934, or the various companies that have evolved into the New York City Ballet. But it is possible to speculate why Kirstein brought Balanchine to America when Fokine, for whom he obviously had so much respect, and whose 1913 ballet *Les Preludes (for Anna Pavlova)* he once called the first of the modern ballets, had already been here for so long. In the process, one is forced to make some assessment of Fokine's position in America.

In 1933, George Balanchine was twenty-nine years old and Michel Fokine was fifty-three. They had both been trained at the Imperial School in St. Petersburg, Fokine graduating in 1898 and Balanchine in 1921, by which time it had changed its name to the Soviet State School of Ballet. When Fokine returned to Russia just after the start of World War I, Balanchine actually danced in one of the ballets he created at the time, *Jota Aragonese* (1916). When the very young Balanchine left Russia and went to work for Diaghilev in 1925, he learned the Fokine ballets, most of which were still in the repertory, and even helped to stage some of them for the Ballet Russe de Monte Carlo.[23]

Michel Fokine and George Balanchine shared a deep interest in music and its direct relationship to the dance, and both were accomplished musicians themselves. When it came to art, Balanchine was interested neither in the graphic arts nor, particularly, in color, whereas Fokine did much of his research in museums and was an accomplished painter. Fokine had performed a great deal as a dancer, was a technically good one, and had created strong roles for men; Balanchine danced little himself, and his attitude toward males was more akin to Petipa's—they are there to support the females. Both stressed the beauty of the body line, but Balanchine's approach was more austere and abstract, while Fokine was more inclined to fill the theater. There was a strong strain of romanticism in both, although it was stronger in Fokine, whose dances were more emotional, while Balanchine was really closer to Petipa. Balanchine used no mime and practically no story or plot; Fokine did the opposite. Balanchine dancers had speed, force, and attack; Fokine dancers were lyrical, with a softness in the arms and body. Balanchine accepted modern dance as dance, with the judgment of bad or good kept to himself; Fokine felt impelled to speak out against it.

From the very beginning, however, Balanchine incorporated many of Fokine's reforms—especially his use of music and the corps de ballet—and went on to create dances that reflected the American national character as he saw it. Over the years he even did his own versions of *Firebird*, *Chopiniana*, and *Schéhérazade*. Antal Dorati says that "Balanchine started where Fokine left off."[24]

Lincoln Kirstein probably chose Balanchine over Fokine because of the age factor and because he wanted a young talent who did not have so much tradition and success behind him. Balanchine did not have a great many world-renowned successes he could restage, and thus had to create new ballets.

When Fokine arrived in America, he had already absorbed and experienced much in the old world, and his avant-garde sensibility was that of pre–World War I Russia and, to some extent, Paris. Balanchine, who was exposed to the synthesis and maturity of many of these new ideas as they came and went in Europe during the 1920s, was more at home with them, and was still young enough to be able to absorb a great deal of American culture. Also, he and Kirstein were closer in age, which, from Kirstein's point of view, would have made the relationship one of greater equality. There is, in addition, the strong possibility that, aesthetically, Kirstein favored Balanchine's stress on abstraction and his emphasis on pure dance over expression.

When Fokine arrived in this country, there were few dancers trained in classical ballet techniques. By the time Balanchine came there were many more—students not only of Fokine, but of Adolph Bolm, Theodore Koslov, Mikhail Mordkin, and others. Both Fokine and Gest realized from the beginning the necessity for the kind of organization that Kirstein created, one in which primary emphasis was on a school, thereby giving the potential creator of American ballet an opportunity to train the American body and personality, and to observe it as well. But Fokine and Gest were never able to create such a school. It was the lucky, perhaps fortuitous combination of Kirstein and Balanchine that worked, resulting in the creation of a very significant aspect of American ballet—the development and teaching of an American technique.

A major difference between Balanchine and Fokine lies in how each saw and observed certain American characteristics: the strong, long-legged bodies; the tendency to regard space as a vast expanse to be conquered; the instinct for speed; the affinity for syncopation; the indigenous quality of jazz; and the fact that American dancers stress rhythm and technique before drama.

Balanchine worked in musical comedy fifteen years later than Fokine, when it was a more developed form, which he in turn helped to define. Balanchine was also exposed to more jazz, instinctively understood it, and was able to incorporate some of its qualities into his own very classical ballet style. Fokine either could not or would not do this. He gave lip service to the importance of jazz and its various dance manifestations, after initially denigrating it, but it is doubtful if he ever truly understood it. In all fairness to Fokine, his role in the musicals and revues in which he was involved was a very isolated one, giving him little opportunity to work within or observe the entire structure. Balanchine, however, was not only the choreographer for many musicals but the director of several as well. Here, timing is a factor: America in 1919 was not ready for Fokine, even in its musicals. By 1935, when it was, he had largely given up, and was concentrating his work in Europe once again.

Although Fokine was considered a radical in the context of Russia in 1905, he was never really a revolutionary but rather an evolutionary. He saw the need for reform and he voiced it; but he was always a conservative, operating within the boundaries of tradition. Artistically he was a humanist, albeit a romantic one, and he possessed certain affinities with the Renaissance man; personally he was, in many ways, an Old World aristocrat. These qualities, plus the fact that he was forty-one when he decided to settle permanently in America, left him totally unprepared to face the eccentricities of American life. The tremendous effort he made to do so—from the countless interviews to the grueling work for vaudeville and motion-picture theaters—must have been degrading to him. Added to this was the constant illegal presentation and plagiarism of his ballets throughout the world. His frustration with America was further exacerbated because he had no one to act as a buffer between him and this strange culture he was trying to understand and conquer.

Fokine realized that an American national character existed, but he seemed to wish to impose a Russian mold upon it, rather than to absorb these attributes into the classical ballet. He never fully understood that, since America was not a traditional society as he knew it, his art form would have to undergo a certain amount of alteration. He probably also had difficulty in understanding that Graham, having no American dance tradition against which to rebel, turned her energies against ballet instead.

Although Fokine could, at times, be as pragmatic as his adopted countrymen—his work in popular entertainment is proof of this—his strongly romantic nature would not permit him to accept abstraction for its own sake. His antipathy toward modern dance came about not because he was incapable of thinking abstractly or of creating abstract movement; it happened because he had already formulated and expressed these same ideas in his outline for the new ballet, thus expressing them creatively without abandoning the training techniques of the past. The fact that he was a romantic and a storyteller did not put him in opposition to the American character, but during the 1920s and 1930s these qualities were being denied by many of the dance rebels. His ideas were ignored by these new revolutionaries, which undoubtedly frustrated and angered him.

The fact that Fokine probably appealed to large segments of the American public because of his reputation rather than his artistry would have appalled him. His actual influence on that public cannot be measured, yet

Vera and Michel Fokine in the dining room at 4 Riverside Drive. *Courtesy Phyllis Fokine Archive.*

the thousands who saw his work must have been affected by their contact with his art, and they were surely being prepared for what was to develop later.

Fokine remained a creative genius to the end of his life. The new works he choreographed for Ballet Theatre and three of those he created in Europe between 1935 and 1939—*Don Juan, Paganini,* and a new *Coq d'Or*—seem, judged by the critical acclaim they received, to attest to his continuing creativity. Had he lived another ten or fifteen years, he would probably have made additional contributions to Ballet Theatre, both in restaging his old ballets and creating new ones.

In America, Michel Fokine was honored and respected for what he had already done in Europe; what he currently did was inevitably regarded in that past light. His ideas and working methods were so firmly set that he never escaped an Old World aura, although he did talk and write about the life and spirit of the New World. His influence on the many whom he taught and with whom he worked was involved with style, philosophy, and inspiration—a kind of sensibility that remained with them throughout their lives. His attempt to create an American ballet failed because of circumstances, human and historical, outside his control. His role in bringing ballet to the average American was considerable. His contribution to Ballet Theatre was to help provide it with a solid foundation. Had he lived, he would probably have continued in this manner, serving as an example to young choreographers—who were exploring dance in ways alien to him—and creating new ballets with the instinct of the master he was.

Michel Fokine was a true genius—both in path breaking (there seems little doubt that without his pioneering work those who followed would have had no guidance) and in his ability to create ballets that could range from fantasy to humanity to pure technical skill. His passion, his integrity, his refusal to be precious, his concept of form, and his struggle against outworn traditions are sufficient to insure him a place of highest importance in the history of dance.

His major contributions to the literature of great works of dance were, without doubt, made just prior to and during his years with the Diaghilev company. To those who might argue that he never again achieved the magnificence of *Les Sylphides, Firebird, Schéhérazade, Le Spectre de la Rose, Carnaval,* or *Petrouchka,* one can answer that these works alone, in their conception, invention, and integrity, are enough. They have influenced the entire creative world of the twentieth century and, as works of art, will endure. *Les Sylphides* was the first modern abstract ballet, and its profound influence on Balanchine, as well as countless other choreographers, is indisputable. His use of the exotic (*Schéhérazade*), the mythic (*Firebird*), and the dramatic (*Petrouchka*) gave all who followed him a model and a source.

If Michel Fokine did repeat and reuse his own dance themes during many of his years in America, he, of all people, was certainly entitled to do so. He created more during his Diaghilev years alone than most artists produce in a lifetime. In fighting artistic battles and wooing both a dance audience and financial backers in middle age, he may have found little energy for any really new endeavors—or perhaps he had already expressed and developed all that was in him.

In his later years he remained a figure of inspiration and stability in the emerging ballet scene, and almost every company saw the need to include his works in its repertory. The respect he engendered until his death and the light in which those who knew him still regard him seem to tell us that Michel Fokine is, in overall assessment, a great figure in twentieth-century dance, whose contributions, both conceptual and artistic, are of lasting importance.

Notes

Chapter One

1. This article is reprinted in translation in Cyril W. Beaumont's *Michel Fokine and His Ballets* (London, 1935) (hereafter referred to as *Michel Fokine*) and there is another translated version in the Fokine Papers of the Dance Collection of the New York Public Library at Lincoln Center. The editor's note is found with the latter. The Dance Collection will hereafter be referred to as DC.

2. *Memoirs of a Ballet Master* (London, 1961). All future references to Fokine's writings are from this book unless otherwise noted.

3. Lincoln Kirstein, *Fokine* (London, 1934), 21.

4. Tamara Karsavina, *Theatre Street* (New York: E. P. Dutton & Co., 1950).

Chapter Two

1. Among the memoirs are those by Benois, Gregoriev, Lieven, Karsavina, Nijinska, and Fokine. Beaumont, Buckle, and Haskell are a few of the historians. It is often difficult to ascertain whether different versions are due to different perceptions or to forgetfulness (or other motives) years later. Buckle, for instance, questions Gregoriev's memory when he claims Karsavina and Nijinsky were "brilliant" in *Carnaval* in Paris, when, in actuality, neither ever danced it there.

2. Fokine refers to this as the Krivoye Zerkalo Theatre. Others just call it Catherine (Ekaterinsky) Hall on the canal of the same name.

3. A plot, as Grace Roberts, *The Borzoi Book of Ballets* (New York: Knopf, 1949), points out, very similar to that of the later *Paganini*.

4. This second version of *Chopiniana* is sometimes referred to by Fokine as having been called "Reverie Romantique" and other times as "Danses Sur La Musique de Chopin." Bronislava Nijinska says that some of this second version was actually first seen in February 1908, when Fokine mounted some of the scenes to a piano score in order to stay out of a quarrel between Pavlova and Kchessinska over which one was to dance one of his solos.

5. *Le Figaro,* May 5, 1909, as quoted in Richard Buckle, *Diaghilev* (London: Sidwick & Jackson, 1955), 137.

6. Cyril Beaumont, *Complete Book of Ballets* (London, 1937).

7. The musical score was very difficult for the members of the orchestra, who initially laughed at it. Pierre Montreaux, the conductor, had a difficult time working with them.

8. Beaumont, *Michel Fokine.*

9. This statement is made in *Protiv Techeniia* (Against the Tide) Yuri Slonimsky, ed. (Leningrad, 1962). This book will hereafter be referred to as *Against the Tide.* All material used from it was translated for this writer by Natasha Miheyev.

10. Fokine first went to Sweden in 1913 to direct the Operaballet, at which time he staged *Cléopâtre* and *Les Sylphides,* and brought Boris Anisfeldt with him to design the decor and costumes. He was asked back in 1914 and mounted *Spectre, Carnaval,* and *Schéhérazade,* all with their original sets and costumes. A visit scheduled for 1917 was canceled due to the October Revolution in Russia, but in March 1918 he, Vera Fokina, and Vitale crossed the Baltic on sleds packed with all their belongings. Mary Skeaping, the Swedish dancer/director, in *Dance and Dancers,* London, May 1957, recalls with pleasure an open-air spectacle, *The Four Seasons,* which Fokine staged in Stockholm on 21 September 1918. The cast of eight hundred dancers performed Spring to part of Grieg's "Peer Gynt Suite," Summer to Schubert's "Moment Musical," Autumn to Tchaikovsky's "Autumn Song," and Winter to the snowflake section of his "Nutcracker Suite." This was certainly excellent preparation for what awaited him in America.

Chapter Three

1. Typewritten script for *Aphrodite* in the Theatre Collection, Museum of the City of New York.

2. Charles D. Isaacson, "Fokine—Sculptor of Human Beings," *Physical Culture,* September 1920. A typewritten copy of this article is in the Fokine Folder in the General Dance and Theatre Collection of the New York Public Library at Lincoln Center. Isaacson does not indicate the context of the Fokine remarks.

3. "Sex Appeal in Dance," Fokine Papers, Dance Collection, New York Public Library at Lincoln Center.

4. Nathalie Krassovska was dancing with Col. de Basil's Ballet Russe when this happened and she recalls that she made her entrance late because Fokine was in the way.

5. *Town and Country,* 20 December 1919.

6. Typewritten script of *Mecca,* Theatre Collection, Museum of the City of New York.

7. Burns Mantle, *Minneapolis Journal,* 16 October 1920. The article indicates that it was sent from New York.

8. *New York Telegram*, 16 July 1923. This was an article on Martha Lorber and it is possible that the unidentified author confused *Mecca* with *Aphrodite*, since there is no other mention of rose petals in the former.

9. Gerald Bordman, *The American Musical Theatre* (New York: Oxford University Press, 1978), 354.

10. *Theatre Magazine*, December 1920, 370.

11. *New York Review*, 5 February 1921.

12. Whether or not she is the same person as Rosa Rolland, who was a dancer at the Metropolitan Opera, and supposedly a student of Fokine's, is unknown.

13. Fokine made a list of ballets he would like to forget when he was preparing the material for his memoirs. The list appears in *Against the Tide*, 555. On it are *Rose Girl, Fra Mino, Faust, Casanova, Samson and Delilah, Hassan, Midsummer Night's Dream, Shayton, Santa Claus, La Valse, Bolero,* and *Pisanelle*.

14. *New York Herald*, 5 September 1921.

15. *New York Herald*, 6 June 1922; Darnton, *New York Evening World*, 6 June 1922.

16. The last of these is on Fokine's list of works to be forgotten and is also included on the various lists of his works. The two major lists of Fokine's ballets are in Appendix C of Beaumont, *Michel Fokine,* and the appendix of Fokine, *Memoirs*. The documentation in *Les Saisons de la Danse* (February 1973) appears to be based on the other two, including errors in dates.

17. Sam McKee, *New York Telegraph*, 4 October 1921.

18. *St. Louis Dispatch*, 8 November 1921.

19. Scrapbook in the Gertrude Hoffmann Archives, Brooklyn Collection, Brooklyn Public Library, Grand Army Plaza. Neither these Archives nor any other source validates a ballet that Fokine supposedly choreographed for Hoffmann and is listed in both Beaumont and *Memoirs* as *Santa Claus* and dated December 1923. The Newark Public Library has one clipping from January 1924 that talks of Hoffmann rehearsing a ballet about a toy shop. Liadov is credited with the music for *Santa Claus*; he did write a piece called "Kolyada" (Christmas Carol), which is a comic symphonic miniature about a group of mummers.

20. *Patterson* (N.J.) *Call*, 6 August 1924.

21. *New York Morning Telegraph*, 9 July 1923.

22. *Philadelphia North American*, 25 January 1921. The performance took place on 24 January, but no further details of the program are available.

23. This ballet seems to have been presented on other occasions under the title *Oriental Ballet*. Beaumont lists it, but it is not included in *Memoirs*.

24. *New York Evening Telegram*, 15 February 1924. No composer is given. This was probably a version of the same ballet to music by Dvorak that the Fokine dancers gave in 1922 at the Strand Theatre, N.Y.C. Either the newspaper was in error or the spelling of Beatrice Belreva's name was purposely changed.

25. The *New York Times* listed Ippolitov-Ivanov on 16 November and Rimsky-Korsakov on 23 November.

26. Hugo Ball, *Flight Out of Time*, ed. John Elderfeld, trans. Ann Raimes (New York: Viking Press, 1974), 10.

27. *Shadowlane*, December 1922, 47; *New York Times*, 21 January 1923.

28. *New York Globe and Advertiser*, 26 December 1922.

29. *New York Sun*, 26 September 1923.

30. Vitale Fokine used the photograph of his mother as a nun on the Christmas card his family sent out the December after her death (1958).

31. Leo A. Marsh, *New York Telegraph*, 23 September 1924.

32. Percy Hammond, *New York Herald Tribune*, 23 September 1924.

33. Lillian Shapero, "The Dance," in *Ten Years of Artef*, Theatre Collection, Yivo Institute for Jewish Research, New York City. Translated verbally by Dina Abramsowicz.

34. *Theatre Arts Monthly*, February 1927.

35. *Jewish Daily Forward*, 19 November 1926. Translated verbally by Diane Cypkin.

36. "Rhythmic Superstition," *Birjevye News*, 29 February 1915. Reprinted in *Against the Tide*, 354–56.

Chapter Four

1. Liadov, who died in 1914, is remembered for his folk-inspired compositions. He had been a pupil of Rimsky-Korsakov. "I Dance with a Mosquito" is a comic song in which there is the musical imitation of the drone of a mosquito. Fokine obviously remembered and liked Liadov's music.

2. Hurok *(S. Hurok Presents* [New York, 1953]) lists the other dances as *The Dying Swan, The Moonlight Sonata* (originally created in 1918 in Stockholm), *Danses Tziganes* (Nachez), *Sapeteado* (Hartman), two Caucasian dances to folk music, and four of Liadov's Russian folk dances.

3. In the Phyllis Fokine Archive.

4. *Washington Times*, 19 February 1922. This is the only reference to this proposed tour, which seems never to have materialized.

5. *Boston Traveler*, 19 April 1922.

6. *Tatler* (London), 8 August 1923. The dependability of this report is questionable since it identified the Fokines as brother and sister and was actually publicity for the production of *Hassan*, which opened in London in September. The article also said that both Fokines would appear in *Hassan*, which was an impossibility, if only because Mme Fokina was in New York overseeing the final rehearsals of the prologue to *Casanova*.

7. *Dayton Daily News*, 31 October 1920.

8. There are photographs in DC and in Beaumont, *Michel Fokine*. A rehearsal film of the Ballet Russe version without sound, DC, reveals an abstract dance that resembles *Les Sylphides* at times. *A Midsummer Night's Dream* (1906) not only used the same music but also had elves in it.

9. Danford Barney, "Will He Ever Have an American Ballet?" *Dance Lovers Magazine*, March 1924.

10. *Memoirs*, 266. The last section of the book was written by Vitale Fokine.

11. There is a program for one performance, which took place at Bay Shore High School on Long Island, 24 May 1940, with Vitale Fokine listed as the director. Among the works performed by Viola Essen, Leon Varkas, Lillian Moore, and others were *Les Sylphides*, *Russian Toys*, and *Prince Igor*, plus a solo and a duet with no choreographer credited. Christine Kriens danced the former and she and Peter Birch the latter. Vitale Fokine was probably the unlisted choreographer. Fokine Folder, Theatre Collection, Museum of the City of New York.

12. The *New York American*'s description of the former as festivities created by Columbine and Harlequin heralding the arrival of a great potentate, plus the fact that Deems Taylor wrote the music, suggest that this ballet was a version of the 1923 Prologue to *Casanova*, discussed in chapter 3. Beaumont concurs, calling it a new version of the Prologue (*Michel Fokine*, 164).

13. S. Jay Kaufman, "Round the Town," *New York Telegram*, 11 February 1926.

14. Lillian Moore, the dance historian, compiled one typewritten sheet concerning these performances (Fokine folders, DC). Renee Wilde and Lora Vinci both performed with this group. Desha became well known (there is a statue of her in the American wing of the Metropolitan Museum of Art), and Dorothy Lee and the Mlles Hunter and Bauer performed with the Fokine dancers on many other occasions. Maria Korolova became Vitale Fokine's first wife, although many years his senior.

15. It is possible that *Danse Classique* is the same ballet later presented as *Antique Frieze*, since the composer is the same and the title suggests the same atmosphere.

16. *Against the Tide*, 484.

17. Helen Caldwell, *Michio Ito* (Berkeley and Los Angeles: University of California Press, 1977). There is also a record of a letter to Fokine from Troy Kinney, dated 5 August 1920, which introduced Ito, in the pamphlet "A Collection of Material from the Estate of Michel Fokine," Theatre Collection, Harvard University.

18. *Variety*, 26 May, 1926, mentioned the Keith-Albee tour while also announcing that they would commence one in the Loew houses. The *Brooklyn Citizen*, 25 April 1926, announced the Brooklyn appearance.

19. *Memoirs*, 269.

20. Ibid., 268. John Martin in the *New York Times*, 12 August 1934, said the ballets were staged in ten days.

21. There seems to be some discrepancy about the date of this ballet. It is listed on the Lewisohn Stadium program for August 1934, yet *Memoirs* lists it as having been created for Ida Rubinstein in 1935. It seems most likely that it was created for Rubinstein in 1934, prior to its appearance at the stadium.

22. Pitts Sanborn, *New York World Telegram,* 14 August 1934. This description makes the ballet sound very much like the one Maurice Bejart created to the same music.

23. Fokine said that it was from this ballet that Nijinsky got several of his movement ideas for *L'Après Midi d'un Faune.* Fokine had staged it at the Hollywood Bowl in 1929.

24. The group also included Christine Kriens (who became Vitale's second wife), Nancy Knott, Gemze de Lappe, Peter Birch, Muriel Bentley, Orest Sergievsky, Dorothy Danton, Aussie Wilde, and Mary Karnilova, who in later years listed her first name as Maria.

25. This is Patricia Bowman's description of it.

26. John Gruen, "Patricia Bowman," *Dance Magazine,* October 1976.

Chapter Five

1. There is no indication that he created anything new at this time.

2. Igor Schwezoff states emphatically that Vitale really hated to dance but that his father insisted. Others have also expressed this opinion. Keith Lester, who made his dancing debut in the London production of *Hassan,* also partnered Tamara Karsavina, with whom he danced for three years throughout Central Europe. He danced several principal roles in Buenos Aires. In 1935 he was in the ballet *Semiramis,* which Fokine created for Ida Rubinstein. Anton Dolin also mentions that the management of the Teatro Colón wanted Fokine to stage Stravinsky's *Apollo Musagetes* but that, after hearing the music, he said he was not interested.

3. Eglevsky says that Blum, the quieter business partner, once told him that he looked around after he and de Basil dissolved their partnership, and seeing so many well-trained dancers unemployed, decided to start another company.

4. There were several later appraisals of this season, most of them positive. A. V. Coton in *A Prejudice for Ballet* (London: Methuen & Co., 1938) called the resurrection of Fokine the "major happening" of the spring of 1936. A writer identified as "R.H." in *Life and Letters,* Autumn 1936, noted that Fokine had arrived "somewhat defiantly" to show how his works should be danced and was not always helped by his dancers.

5. Horst Koegler, *The Concise Oxford Dictionary of Ballet,* 182. The standard music references and several books on Mozart do not discuss this work at all in relation to the composer.

6. There is no consensus of opinion regarding the fact that Fokine rehearsed the de Basil company while he was still officially with Blum. Osato cites several instances and particular ballets, Danilova recalls that he watched her rehearse *Les Sylphides* and corrected the lines of movement, and Platt, who danced in *Petroushka, Firebird,* and *Schéhérazade,* has absolutely no memory of rehearsing anything but *Coq d'Or* with him.

7. Sona Osato says the score was cut to forty-five minutes, which was the longest de Basil would allow a ballet to run, but an Ohio newspaper said it was sixty minutes in length.

8. In fact, de Basil had financial problems as well as trouble with the legal name of the company, and the organization, which temporarily changed its name to Educational Ballet, although also known as the Covent Garden Russian Ballet, was run for an interim period by German Sevastianov and Victor Dandré. Later, when de Basil returned, the company became the Original Ballet Russe, which was its name when *Paganini* opened in London.

9. Three of Fokine's letters to Rachmaninoff are reproduced, in part, in *Memoirs*. The Library of Congress has their correspondence on microfilm and it appears in *Against the Tide*.

10. Rachmaninoff was not the only individual to whom a ballet about Paganini was appealing, and the subject of the psychological ramifications of genius was not new. After the formation of the Denham company there was talk of Balanchine creating such a work to a piece by the composer Vincenzo Tommasini, which used some of Paganini's variations. It was Frederick Ashton, however, who choreographed *Le Diable S'amuse*, which was begun in the summer of 1939 and featured the devil as the chief protagonist. David Vaughn discusses this at length in *Frederick Ashton and His Ballets* (New York: Alfred A. Knopf, 1977) and suggests that the libretto of the Ashton ballet (over which Ashton had no control) may have been changed because of the Fokine/Rachmaninoff ballet.

Chapter Six

1. The Mordkin Ballet, composed of students of Mikhail Mordkin, the Russian dancer and choreographer, was organized in 1937.

2. Charles Payne makes this point in *American Ballet Theatre* (New York: Alfred A. Knopf, 1977), 16. History appears to sustain it. This book will hereafter be referred to as *ABT*.

3. Richard Pleasant in a letter to Anton Dolin dated 22 December 1959, New York City. William Seymour Theatre Collection, Princeton.

4. Payne, *ABT*, 28. Payne also indicates that there were various personalities and a considerable amount of backroom politics involved in this great collaboration. Fokine seems to have learned his lesson by then, and stayed out of it, after making sure that his contract guaranteed him autonomy in staging his works and the billing he desired. Money was evidently not a consideration for him at this point, since he received only $2,000 for staging both ballets, plus a per diem of $25 if he went out of town. Mordkin might have been paranoid, but it seems to have been justified. He had assumed he would be the artistic director, but it is obvious that his organizers—Richard Pleasant, Rudolf Orthwine, Alexander Kahn, and Lucia Chase—never intended this to be.

5. Ballet Theatre did not use the original Benois scenery until 1972,

when they obtained the designs from the Royal Ballet. Payne says Fokine was at odds with Pleasant over this.

    6. Annabelle Lyon recalls Fokine's astonishment. Every critic who reviewed Miss Conrad then and subsequently commented on her amazing style and technique in this ballet.

    7. Marilyn Hunt, Interview with Donald Saddler, May 1978–March 1979, Oral History Project, DC.

    8. Antal Dorati, letter to the author, 10 January 1981.

    9. Interview with Nora Kaye by Ara Guzelimian, 1978, DC.

    10. Annabelle Lyon, in fact, assisted André Eglevsky in restaging this work for American Ballet Theatre in 1975.

    11. Copy of letter of agreement to Antal Dorati, dated 25 June 1941, and signed by G. Sevastianov, Ballet Theatre Foundation production files. Nijinska comments in her memoirs that operas by Offenbach, including *Barbe Bleu*, were very popular in summer theater in Russia in the 1890s. It is therefore possible that Fokine was already familiar with it.

    12. Letter of agreement from German Sevastianov to Michel Fokine dated 26 March 1942. Copy in Ballet Theatre Foundation files.

    13. Many of those interviewed, including Lazowski, said that American Ballet Theatre all but forgot Fokine's staging of *Petrouchka* and *Les Sylphides*, which is not surprising considering the number of intervening years and cast changes.

    14. This appears as a typewritten statement signed by Fokine, undated, DC. It can also be found in a different version in Fokine, *Memoirs*, 294, where the date is given as 28 April 1942, and the paragraph quoted is not included.

    15. Letter of agreement from German Sevastianov to David Lichine dated 1 October 1942. Copy in Ballet Theatre Foundation files.

    16. Letter from Herman Sevastianov to Harry M. Zuckert dated 7 April 1943. Copy in Ballet Theatre Foundation production files.

    17. Dale Harris, interview with Irina Baronova, 17–18 November 1977. Oral History Project, DC.

    18. Antal Dorati, letter to the author, 10 January 1981.

    19. Saddler, interview by Marilyn Hunt, p. 50. May 1978–March 1979, Oral History Project, DC.

Chapter Seven

    1. Agnes de Mille in a letter to the author, 15 August 1977.

    2. Kirstein, *Fokine*, 64.

    3. Anton Dolin, quoted in the obituary on Michel Fokine, *Dancing Times*, London, October 1942.

    4. These plans are owned by Phyllis Fokine.

    5. Antal Dorati, letter to the author, 10 January 1981.

    6. Irina Baronova recalls him once demanding a variation be done on the left and then saying it was all right to perform it on the right.

7. Helene Saxova, "At Work with Fokine—A Rehearsal Impression," *Dancing Times*, London, November 1923.

8. *New York Morning Telegraph*, 12 March 1923. Beaumont lists this as several lectures taking place at the Al Jolson Theatre. Since the month and year agree, this is either one of several or they are the same.

9. *New York American*, 22 December 1926.

Chapter Eight

1. *New York Herald, New York Times, New York American*, 23 March 1923.

2. In *Against the Tide*, 485. The letter was excerpted from the Soviet publication *Red Panorama* 4 (1923). A note on page 601 of *Against the Tide* says that Vitale Fokine reports that his father kept a special folder of documents concerning lawyers and entrepreneurs. To date, this has not been located.

3. "Routine for Sat. and Sun., Feb. 25 and 26, 1922," Press Copy, Private collection.

4. There is a note from J. J. Shubert to William Klein, dated 14 July 1922, making this statement. Private collection.

5. *New York Times*, 1 November 1924. The same page of the newspaper also contained advertisements for forthcoming appearances by Anna Pavlova and Tamara Karsavina.

6. Unidentified newspaper clipping, Theatre Collection, Museum of the City of New York. The article mentions that the Diaghilev Ballet will appear the next season, so it was probably in 1915.

7. *New York Star*, 16 January 1921.

8. Letter to Morris Gest from Michel Fokine dated 8 May 1929, copy in Phyllis Fokine Archive.

9. *American Dancer*, July 1929.

10. Olga Maynard, *The American Ballet*, (Philadelphia: Macrae, Smith Co., 1959).

11. "A Sad Art," *Novoe Russkoe Slovo* (The New Russian Word), New York, 1 March 1931. A translation entitled "A Melancholy Art" appears in the Fokine Folders, DC. It was reprinted in translation in *Dance Magazine*, May 1931, as "A Sad Art," and appears in *Memoirs* under that title.

12. She also points out that in *Schéhérazade*, when Zobëide is pleading for her life, she does a contraction.

13. Letter from Agnes de Mille to the author, 15 August 1977.

14. Peter Williams, in *Dance and Dancers*, London, January 1962.

15. "Dilettantism in the Dance," 20 November 1932. Fokine Papers, 11–10, DC.

16. "The American Ballet Today," *Dance Magazine*, November 1928.

17. John Martin, "The Dance: Creating The New Ballet," New York *Times*, 15 November 1931. Historians are still debating the actual extent of Duncan's influence on Fokine prior to 1909. An interesting discussion on this is Debra

Goldman's, "Mothers and Fathers: A View of Isadora and Fokine," *Ballet Review* 6, no. 4 (Winter 1977–78).

18. Kirstein, *Fokine.*

19. "What Dancers Think," *Dance Magazine,* May 1931, 14.

20. "The Central European Dance: Is Modernism Modern?" March 1931, Fokine Papers, 11–8, DC.

21. Fokine, "The American Ballet Today," *Dance Magazine,* November 1928, 55.

22. Kirstein, "Homage to Michel Fokine," *New England Weekly,* 27 July 1933, General Fokine Files, New York Public Library at Lincoln Center.

23. Dale Harris, interview with Irina Baronova, 17–18 November 1977, Oral History Archives, DC, 39.

24. Antal Dorati, letter to the author, 10 January 1981.

Selected Bibliography

Books

American Ballet Theatre. Text and commentary by Charles Payne. New York: Alfred A. Knopf, 1978.

Anderson, Jack, *The One and Only: The Ballet Russe de Monte Carlo*. New York: Dance Horizons, 1981.

Atkinson, Brooks. *Broadway*. New York: MacMillan Co., 1970.

Baral, Robert. *Revue*. New York and London: Fleet Press Corp., 1962.

Beaumont, Cyril W. *Complete Book of Ballets*. London: Putnam, 1937; reprint. with additons, 1951.

———. *Michel Fokine and His Ballets,* London: C. W. Beaumont, 1935; reprint. 1945.

———. *Supplement to Complete Book of Ballets*. London: C. W. Beaumont, 1942.

Benois, Alexandre. *Reminiscences of The Russian Ballet*. London: Putnam, 1941.

———. *Memoirs*. London: Chatto & Windus, 1964.

Buckle, Richard. *In Search of Diaghilev*. London: Sidwick & Jackson, 1955.

Dean, Basil. *Seven Ages*. London: Hutchinson, 1970.

Dolin, Anton. *The Sleeping Beauty*. London: Frederick Muller, 1966.

Flecker, James Elroy. *Hassan*. London: William Heinemann, 1924.

Fokine, Michel. *Memoirs of a Ballet Master*. Translated by Vitale Fokine. Edited by Anatole Chujoy. London: Constable & Co., 1961.

Grigoriev, S. L. *The Diaghilev Ballet 1909–1929*. London: Constable, 1954.

Haskell, Arnold. *Balletomania Then and Now*. New York: Alfred A. Knopf, 1977.

———. *Diaghileff, His Artistic and Private Life*. In collaboration with Walter Nouvel. London: Gollancz, 1935.

Hurok, Sol. *S. Hurok Presents*. New York: Hermitage House, 1953.

Kirstein, Lincoln. *Fokine*. London: British-Continental Press, 1934.

———. *Movement and Metaphor: Four Centuries of Ballet*. New York: Praeger, 1970.

Lieven, Prince. *The Birth of the Russian Ballet*. London: Allen & Unwin, 1936.

Martin, John. *World Book of Modern Ballet*. Cleveland and New York: World
    Publishing Co., 1952.
McDonald, Nesta. *Diaghilev Observed*. New York: Dance Horizons, London:
    Dance Books, 1975.
Nijinska, Bronislava. *Early Memoirs*. New York: Holt, Rinehart & Winston,
    1981.
Osato, Sono. *Distant Dances*. New York: Alfred A. Knopf, 1980.
Propert, W. A. *The Russian Ballet in Western Europe 1909–1920*. London: 1921;
    reprint. New York: Benjamin Blom, Inc., 1972.
Rambert, Marie. *Quicksilver*. London: Macmillan, 1972.
Sergievsky, Orest. *Memoirs of a Dancer: Shadows, Dreams, Memories*. New
    York: Dance Horizons, 1979.
Slonimsky, Yuri. *Protiv Techeniia* (Against the Tide). Leningrad: Fine Arts, 1962.
The New Grove Dictionary of Music and Musicians. 20 vols. Edited by Stanley
    Sadie. London: MacMillan Publishers, 1980.

Articles

Barnes, Clive. "Fokine: Ballet Revolutionary." *New York Times*, 27 August 1967.
Beriosoff, Nicholas. "Remembering Fokine Ten Years after His Death." *Ballet*
    (London), August 1952.
Cohen, Selma Jeanne, and Pischl, A.J. "The American Ballet Theatre: 1940–
    1960." *Dance Perspectives* 6. Brooklyn, N.Y.: Dance Perspectives.
Goldman, Debra. "Background to Diaghilev." *Ballet Review* 6, no. 3 (1977–78).
———. "Mothers and Fathers: A View of Isadora and Fokine." *Ballet Review* 6,
    no. 4 (1977–78).
Gruen, John. "Patricia Bowman." *Dance Magazine*, October 1976.
Haskell, Arnold. "Further Studies in Ballet: A Study in Romanticism." *Dancing
    Times* (London), December 1929.
———. "Some Memories of Fokine." *Dancing Times* (London), December 1961.
Horwitz, Dawn Lille. "A Class with Michel Fokine." *Dance Chronicles* 3, no. 1
    (1979).
———, and McDonagh, Don. "Conversations with Eglevsky." *Ballet Review* 8,
    no. 1 (1980).
Karsavina, Tamara. "Fokine's Two Great Careers." *Dance and Dancers* (London),
    May 1932.
Kirstein, Lincoln. "Homage to Michel Fokine." *New England Weekly*, 27 July
    1933.
———. "Crisis in Dance." *North American Review*, March 1937.
Levinson, André. "A Crisis in the Ballets Russes." *Theatre Arts*, November 1926.
Lloyd, Margaret. "Conversation with a Legend." *Christian Science Monthly*, 23
    February 1938.
Martin, John. "Father of the Modern Ballet." *New York Times Magazine*, 15 De-
    cember 1940.

Perugini, Mark E. "Fokine and the Future." *Dancing Times* (London), June 1933.

Rambert, Dame Marie. "Petipa and Fokine." *Dancing Times* (London), May 1942.

Ross, Betty. "Answer Number Ninety Nine." *Dance,* May 1926.

Svetloff, Valerian. "The Old and the New." *Dancing Times* (London), July 1929.

Vaughan, David. "Fokine in the Contemporary Repertory." *Ballet Review* 7, nos. 2 and 3 (1978–79).

Interviews by Dawn Lille Horwitz

Anchutina, Leda. Massapequa, New York, 8 July 1976.

Bird, Dorothy. Via telephone, Merrick, New York, 20 November 1980.

Bowman, Patricia. New York, New York, 9 February 1976.

Chaffee, George. New York, New York, 23 April 1976.

Chase, Lucia. New York, New York, 17 June 1980.

Danielian, Leon. New York, New York, 17 October 1977.

Danilova, Alexandra. New York, New York, 30 December 1982.

De Lappe, Gemze. New York, New York, 21 February 1977.

Eglevsky, André. Massapequa, New York, 8 July 1976.

Ehrenreich, Belle Didjah. Via telephone, New York, New York, 5 January 1981.

Fokine, Phyllis. Jackson Heights, New York, March-August 1981.

Gibson, Ian. Via telephone, Alpine, New Jersey, 26 October 1981.

Goya, Carola. New York, New York, 11 February 1977.

Haakon, Paul. New York, New York, 2 June 1976.

Koner, Pauline. New York, New York, 18 November 1976.

Krassovska, Nathalia. New York, New York, 25 July 1980.

Lazowski, Yurek. Wantagh, New York, 15 August 1977.

Low, Betty. New York, New York, 12 January 1983.

Lyon, Annabelle. Great Neck, New York, 9 July 1976.

Mauret, Virginie. Via telephone, New York, New York, 15 October 1981.

Nemchinova, Vera. New York, New York, 13 January 1983.

Page, Ruth. Chicago, Illinois, 26 November 1977.

Platt, Marc. Via telephone, Florida, 10 December 1982.

Poliakoff, Miriam Weiskopf. Great Neck, New York, 27 January 1977.

Schwezoff, Igor. New York, New York, 18 May 1978.

Sergava, Katherine. New York, New York, 15 July 1977.

Sergievsky, Orest. New York, New York, 21 November 1977.

Shurr, Gertrude. New York, New York, 15 September 1980.

Spencer, Virginia Comer. Via telephone, Stamford, Connecticut, 29 March 1981.

Taras, John. New York, New York, 22 November 1977.

Trueman, Paula. New York, New York, 14 October 1980.

Wilde, Renee. Via telephone, Miami, Florida, 2 June 1981.

Wilson, Anne. New York, New York, 13 October 1977.

Interviews by Others

Gruen, John. Interview with Cyril Beaumont, London, 28 July 1974. Oral History Archives, Dance Collection, New York Public Library at Lincoln Center.

Guzelimian, Ara. Interview with Nora Kaye, 1978. Dance Collection, New York Public Library at Lincoln Center.

Harris, Dale. Interview with Irina Baronova, 17 and 18 November 1977. Oral History Project, Dance Collection, New York Public Library at Lincoln Center.

Horosko, Marion. Interview with Vitale Fokine, New York, 1965. Oral History Archives, Dance Collection, New York Public Library at Lincoln Center.

———. Interview with Caird Leslie, New York, n.d. Oral History Archives, Dance Collection, New York Public Library at Lincoln Center.

Hunt, Marilyn. Interview with Donald Saddler, May 1978–March 1979. Oral History Project, Dance Collection, New York Public Library at Lincoln Center.

Manchester, P. J. Interview with George Balanchine, 1975. Oral History Archives, Dance Collection, New York Public Library at Lincoln Center.

Matheson, Katy. Interview with Tatiana Leskova, 21 February 1979. Oral History Archives, Dance Collection, New York Public Library at Lincoln Center.

Articles by Michel Fokine (arranged chronologically)

"The New Ballet." *Argus* (Russia), 1 November 1916. Typewritten translation in Fokine Papers 1914–1941, Dance Collection, New York Public Library at Lincoln Center.

"The Ballet's Rise from Pink Frills and Satin Slippers." *Musical America*, 29 April 1922.

"The Dance Is Poetry without Words." Typewritten manuscript, 1924. In Fokine Papers 1914–1941, Dance Collection, New York Public Library at Lincoln Center.

"The American Ballet Today." *Dance Magazine*, November 1928.

"A Sad Art." *Dance Magazine*, May 1931. (This is an English translation of an article originally published in New York in the Russian periodical *New Russian Word*, March 1, 1931.)

"What Dancers Think." Opinions by several dancers on the art of Mary Wigman. *Dance Magazine*, May 1931.

"Fokine Choreography." Lucille Stoddart Teachers Course, New York, Hotel Astor, 1931. Typewritten manuscript in Fokine Papers 1914–1941, Dance Collection, New York Public Library at Lincoln Center.

"Michel Fokine Remembers Anna Pavlova as She Was in the Beginning." *Dance Magazine*, August 1931.

"Sex Appeal in Dance." Typewritten manuscript, 1 September 1932. In Fokine Papers 1914–1941, Dance Collection, New York Public Library at Lincoln Center.

"Dilettantism in the Dance." Typewritten manuscript, 20 November 1932. In Fokine Papers 1914–1941, Dance Collection, New York Public Library at Lincoln Center.

"Lifar—His Books and Theories." *Dancing Times* (London), August 1938.

"How a Legend Is Created." Unpublished manuscript, 27 March 1940, dictated to *Dance Magazine* in 1967 by Vitale Fokine. Galley in Fokine Papers 1914–1941, Dance Collection, New York Public Library at Lincoln Center.

"How Diaghilev Became the Creator of My Ballets." Unpublished manuscript, 28 March 1940, dictated to *Dance Magazine* in 1967 by Vitale Fokine. Galley in Fokine Papers 1914–1941. Dance Collection, New York Public Library at Lincoln Center.

Major Collections and Archives Consulted

Ballet Theatre Foundation, New York, New York.

Dance Collection, New York Public Library at Lincoln Center, New York, New York.

Gertrude Hoffmann Archives, Brooklyn Collection, Public Library, Grand Army Plaza, Brooklyn, New York.

Michel Fokine Archive, Phyllis Fokine, Jackson Heights, New York.

Metropolitan Opera Archives, New York, New York.

Theatre Collection, Harvard University, Cambridge, Massachusetts.

Theatre Collection, Museum of the City of New York, New York, New York.

Theatre Collection, New York Public Library at Lincoln Center, New York, New York.

William Seymour Theatre Collection, Princeton University, Princeton, New Jersey.

Yivo Institute for Jewish Research, New York, New York.

Index

About the Author

Dawn Lille Horwitz is trained in ballet and modern dance and has worked as a performer and rehearsal coach. A graduate of Barnard, she holds masters degrees from Columbia and Adelphi and the Ph.D. from NYU. She has taught dance history, technique, theater, and Labananalysis at many schools including Barnard and Brooklyn colleges, the High School of Performing Arts, and the Kibbutz Regional School at Gaaton, Israel. She has researched and written sections of books and her articles have appeared in *Ballet Review* and *Dance Chronicle,* among other publications.